WEST GERMANY
A Contemporary History

MICHAEL
BALFOUR

ST. MARTIN'S PRESS   NEW YORK

All rights reserved. For information, write:
St. Martin's Press, Inc., 175 Fifth Avenue, New York, NY 10010
Printed in Great Britain
First published in the United States of America in 1982

Library of Congress Cataloging in Publication Data

Balfour, Michael Leonard Graham, 1908-
    West Germany, a contemporary history.

    Bibliography: p. 293
    Includes index.
    1. Germany (West) – History. 2. Germany (West) –
    Politics and government. I. Title.
    DD259.B34   943.087   81-21293
    ISBN 0-312-86297-0   AACR2   5/31/8~

CONTENTS

PREFACE

In 1966-7 I wrote a book with the same title as the present one, which was duly published in the 'Nations of the Modern World' series. This book, however, differs from it in three important respects. First, I have added three chapters to cover the period 1967-80 and written a completely new conclusion. Secondly, to keep the length of the book within reasonable limits, I have considerably shortened the original Chapters 1 to 4 and cut to a lesser extent Chapters 5 to 6. Thirdly, I have tried to take account of all that has been published in the last fourteen years about the history of Germany up to 1966, while there are a number of matters on which I have modified or changed my views. The total result is tantamount to a new book.

There are of course many histories of Germany already in print. There are also a number of books about the contemporary Germanies, most of which begin with a short historical survey. The aim of this one, however, is to use the past to explain the present. Thus it is important to know what happened to Germany in the Middle Ages in order to understand her relative backwardness in the nineteenth century, while the descriptions of the 1871 and 1919 Constitutions go far to explain why the Basic Law of 1949 took the shape it did. But this is not a normal history in that the amount of space devoted to an epoch gets progressively greater as the present day approaches. On the other hand, such features as co-determination and terrorism are described in their historical setting rather than viewed purely as current phenomena.

I have interpreted my subject as entitling me to deal with Germany as a whole up to the point at which the division into East and West took place and have thereafter only written about the Democratic Republic when I thought this necessary to explain what was happening in the Federal Republic.

To make the book easier reading for those who know little about its subject, I have avoided footnotes and given virtually no references, but I have tried to widen my description of the Federal Republic today and yet economise on words by providing a number of tables. I hope that they will be regarded as an integral part of the book.

I would have found the last third of the book far harder to write if I had not been for a long time a regular reader of *Die Zeit*. I am most grateful to Dr Childs for commenting on my typescript; to Professor

Wolfgang Freiherr von Marschall for checking my Annexe on the voting system; to Professor Kurt Koszyk for help over Table 20; to my wife, for help in typing; and to my great-niece Morwenna Wood of Balliol College, Oxford for making a number of valuable criticisms from the student's point of view.

M.L.G.B.
Burford
1 September 1981

Key
- Frontier of WEST GERMANY
- Frontiers of adjoining countries
- West Germany LÄNDER (provinces)
- German frontier in 1937
- Towns of over 1 million inhabitants
- Towns of between 1 million and 400,000 inhabitants
- Other towns
- Land over 1500 feet

1 FROM TRIBE TO NATIONAL STATE: THE FIRST REICH

Origins

How the name 'German' originated is a matter about which nobody seems sure. According to one theory it means 'one who shouts' and thus a warrior; according to another, it means 'a neighbour'. (As neighbours long tended to be warlike, the two meanings perhaps came to much the same thing.) The earliest people to be so called were tribes living in Denmark and South Scandinavia in the first millennium BC. The individual tribes had different names, such as Teutons and Cimbrians, but the facts that the name 'German' was applied to them all collectively and that they all spoke the same language point to a common origin further back.

During the second and first centuries BC these tribes shifted southwards and westwards, presumably under pressure from nomadic groups arriving from the North and East. They pushed the Celts, who had previously inhabited the area between the Elbe and Rhine, over the latter river and in some cases followed them across it. When, about 98 AD, the Roman historian Tacitus set out to shame his decadent fellow countrymen by comparing them with the noble savages in 'Germania', he defined that area as lying between on the one hand Gaul and the Alps, from which it was separated by the Rhine and the Danube, and on the other the Sarmatians and Dacians from whom it was separated by 'mountains and mutual terror'! The two Roman provinces of High and Low Germany hardly came into this area at all. Their eastern boundary lay along the Rhine from its mouths to the neighbourhood of Mainz and then cut across to the upper Danube. A move to press forward met with disaster in 9 AD when the Cherusci, under a chief whom the Romans called Arminius (a name which later Germans have transliterated into Hermann), annihilated the Roman general Varus and a couple of legions at the battle of the Teutonic Wood, probably near Detmold. The result was that much of modern Germany and most of the peoples who were to settle there never came under Roman law or absorbed Roman culture. Some later writers have blamed upon this omission many of the faults, and others some of the virtues, which they found in German behaviour; at the very least it made the Germans different from their Latinised neighbours.

As the Roman Empire staggered to its collapse, its armed forces grew incapable of keeping at a safe distance the tribes from whom they were increasingly recruited; north-western and western Europe saw successive inroads of the Germani. Thus the Franks (or free men) went to France, the Lombards to Italy, the Visigoths to Spain. But as soon as one group moved off, another emerged to replace it from the vast reservoir of the northern plains. As a result present-day West Germany came to be inhabited by Bavarians, Swabians (or Alemanni), Thuringians, Franconians, Frisians, Saxons and Lorrainers, loose agglomerations with little apparent cohesion or political connection. About the sixth century an adjective derived from *thiod* (i.e. people) began to be applied to the language of the tribes between the Rhine and Elbe. In Old High German *thiod* became *diutisk*, which gradually developed into *diutsch* and so into *deutsch* — the name used to describe themselves by the people whom this book is about.

In the eighth century the seven tribes were converted to Christianity, largely by the efforts of Boniface from Devonshire. Soon afterwards they fell under the overlordship of the Emperor of the Franks. Such cohesion as this involved was threatened when the Frankish Empire broke up after Charlemagne's death in 814, but the eastern part of it remained united under King Louis, who although a Frank used the title Germanicus. In 843 his domains were given recognised form by the Treaty of Verdun which (in view of the fact that the Franks and *Diutisks* could no longer understand one another) had to be drafted in both languages. It is this Treaty which is generally taken to mark the beginning of what we, looking backwards, can see to have been German history. Then in 911 the seven tribes, tired of being ruled by outsiders, made Conrad of Franconia their King. Almost immediately we find his realm being described in Latin as *regnum teutonicorum* — the Kingdom of the Teutons.

Up to this point, and indeed for another century, the history of Germany did not basically differ from that of areas further west. In all cases loose tribal groupings were being consolidated under the domination of strong and ambitious kings.

By 1075 Germany had far outstripped France and England . . . and was already on the path leading to more modern forms of government. Had this process proved durable, it is scarcely doubtful that Henry IV (1056-1106) would have created a great German state coeval with Norman England and [the France of] Philip Augustus.[1]

The process was successful enough for the consciousness of common interest which the rulers instilled into their subjects never to become altogether effaced; Germany remained a cultural entity even after there ceased to be a single effective political ruler.

For, in spite of the initial success, political consolidation failed to be realised. This was not due simply to the fact that Germany lacked the clear-cut frontiers of France and Britain, though the resulting exposure to invasion was certainly a distracting factor. The main cause of the failure had begun by making a major contribution to the success. In 962 Otto, King of the Germans, was elected King of the Romans and thus heir to the Emperors (though the title Roman Emperor was not used till later). This ensured him the powerful support of the Church, many of whose dignitaries in Germany and North Italy acted virtually as imperial officials. But in 1075 the great Pope Gregory VII (Hildebrand) decided to put an end to this practice and immediately clashed with Henry IV. The struggle which led to the penitent Emperor standing barefoot in the snow at Canossa may have served the cause of liberty and true religion by preventing the Popes from degenerating into imperial lackeys, but its effects upon Germany were disastrous. Instead of devoting themselves to consolidation of their hold on that country, successive Emperors were tempted or forced to assert themselves against the Papacy; the church, instead of acting as their ally in maintaining law and order, only too frequently sought to undermine their authority.

One step to this end was the claim that succession to the imperial throne did not go by hereditary right but that each new occupant had to be elected by his immediate vassals. The result was a series of disputed successions and debilitating bargains; the central authority grew weaker rather than stronger. In their search for allies, the rulers of the First Empire (*Reich*) were drawn into controversies all over Europe but particularly in Italy. Attention was distracted from the task of ruling Germany by the fear of losing ground against Rome. The people who profited most from this situation were the elector princes who should have been subordinate. In the end it was one of these princely families, the Habsburgs, who in 1438 succeeded in appropriating the imperial throne and, by dint of judicious marriages, keeping it as family property. In their hands the Empire regained a good deal of its glory but lost the closeness of its connection with Germany. For it was in the basin of the middle Danube and in Northern Italy that Habsburg possessions and interests were concentrated. Many of their subjects were not German at all, in many of the areas inhabited by Germans their authority was slight, and many of the ends to which the imperial resources were devoted brought to Germany little or no benefit.

The later history of Germany has been dominated by the fact that during the Middle Ages the process of political consolidation was not carried through. The thing which gave Britain her outstanding advantage and made her the scene of that technological breakthrough known as the 'Industrial Revolution' derived from the achievements of the Normans, Plantagenets and Tudors. The three main spurs underlying that Revolution are accumulation of capital (with means of transferring it from savers to effective spenders); its use to put into effect technical invention (which presupposes the accumulation of knowledge and is particularly important in its application to communications); and growth of population (to provide both manpower for the machines and consumers for the products). The vital pre-condition for all three developments is stable and effective government with all that this can bestow in the way of peace, security, ease of movement and a reliable undiscriminating legal system. The accidents or, if one prefers, the destiny of history, and particularly the fact of being insulated by the sea, placed Britain in a specially favourable position for establishing such government and its accompaniments. Their progressively accelerating development involved an early swelling in the numbers of merchants, well-to-do landed gentry, professional men and craftsmen. This in turn meant that the crucial conflict between a monarchy tending to absolutism and the various elements composing the 'middle classes', who had within them the seeds of the democratic state, was in Britain fought out at a relatively early date and settled decisively in favour of the popular side. This shift of power intensified the awareness of common interest which had been growing under a relatively benevolent royal government since medieval days; the resulting cohesion (or to use a simpler term, patriotism) considerably increased the international effectiveness of the state. True, the power of the king was during the seventeenth century replaced by that of an oligarchy, but the oligarchy was never a closed one (the younger children of an English peer relapse into being commoners whereas in Germany they all retain their father's title). It owed much of its resources to its connection with commerce and took care to see that commercial interests got free play. Moreover the doctrines evolved to justify the political revolution continued to dominate orthodox thought. The result was that, when the social transformations caused by the industrial revolution began to gather way, there were within the ruling classes enough believers in the principles of liberty to provide a focus for the dissatisfied and to offer them hope that the necessary adjustments could be made without having the social fabric again torn apart by the spiritual and material destruction of revolution.

In Germany, by contrast, the pre-conditions for these developments were lacking. At the end of the Middle Ages the land of the *Deutsch* was an idea rather than a political reality. A dawning awareness of this fact and a consequent sense of frustration may have been responsible for a wave of interest which arose in the fifteenth century about the distinctive features of German culture. Historical studies flourished as never before; several of the first books to be printed were concerned with the German past. This was also the time that the words 'of the German nation' were added to the title 'Holy Roman Emperor'. The towns were growing in wealth and enterprise. Already the dominant economic force in Central Europe, they might soon have seized the political initiative. From the Low Countries a cultural flowering comparable to the Italian Renaissance spread at the end of the fifteenth century all the way up the Rhineland and into southern Germany. For a moment Germany seemed to have a chance of catching up on her omissions. In fact, the full damage done by those omissions was just about to be revealed.

The Reformation and Religious Wars

The ferment of new thought awoke in Martin Luther (1483-1546) an intense religious experience which spread from theology to morals and thence to politics. The success of the Reformation owed not a little to a widespread dissatisfaction which projected onto the venal and decadent leaders of the Catholic Church the blame for the weakness and misgovernment of which the Germans were becoming so conscious. But a substitute had to be found for the Papal authority which was being rejected and this was almost inevitably the local secular power. In England, where this power had already been established on a national plane, the extra title of Head of the Church made the single central ruler even stronger. But in the lands of the Germans, where effective power was split between many princes and each was free to choose his creed, this process of secularisation had a disintegrating effect, especially as the minority remaining true to the old faith included the Habsburg Emperors.

The introduction of religious differences added a new dimension to the political rivalry already existing between the princedoms and, in the absence of a dominating authority, there was no way of settling these differences except by arms. Luther revived and extended the Pauline and Augustinian doctrine that it was faith alone which could save souls from damnation. In the hands of his successors this tenet degenerated into an intense preoccupation with the details of the correct faith. A disposition to abstract argument was fostered at the expense of humanist culture. It was not an accident that in Germany the Wars of Religion lasted for thirty years, reduced the population by some thirty-five per cent and at their end left the country divided into 234 territorial units. The endemic fighting made lives and property insecure. Justice was hard to be had; saving, learning and invention languished. Awareness of common interest and the sense of being master of one's own fate, along with belief in ability to control one's own environment, were all weak. The new Atlantic trade-routes, which brought so much stimulus to Western Europe, turned Germany into an economic backwater. The middle classes lost ground instead of advancing. While Britain and France were entering on the most eventful period in their history and expanding in all directions, Germany was at best stagnating. Later generations were to describe these as 'the lost centuries'.

Emphasis on the direct responsibility of the individual to God might have been expected to foster a critical attitude towards the state. But Luther's belief in original sin led him to a pessimistic view of human institutions and a distrust of the masses, which was intensified when in 1525 the excitement of defiance to the existing order spread from the religious to the secular field and burst out in the Peasants' Revolt. By throwing his authority against the rebels, Luther may have lost a chance of making Protestantism a religion of the masses. But in the long run the support of the princes was more important; without it, the Reformation might have petered out as earlier movements had done. Yet by taking their side, he put control into their hands. The Lutheran Church grew into a branch of the state, teaching that God had ordained princes to rule their peoples as fathers rule their families; the business of pastors was to save souls for a heavenly kingdom rather than to influence the policies of earthly ones. As all a ruler's subjects had to conform with his religious views, it was natural for his officials to collect from them along with other taxes the dues on which that Church depended. Those who disliked the religion of their ruler could usually find near at hand an alternative more to their taste. All of which goes to explain the virtual absence in Germany of the nonconformist dissenting tradition which has proved in Britain and America so potent a source of politics which were radical without being irreligious. Even in 1914 there were only 15,000 people in the whole of Germany claiming to belong to 'Free Churches'.

Germany's Eastern Face

To say that Germany, being in the centre of Europe, has an eastern as
well as a western frontier may seem a glimpse of the obvious but is all
the same a truth of the first importance. For her history has been as
much affected by the lands to the one side as by those to the other and,
as conditions in the two directions differed vastly, her people have had
continually to reconcile dissimilar influences and problems.

When, in the second century BC, the Germanic tribes moved west
and south, their place on the great plain east of the Elbe was taken by
Slavs. These people remained little affected in religion, society and farming methods by Mediterranean culture. As central Germany developed,
the Christian duty of converting the heathen on the east combined with
a desire to get the land put to better use.

In Bohemia and Silesia, the operation of conversion and colonisation
went ahead fairly smoothly, but farther north the Prussians, a Slav
people akin to the Latvians and Lithuanians, offered the fiercest resistance. A prominent part in subduing them was played by the Teutonic
Knights, an order originally formed to free the Holy Land from the
infidel which, after the distraction of the Fourth Crusade, decided to
seek other areas for applying the techniques of the Church Militant. In
1225 they moved to north-east Germany and in fifty years of struggle
succeeded in imposing on the Prussians German habits even where they
could not impose German names. Nor was it only in Prussia that the
original inhabitants became Germanised. In spite of a Slav counter-
attack in the fifteenth century, a parallel assimilation was achieved
widely in the conquered territories, though more among the owners
of the lands than among the tillers of them, thus complicating the task
of anyone so rash as to try and decide on strictly historical grounds to
which state it is that they should now belong. All these lands remained
outside the Empire.

The process left a lasting mark on the men who conducted it. They
came to regard as inferior beings all those — chiefly peasants — who
kept any of their original characteristics, until the habitual attitude of
the German to the Slav became one of disdain. On numerous occasions
in coming centuries German and Slav were to co-operate, but this co-
operation was never, in German eyes, between equals. Secondly their
goal of obtaining and keeping the upper hand was almost beyond their
resources and they never felt secure against the possibility of a Slav
counter-attack. In consequence great emphasis was laid on discipline,
sacrifice, vigilance and valour. But these are secondary virtues, whose

value depends on which primary objectives they are invoked to serve.

In the twelfth century the Emperor Conrad III entrusted to a man called Albert the Bear the responsibility of turning part of Brandenburg into a strong point and as a result peasants from further west were encouraged to settle in the swamps surrounding a village which was called Berlin. Three centuries later in 1415 a new ruler of Brandenburg became needed and the Emperor Sigismund gave the job to his friend Frederick von Hohenzollern whose family, after originating on a Swabian hilltop, had for generations held an important post in Nuremberg.

At the time of the Reformation a junior member of this family was Grand Master of the Teutonic Knights. He was advised by Luther to renounce his views, abolish the Order, marry and found a dynasty. This comprehensive programme he executed in full. But early in the seventeenth century the direct line of his descendants died out and his Lutheran Prussian Dukedom was as a result inherited by the Calvinist Elector of Brandenburg. And whereas the German peasants needed to colonise the Slav lands had originally had to be allowed exceptional privileges, a variety of forces had combined towards the end of the Middle Ages to turn them back into serfs bound to the land and dependent on the landlord for justice. The towns decayed in the religious wars, except for a few ports through which the surplus corn, grown by large-scale farming on the noble estates, was shipped to remedy bad harvests further west. Manufacturing was almost non-existent. The net result was that from 1400 to 1650 the landowners, or 'Junkers', dominated the country.

They began, however, to lose ground under Frederick William, who was known as 'the Great Elector' and reigned from 1640 to 1688; in 1701 his son Frederick ventured to take the title of 'King in Prussia'. The Hohenzollern family held the view that a medium-sized state such as theirs could only prosper by exploiting the differences between its bigger neighbours. In view of Prussia's limited resources, the essential minimum of strength which this aim required could only be achieved by the strictest care and control in the use of those resources. But the basic industry to which the fruits of economy were devoted was war, and since mercenaries were on the whole too expensive, Prussia anticipated revolutionary France by creating a conscript army. On this, Frederick II (the Great, 1712-86) spent two-thirds of his revenue and in it one-sixth of the adult male population was required to serve; by his death it was practically as big as the French. Its officer corps was imbued with a high sense of duty —

a moral compulsion which forced them, out of respect for themselves and their calling, to bear hardship, danger and death without flinching and without hope of reward. This feeling of honour, the King believed, could only be found in the feudal nobility, not in other classes and certainly not in the bourgeoisie.[2]

A bargain was accordingly evolved by which the King was given the right — and the money — to maintain a standing army while the supply of officers became a monopoly of the nobles. A further innovation was the development of a General Staff to plan and conduct campaigns.

To raise the money and men, however, a civilian service was needed and it was to the bourgeoisie that the kings originally turned for staffing this. In more than one respect it set the pattern for later bureaucracies. As early as 1700 the principle of entrance by examination was established (though some posts went on being sold to the highest bidder) and in 1723 it was laid down that applicants for senior grades must have had a university education. By the end of the eighteenth century, officials had acquired security of tenure against arbitrary dismissal. They, like the officers, were expected to serve the King rather than the public and to hold their tongues about work which so often had military implications. Such servants proved their value in enabling the monarchy to assert itself against the aristocracy, but once the struggle was over, nobles too were taken into service, particularly at the local level. The pillar of Prussian administration became the *Landrat*, or District Counsellor, who tended to be at one and the same time a local magnate nominated by his peers and a permanent official appointed by the King. This absolutism was tempered in three ways. First the Government was among the most up-to-date in Europe, inspired by the advanced ideas of the Enlightenment and tolerating almost any form of religious view; the King encouraged his subjects to reason for themselves, provided only that they obeyed his orders. General education was established in Prussia in 1717, 21 years later than in Scotland but 150 years ahead of England and France. The *Allgemeines Preussisches Landrecht*, promulgated in 1794, provided a comprehensive, clear, uniform and impartial code of justice which was not superseded for over a century. It exemplified the concept that all public activities should be regulated by legal rules rather than by the changeable views of individuals; this was to become the core of the German approach to politics.

Secondly the King accepted the same standards as he imposed and regarded himself as the first servant of his people, even if he took his own decisions as to where their interests lay. Finally Prussia was successful, growing rapidly in size and international reputation. In 1740 it seized Silesia from the Habsburg Empire. In 1772 and 1793, it acquired large areas of Poland. The human tendency to identify with success would by itself be enough to explain why the most autocratic state in Germany was also the only one to evoke among its subjects an effective loyalty as well as a sense of corporate identity.

This was the austere and elevated climate in which was formulated the philosophy of Kant, the descendant of a Scottish immigrant and Germany's most profound thinker (1724-1804). Kant struggled to reconcile in the circumstances of eighteenth century Prussia the two values of freedom and order, just as in the field of knowledge he sought to reconcile freedom with the universal law of cause and effect. The starting point of Kant's thought may have been his hatred of tyranny. But in the effort to render external tyrants unnecessary, the individual was required to impose on himself an even more rigorous code of duty than the King of Prussia imposed on his people. A man could be allowed to be free only if he was completely subject to an inner control. In this way the tenets of the Prussian state were provided with an intellectual justification derived in part from the liberal tradition of Western Europe but capable of independent development.

Germany and the French Revolution

Germany as a whole took over a century to recover from the Thirty Years' War (1618-48). During the period French influence was persistent in politics and literature, while artists, architects and musicians drew their inspiration from Italy. It was the age of despotic rulers, supported by mercenary armies, a necessary episode in the rebuilding of the social fabric but hardly an inspiring one. In the north and east the Protestants held their ground. In the south and west Catholicism succeeded under Habsburg leadership in re-establishing its hold and these areas were in consequence brought within the orbit of the Mediterranean Counter-Reformation, having baroque as its distinctive art accompaniment.

With the major exception of Prussia, none of the German states had a sufficient record of success to inspire its subjects with any strong feelings of pride or loyalty. The middle classes grew only slowly and were composed more of officials, lawyers, teachers, clergy and merchants than of manufacturers. They it was who provided the protagonists of a slow cultural revival which was at first largely rationalist in character and regarded the enlightened individual as a citizen more of the world as a whole than of the principality in which he happened to live.

Gradually, however, signs of a national revival appeared, starting with an academic reassertion of the values of German learning and the German cultural heritage. The common language, enshrined in Luther's Bible, and the memory of a common history, the two great legacies of the medieval Reich to modern Germany, began to be recognised as the essential links uniting the inhabitants of the many and varied political fragments into which the area had been splintered. Looking round the outside world, those inhabitants of the area who had attained the level of self-consciousness needed for effective reflection could not help noticing that elsewhere links of language and culture had become the keystones of the most successful political societies yet evolved. In France and Britain, and to a lesser extent in Spain, Holland and Scandinavia, national feeling had grown spontaneously as a loyalty to a homogeneous social structure evolved under a settled central government and enjoying the highest level of prosperity yet known to man. From this observation it was but a step for Germans to conclude that, since they had a common language and history, they ought also to have a common government and that lack of such a government might be a major reason for their relative backwardness.

German national spirit was thus a self-conscious growth, based on a deliberate imitation of what had happened unintentionally elsewhere, and drawing its emotional drive from a sense of deprivation. In France and Britain the facts preceded and formed the basis for the theory; in Germany the theory was taken over ready-made by the intellectuals in the population and adopted as an ideal which the facts must be altered to fit.

The execution of this process was notoriously accelerated by the French Revolution. This movement provided the world with an unprecedented demonstration of what could be achieved by a resolute and fanatical government able to fire its people with enthusiasm and thus mobilise the full resources of the nation. In face of the whirlwind, the cosmopolitan rationalism of Goethe's Weimar and the Spartan discipline of Frederick's Potsdam alike proved inadequate. The Germans were first inspired and then humiliated. One result was a wave of romantic dissatisfaction with rationalism, another a widespread desire to emulate France in exploiting the national idea for political purposes and in securing popular support for a war to liberate and unify Germany. The Revolution must be fought with its own weapons.

It was as a step towards this end that, in the years following their defeat by Napoleon at Jena (1806), the Prussian authorities put in hand an overhaul of their society – principally accomplished by non-Prussians in the King's service such as Stein, Hardenberg, Scharnhorst and Gneisenau. Outmoded economic restrictions were removed, the towns were given a certain amount of self-government and in the countryside the serfs were emancipated. The professional standing army was reorganised and supplemented by a popular short-service 'Home Guard' (*Landwehr*). The responsibilities of the General Staff were increased. The reformers sought to sacrifice all other values to the re-establishment of Prussia as a major European power. The resulting excitement carried the country into the coalition which overwhelmed Napoleon in 1813 and again two years later.

An atmosphere of this kind favoured the development of that emphasis on the individuality of peoples which distinguished German thought for the following 140 years. Each people was conceived of as a separate entity with distinct characteristics and capacities; the differences were as significant as the similarities. Moreover the state rather than the individual became in the philosophy of Hegel (1770-1831) the embodiment of the national identity and as such the repository of ultimate values. As a result there could be no higher authority than the individual state; the final arbiter in inter-state affairs must therefore be force (though the road to this conclusion was often smoothed by a facile optimism which suggested that, once the national will rather than the ruler's whim was everywhere sovereign, states would share the same views on all questions of mutual interest and thus live in peace with one another).

It may be that, because in Western Europe government was on the whole well established over wide areas, political theorists tended to emphasise freedom and individual rights; in central and eastern Europe where the defects caused by division were easier to see, they gave priority to order and the rights of the state. Now the exaltation of individual rights at the expense of government authority leads to selfishness and anarchy, while the opposite process leads to despotism and injustice. The idea of holding the two in balance is easier to express than to execute. Equilibrium can be achieved verbally by saying, with Hegel, that the highest freedom consists in obedience to law as the embodiment of reason and that social liberty is a consequence of, rather than a check on, the power of the state. But in practice this formula tends to be given one of two slants. Either existing law is attacked in the name of freedom as a palpably inadequate embodiment of reason, or else obedience is demanded, in the name of reason, to law equated with the current demands of the government, even where this appears to be at the expense of the individual. Germany was to exhibit examples of both deviations.

Hegel was a professor at the University of Berlin, founded in 1812 by William von Humboldt as an integral part of the Prussian revival. In a country where nationalism began as an intellectual exercise and all professors are appointed and paid by the state, universities have an obvious political role. Berlin in particular deserved its description as the '1st Guards Brigade of Learning'. For this was the intellectual power-house where not only Hegel but such historians as Ranke and Treitschke generated the distinctive view of the world and of Germany's place in it which the country was to offer as its gospel, a coherent and comprehensive alternative to the rational individualism stemming from the Graeco-Roman tradition.

Yet paradoxically von Humboldt, far from designing the university as a political weapon, made the freedom of the professor to teach and of the student to learn into one of the fundamental principles of his system. He also reinforced the tradition that research, the advancement of learning, is not merely the primary function of a university but an ideal means of stimulating students to independent thought. A school course based upon the principle that no branch of human activity should be alien to the educated man was followed by narrow specialisation, with the doctorate as virtually the only degree. Precision and thoroughness thus gained status in public life, perhaps at some cost to a sense of proportion. This trend was reinforced by the requirement that almost all candidates for administrative posts should pass an examination in law, so as to ensure that they understood the principles of the system which they would be called on to apply.

The Failure of the Liberals

In 1803 Napoleon rationalised Germany, apart from Prussia, by expelling Austria and reducing the remaining units from three hundred to thirty; three years later he prevailed on the Habsburg Emperor to abolish the Holy Roman Empire. The statesmen who met in 1815 at the Congress of Vienna found it difficult to put the clock completely back and accordingly confirmed these changes with minor variations, linking the German states (including Austria) in a loose Confederation with a weak Federal Council. At the last moment Prussia was given considerable areas of the Rhineland and Westphalia which she did not welcome (since they meant that her territories were divided into two large blocks with

no geographical connection) and in which she was not welcomed (since
her dour methods contrasted unfavourably with twenty years of French
rule). As a result of this and earlier transactions her predominantly
Protestant population of six million was increased to ten, of whom
five, including a million Poles, were Catholic. But Prussia's victory over
France had been won by government action and the popular movement
was allowed little share in its fruits.

The problem for German nationalists prior to March 1848 was to
find a rallying-point. The obvious leader for a united Germany might
seem to be the Austrian Emperor, but less than a third of his dominions
was included in the German Confederation and of the twelve million
people who were so included almost half were Slav. His predecessors
had signally failed to rouse an adequate consolidating loyalty in the
days when this might have been done spontaneously and nobody could
rate very highly the chances of holding together a population still retaining cultural badges of membership in so many different national groups.
Clearly however an identification of the Habsburg Empire with Germany
would be bound to alienate the Emperor's non-German subjects, and
the interests of the dynasty were for that reason only partially German.
The Habsburg Emperors and Prince Metternich, who was their Chief
Minister from 1809 to 1848, were therefore unwilling to risk the loss
of their non-German possessions by taking a lead in unifying Germany.
At the same time they realised that for Germany to become united
would involve the splitting-up of their domains. They were as a result
wedded to the existing order because any change must be to their disadvantage.

The nationalists were thus left with two choices. One was to bring
about a revolution which would expel all the reigning families and unite
in a single state as many as possible of the lands in which Germans lived.
The other was to build the new state round Prussia. From 1815 onwards,
two-fifths of those Germans who were not Habsburg subjects lived in
Prussia so that a united nation-state which left them out would have
made nonsense. But the leaders of the national movement, basing themselves on English and French examples, took it for granted that a national
state must have a liberal constitution and therefore associated unification with the establishment of responsible representative government.
The demand for this also reflected the early stirrings in Germany of
the Industrial Revolution and the pressure of groups whose economic
position was improving for a corresponding improvement in social status.
The *Zollverein* or Customs Union set up between 1828 and 1835 under
Prussian leadership (but excluding Austria) did something in the short

run to relieve the pressure for political unification but, by removing economic barriers, and thereby hastening technological change, in the long run increased that pressure. Significantly it was Prussia which, in the Ruhr Valley and Silesia, possessed two of Europe's chief coalfields.

But although there were considerable numbers of liberals in Prussia, particularly in the western parts, the core provinces east of the Elbe were the last parts of Germany to be affected by industrialisation. Here an independent middle class was still small, the ruling class consisting of landowners and of officials closely assimilated to them. Liberalism, so far from attracting the Junkers, was anathema to most of them and rather than pay the price of recasting their society, they preferred, like the man asked whether he would rather be a Christian or a gentleman, to remain as they were.

Many of the leading German liberals had official posts of one kind or another (since teachers and clergymen, as well as many lawyers and doctors, were state servants) which made it unnatural for them to contemplate violent resistance to the government. The respect paid to the rule of law increased their reluctance to break it. Theories borrowed from England and elsewhere fostered the idea that any army beyond a militia was a menace to individual liberty. When in 1848 an economic recession set off a wave of revolutions in Berlin, Vienna and other cities, the leaders failed to see the need to protect what they had won by organising a citizen force which could resist the royal armies. Instead, a self-appointed assembly of the educated middle classes met at Frankfurt and drew up a constitution embodying the so-called 'small German' solution (i.e. excluding Austria). They then offered the crown of the proposed state to King Frederick William IV of Prussia. When he refused it, the gathering broke up. The King's troops had already restored normality in Berlin and went on to suppress a rising in south-west Germany by craftsmen and peasants who were less inhibited about using force but too weak to do so effectively. When the king tried to set up a German union of his own, Austria threatened war and by the humiliating Agreement of Olmütz (1850) forced him to abandon the scheme.

Thereafter the liberal cause might have foundered altogether if the economic tide had not been steadily strengthening its upholders. The groups ranged against them were neither effete nor incompetent nor half-hearted. They believed that they had saved Germany from chaos by standing firm in 1848-9 and were prepared to do so again if necessary. Moreover, as 1848 had shown, the would-be reformers were in two minds about revolution. For the struggle to break the political power of the landowners had been postponed in Germany to an epoch in which working-class consciousness was beginning to stir. Marx, born in Trier in 1818 and educated in Berlin, was doing his best to spread the idea that the proletariat should exploit the bourgeois revolution as a stepping-stone to their own dictatorship. Not for the last time, those Germans best able to put their fellow countrymen in control of their own destiny shrank from the action needed to do so, for fear that, once the impetus was created, it might hurtle beyond the goal. And indeed if the bour-geoisie had had the will to fight, the result might well have been a pro-longed civil war into which most of Europe would gradually have been drawn.

Yet a widespread desire for unity persisted. The failure of 1848-50 deepened the sense of frustration which the years after 1815 had aroused and produced a reaction against what were regarded as the unpractical policies responsible for failure. Many of those reaching manhood be-tween 1850 and 1870 were not only obsessed with the problem of unification but convinced that policies of realism (*Realpolitik*) could alone be expected to overcome the obstacles. Realism involves a hard-headed assessment of values and a readiness to sacrifice subordinate ones to the top priorities. And whereas in the reforms after 1806 internal liberty had been called for in the name of national liberty, it was now denied in the name of national unity. The primacy which these men and women gave to the national cause at the expense, if necessary, of liberties is one of the dominating facts of the next seventy years, since this was the generation which was to provide Germany's leaders between 1880 and 1914.

After 1848 all the indications pointed to Prussia as the focus of German unity and to lack of international influence as the price to be paid for remaining disunited. But the Prussian ruling classes still feared that a united Germany would mean the ruin of all the things which they valued, while the other states were too proud of their own identities to accept a merger reducing them to the level of Prussian provinces. Moreover an all-German government, to deserve the name, would have to be responsible for the defence and foreign policy of its territories. Yet these two prerogatives and the control thereby ensured over the kingdom's destinies were precisely what the Prussian leaders felt least inclined to surrender.

Although the Liberals probably had a majority among the Prussian voters and although a more liberal ministry was called to power in Prussia in 1858, the history of the next four years showed how deeply rooted was the opposition to concessions. The crucial clash came on the question of what form the army was to take and where control over it was to rest. Strategic developments had outmoded the Landwehr and made it an obstacle to the organisation of an efficient striking force. Accordingly the War Minister von Roon wanted to convert it into the regular army's reserve. The change involved the adaptation of the nation to militarism whereas the reforms of 1806-14 had sought to make the army a reflection of the nation. The Prussian Parliament (*Landtag*) proposed amendments to restore the balance and, when it was disregarded, tried to enforce its will by the power of the purse. The men round King William I took the view that military arrangements were his personal concern as commander-in-chief and advised him to stand firm. This he readily did, dissolving Parliament. But even though the constitution divided voters into three classes according to wealth and allowed 3 per cent, 12 per cent and 85 per cent of the total each to elect an equal number of Deputies, the opposition came back in greater strength. Still the royal group would not give way. The King's obstinacy seemed destined to make his name a stock example of the social havoc done by misplaced pertinacity.

From this predicament King William was not only saved but in the short space of eight years raised to the position of German Emperor. The man chiefly responsible for this transformation was, of course, a highly-strung genius with an inordinate appetite and a squeaky voice, called Otto von Bismarck. Bismarck once compared the statesman to a wanderer in a forest who knows the direction of his route but not the precise point at which it will emerge from the woods. He himself showed supreme skill in keeping in sight during his wanderings as many alternative routes as possible and postponing to the latest moment a choice between them. Indeed he often managed to travel by several at once and contrive for them to converge at the same point. Men and ideas alike he regarded more as tools than as ends in themselves and while this goes far to explain his success in solving the problems which faced him, it also helps to explain why he left for those who came after him other problems more intractable still. He understood intimately the dynastic system in which he had grown up, but the new order of society which emerged during his lifetime filled him with foreboding rather than sympathy.

Between 1862 and 1870 Bismarck succeeded in defying the Prussian Parliament for four years, relying on the ingenuity of a Jewish banker Bleichröder to provide the money which it refused to grant. But in addition he had the insight to recognise that German unity in one form or another was inevitable and that the question facing Prussia was not therefore 'whether' but 'how'. Bent on avoiding the acceptance of other people's terms, he engineered by a series of improvisations what was in effect the conquest of Germany by Prussia. In the war of 1866, with the help of von Moltke's strategic gifts and the remodelled Prussian army, he overcame Austrian and Hanoverian opposition to North German unity under Prussian leadership and in the war of 1870 overcame that of France to the incorporation of South Germany within that unity. He further kept these two wars from starting a European conflagration. But in addition he led Prussia to a position in which she could no longer refuse to assume the leadership of Germany and in which neither the other princes nor the Liberals could refuse to accept Prussian predominance. Finally, in the 1866 constitution of the North German Confederation, adapted in 1871 to become that of the German Empire, he evolved a compromise which gave all groups enough of what they wanted to be acceptable to most of them.

Yet it is hard to contemplate this epoch-making result without pondering on the turn of chance or fate which provided that, when a man of genius appeared, he did so on the conservative side. If the Liberals had possessed a Bismarck or a Lenin in 1848, how differently the world might have developed! But was the absence of such a man merely due to accidents of heredity or did the history of Germany prior to 1862 make it impossible for realists to be liberal?

2 THE SECOND REICH, 1871-1918

Internal Affairs under Bismarck

In January 1871 the victorious King William of Prussia was proclaimed 'German Emperor' (not 'Emperor of Germany') at Versailles. He thus became the senior rather than the superior of the other German princes. Bismarck indeed maintained that the princes were subordinated to the Empire rather than to the Emperor, and in particular to the Federal Council or *Bundesrat*. To this body, which in name was nothing new, each of the twenty-five member governments sent a delegation proportionate to its importance. Though all the votes of each delegation counted, each voted as a block (on the logical if questionable principle that no government can be of two minds). Of the fifty-eight members, seventeen came from Prussia (which after her victories comprised in area and population about five-eighths of the Federation and completely surrounded twelve of the smaller states), six from Bavaria and four each from Saxony and Württemberg. As no proposal to change the constitution could go forward if fourteen votes were cast against it, Prussia and the South German states acting together were thus in effect given a guarantee against any reforms of which they disapproved. The agreement of the Bundesrat was required before legislation could be submitted to the Imperial Assembly or *Reichstag* (the name habitually used in the First Reich for the body described in English as the 'Imperial Diet') and the Bundesrat was to be consulted on all important questions including declarations of war.

The intention would seem to have been for the Bundesrat to become a sort of Cabinet. But it proved too cumbrous for that purpose and steadily lost influence. Instead power passed progressively into the hands of its chairman the Imperial Chancellor who was almost always Minister-President of Prussia and, as such, head of the Prussian delegation. There was no Cabinet in the English sense of the word (the Emperor's 'Cabinet' being composed of his private secretaries) and the 'State Secretaries' for Foreign Affairs, the Interior, Finance, Justice, Posts and (later) the Navy were not Ministers like British Secretaries of State but, more as in the United States, officials responsible to the Chancellor. There was no Federal State Secretary for War, the Prussian Minister of War acting as chairman of the Bundesrat committee on the armed forces and appearing in the Reichstag to speak on military matters. This was because the

Prussian Army remained directly responsible to its King, while absorbing
the troops of all the smaller states; the armies of Bavaria and Württemberg retained varying degrees of independence in peacetime. The Prussian
Parliament remained unaltered, including the three-tier voting for the
Landtag (p. 27). Prussian Ministers often doubled their job with that of
the corresponding Federal State Secretary, the Chancellor always being
Prussia's Foreign Minister (since her foreign policy mostly consisted of
her relations with the other states in the Empire).

To this complex and conservative structure, however, Bismarck added
a Reichstag elected by secret universal (male) suffrage, as the Frankfurt
Assembly of 1848 had proposed. This was something which in 1871
few other states in Europe possessed and its radicalism alarmed the
Conservatives. But in practice the Reichstag went far to justify its description by a Socialist as 'the fig-leaf of absolutism'. Apart from the
fact that throughout virtually the whole of its existence it provided a
majority ready to vote for the existing regime, its powers had three
flaws. It could not initiate legislation, it did not appoint the Chancellor
and it was soon compelled to curtail drastically its say about defence
expenditure. Membership was by law incompatible with membership
of the Bundesrat and therefore in practice with the active holding of
official posts, although civil servants could and frequently did stand for
election as Deputies, being given leave of absence while they sat. (It
went without saying that they had to belong to a party supporting
the Government. Once when a nobleman who was a National Liberal
Deputy and aide-de-camp to the Kaiser voted with the Progressives, he
was deprived of the right to wear uniform.)

The Reichstag reflected public opinion and could stop government
proposals, including taxation, from becoming law. But it could not
enforce its own wishes. The parties were allowed to criticise but given
no chance of putting alternative policies into action; they therefore
tended to degenerate into irresponsible pressure groups more prone to
split up than to coalesce. Deputies were unpaid and seldom promoted
so that there was no great attraction in a parliamentary career.

According to the constitution, the Emperor appointed the Chancellor
and the other Federal officials. Their tenure of office depended, not on
the confidence of a majority in the Reichstag but on the will — one might
almost say the whim — of the monarch. What the constitution failed to
lay down with clarity was where the powers of the Emperor ended and
those of the Chancellor began. It is true there was a clause requiring the
Chancellor to countersign and take responsibility for all imperial decrees
and orders. But if a Chancellor had ever shown reluctance to perform

this function, all the Emperor had to do was to replace him with some-one more compliant — there was never any lack of candidates! In theory the Reichstag could have forced on the Emperor a Chancellor of its own choice by refusing to vote for the measures of any holder of the post who did not follow the policies it favoured. But not only had the Prussian Landtag come off worst when it tried to do this in 1863. Most deputies would have recoiled in horror from the very idea. To decide who should run the country was no more part of a politician's business than it had been in the England of 1760. As a result the country was largely run by a virtually uncontrolled bureaucracy.

This bureaucracy was older than the legislature and correspondingly disdainful of it. But bureaucrats have a different approach to problems than politicians and Germany later suffered from having administrative rather than political judgment brought to bear on the formulation of policy. This weakness was aggravated during the 1880s by the gradual elimination of liberally-minded officials from the Prussian service (from which Reich officials were largely recruited) which meant that the people running the country, although diligent, honest and methodical, were often out of sympathy with the ordinary citizens.

Dependence on the Emperor was by no means the only problem facing the man who combined the posts of Imperial Chancellor and Prussian Minister-President. He had to work at the same time with two parliamentary bodies, each chosen on a different basis. How could he hope to do this if the balance of parties in the Reichstag began to differ markedly from that in the Landtag? Moreover, although the Chancellor was largely concerned with foreign policy (since much internal policy remained the preserve of the individual states), he had no right of con-trol over the armed forces which reported direct to the Emperor as King of Prussia. Bismarck, whose policy from 1863 to 1866 had alone enabled this situation to persist, defended it on the ground that, if the Chancellor were allowed a hand in military matters, it might be hard to prevent the Reichstag interfering in spheres vital to national security. Yet if the Chancellor was denied the powers needed to keep military and political policies in line, the only constitutional possibility of recon-ciling them rested with the Emperor. Bismarck was usually able to get William I to do as he wished, but in 1871 William was already 74.

Such then was the form of the Federation into which most people speaking German had been collected, though there were many left out-side, in Switzerland, in Austria and in isolated groups throughout eastern Europe. Bismarck had squared the constitutional circle by a formula which did not admit of easy revision, but the inhabitants of the new

Empire were still far from being an integrated community. Conservatives looked suspiciously at Liberals, aristocrats at the bourgeoisie, industrialists at workers, soldiers at civilians, Protestants at Catholics, north at south, Christians at Jews. In the past, centrifugal forces had often proved too strong. Could they now be held in check? Could the political system be adapted to the consequences of the industrial and social growth which was just beginning to get under way?

A challenge arose almost immediately. The doctrine of Papal infallibility, formulated by the Vatican Council in 1870, was not only a slap in the face to liberal opinion but raised the whole question of the relation of the Catholic Church to the state. In the controversy which followed, laws were passed giving the Imperial and Prussian Governments powers over education and the appointment of bishops, establishing civil marriage and expelling Jesuits and other non-German priests and nuns. Bismarck saw in the Catholics, who composed a third of the population and founded the Centre Party to look after their interests in the Reichstag, the allies of all his enemies – the South Germans and Hanoverians who had opposed Prussian leadership and now wanted to limit the Federal Government's powers, the Austrian Conservatives who resented a German Empire from which they were excluded, the French right wing who longed to avenge the 1870 defeat and the Poles who threatened Prussian security in the eastern provinces. The legislation was thus a logical continuation of the campaign for a unified Germany; the idea of fighting clerical obscurantism was backed with enthusiasm by the Liberals who called it 'the cultural struggle' (*Kulturkampf*).

Before long, however, Bismarck found that the course which his subordinates supported on grounds of principle raised almost as many political problems as he had expected it to solve and by the end of the 1870s he had had enough of it. The accession of a new Pope led to negotiations which in 1887 finally produced an amicable settlement. The state established its right to supervise education and have a say in the appointment of bishops. The Church went a long way to germanise its clergy. The Centre Party, afraid of the attack being renewed, took care to give no grounds for a charge of disloyalty. Bismarck had thus succeeded in neutralising a possible source of disintegration.

One of his motives for relaxing the Kulturkampf was his view that the gravest threat to the state in future was likely to be social rather than religious. In 1875 the two working-class parties founded by Marx and Lassalle had sunk their differences to form the Social Democratic Workers Party of Germany (SPD). In the 1877 Reichstag Election the votes it obtained rose from 350,000 to 500,000. Continued progress at such a rate would mean serious difficulties. In 1878 Bismarck, taking advantage of two attempts on the Emperor's life, introduced a law to impede Socialist activity without going so far as to ban the Party outright. He did not confine himself to repression. In a series of measures between 1883 and 1889 he inaugurated, for the first time in history, an imaginative system of social insurance and labour arbitration designed to reconcile the workers to their conditions.

Events were to show that few people were in fact more orderly and public-spirited than the average German worker, but their leaders continued for a long time to talk in terms of revolution. Bebel had in 1871 pointed to the Paris Commune as a weak prelude to what would happen before long in Germany. The most intense venom was reserved for anyone who challenged the view that revolution was both necessary and bound to come. Indeed the attitude of the ruling class made it hard to see how the workers could get what they wanted without revolution and it was in fact only after a revolution of sorts that their main demands were met. The owners of property can hardly be blamed for taking the threat of revolt seriously. Germany's lack of any tradition of religious radicalism (p. 16) meant that socialism, as generally on the continent, was materialistic, opposed to religion as the 'opium of the masses'. In the eyes of all respectable citizens, this combination put the Social Democratic Party beyond the pale. Nobody belonging to it could be regarded as loyal; its participation in the conduct of public affairs was unthinkable, it was *regierungsunfähig*. The Party in return organised for its members a self-contained world with its own publications, clubs, banks and shops.

The years immediately after the Franco-Prussian War saw a boom in the German economy but in 1873 this overreached itself and was followed by a period in which growth, though still rapid by pre-industrial standards, was slow enough to arouse widespread concern. Moreover the end of the 1870s saw the arrival in Europe of cheap wheat from the American prairies, thanks to investment in communications and the introduction of iron ships. The landowners of the East-Elbian plains were faced not merely with competition at home but with the loss of the exports which had made the lands round the Baltic into the granary of Europe. Free trade therefore ceased to be to their advantage and their political and social position made it hard to disregard their clamour for protection, whereas their counterparts in Britain had no prospect of prevailing against the middle-class free-traders. Heavy industry (though not commerce) was also anxious to be shielded against competition while in the process of establishing itself. A tariff also suited Bismarck, since he needed money for various projects and the constitution only empowered the Federal Government to raise money by indirect taxation. This led him to a change of policy which has been described as 'the second founding of the Empire'. Whereas his solutions to his problems had hitherto, in accordance with his forecast of 1862, been based on blood and iron, he decided to maintain that settlement by basing it on corn and iron. The alliance between large-scale agriculture and heavy industry was to be the essential foundation of the political system over the next fifty years. Until 1879 it was possible that Germany might make a peaceful transition to modern industrial capitalism; after 1879 that was much less likely.

Bismarck's reorientation split the Liberal Party along the lines of social division which had been visible in 1848 (p. 25). The Progressive left wing refused to vote for the tariff laws and anti-socialist legislation. They continued to demand a constitutional reform which would make the executive responsible to the legislature. Bismarck's need to compensate for the loss of their votes helps to explain his conciliation of the Centre. But unity rather than liberty had been the priority of many among the more prosperous Liberals. When Bismarck demonstrated that it could be achieved without responsible government, they indulged in an uncritical admiration of him and stopped pressing for further reform. The process was justified ideologically by the argument that individual personal liberty and local self-government mattered more than parliamentary and ministerial arrangements. The introduction of laws to secure the former between 1872 and 1883 was claimed to have given Germany her own form of Liberalism; the authoritarian state (*Obrigkeitsstaat*) had been replaced by the state in which law reigned supreme (*Rechtsstaat*), assigning to each citizen his obligations and rights. Various measures relating to currency and commerce helped to adapt the administrative machine to the essential needs of an industrial society. Thus modernisation was imposed in Germany from above instead of being extorted by popular pressure from below.

Bismarck might therefore seem to have achieved considerable success in consolidating German society. By the time of his dismissal his Empire had not only proved able to survive for two decades but Conservatives, Catholics and most Liberals had come to accept it. Moreover the future was to reveal a surprising amount of readiness on the part of the rest of the population to do the same. Dissatisfaction, however, showed itself in two directions.

On the one hand a number of the ruling class succumbed to dreams of aggrandisement and talked of the need for Germany, having established herself as a European Power, to claim her rightful place as a world leader. Like other social groups which gain power by a gradual process rather than a sudden revolution, the German middle classes, on reaching maturity, tended to assimilate themselves to the standards which they found dominant instead of evolving their own. This process was powerfully fostered by many of the institutions of society, notably the student corps in the universities and the much-prized grade of reserve-officer to which the steadily growing appetite of the army for manpower made the admission of well-to-do bourgeois essential. The Prussian General Staff were pioneers in applying to war and the preparations for it the systematic rationalising which underlay the Industrial Revolution, but they failed to apply the same yardstick to their own social and political ideas. The moment when Prussia's efforts had been crowned with success might have been appropriate for relaxing her traditional emphasis upon the martial virtues. Instead these were taken over, often by people from other parts of Germany, and exaggerated to the point of distortion. Compassion became taboo; charity and tolerance were too easily condemned along with it. Violence was exalted and little appreciation shown for its effects on other people. Courage turned into contempt for modesty and common sense, self-reliance into disdain for all who did not belong to the warrior caste, discipline into a demand for unquestioning obedience and patriotism into a lust for domination. The law that material resources are useless without the will to use them became a faith that all things were possible to the obstinate. Such a distortion was not merely to prove a menace to Germany's neighbours; it was also seriously to mislead its practitioners about the realities of the world.

Unfortunately that was not all. For besides the people to whom the Empire had brought success and power, there were others to whom it — or strictly speaking the economic and social changes accompanying it — spelt failure and the need to change. Whereas in the pioneer industrial countries, the innovations stretched over several generations, reducing the risk that individuals with particular skills would find themselves obsolete in mid-career, the faster pace which Germany as an imitator was able to achieve proved a mixed blessing. While it certainly accelerated her rise to Great Power status, it did so at the cost of multiplying internal tensions. A number of people found the world turning against them and, instead of adapting to that turn, preferred to decide that it was wrong. Among them were some who had got through a university education only to find themselves unable to gain the status of a professorial chair. The school-teaching to which they were instead reduced gave them chips on their shoulders and a disposition to prove their ability by abstract theorising. They lacked the alertness of mind needed to criticise the views which their intellectual training equipped them to absorb, and much high-flown nonsense was the result.

The criticisms of such people fastened not simply on the materialism of a world growing rapidly more affluent but on the creeds which had brought this about. They denied the claims of reason, intellect and the critical spirit, preferring instead intuition, imagination, 'history' and faith. They rejected the view that the individual had a right to equal treatment or to freedom, preferring that an idealised élite should have the right to give orders which it was the duty of patriots to obey. In short, they wanted their country to break with Western Europe and return to what they regarded as her distinctive national traditions.

The concessions made to Liberalism and democracy in the 1871 settlement disgusted them. The party system in particular was in their eyes designed to create discord rather than the harmony for which they longed. For they believed that harmony alone would make their country strong enough to take that place in the world struggle for power which the misfortunes of her history had denied to her. But since this harmony was to be a harmony on their own conditions, they rejected the idea of achieving it by discussion and compromise, preferring instead the short cuts of emotion and autocracy. Thus there developed the idea of a national community or *Volk* cemented by a common spirit because it was dominated by attitudes which grew naturally like plants out of their historical background and physical surroundings. Where elements of the Volk refused to fall into line or where other *Völker* got in the way, superficial recollections of Darwin or Nietzsche were invoked to justify an appeal to force. But the general view was that a pure Volk would be a unanimous Volk so that disunity was evidence of an impurity needing to be eradicated. It was in this context that anti-Semitism became important.

The European Jews, having for long been forbidden to own land or ply a craft, had gravitated to towns. Their tendency towards intellectualism fitted them for finance, trade, journalism and the learned professions (particularly law), the very skills which were in demand in an industrialising society. As a result they gained a social position out of all proportion to their numbers; it was reckoned in the 1880s that, while they made up only 1 per cent of the total population of Germany, they amounted to 5 per cent in Berlin where 25 per cent of the grammar-school places were filled by their children. They inclined to the left in politics, partly because it was people on the left who had advocated their emancipation. The net result was that they quickly came to symbolise to those who disliked liberal, rational, industrial society all the things which were dislikable about it -- especially as unsuccessful people are often in debt and creditors are not infrequently Jewish.

Though the peddlers of these sorts of notions were active enough in the Second Reich, its success and respectability deprived them of serious political influence. Moreover, although their views on several aspects of social policy were to diverge from those of the ruling classes, they saw eye-to-eye on the question of extending Germany's authority abroad, a fact which must have enhanced the attractions of that theme in the rulers' eyes. All the same, their existence hung an extra question mark over the future, especially as many of them earned their living in ways which gave them a hold on youth. Indeed, Germany diverged from much of the rest of Europe in that her middle-class youth, though eager for change, was often looking right rather than left. This was not true of the workers, who were inoculated against Volkism by Marxism — which made all the more remote the prospect of evolving a society into which both groups could fit.

Bismarck's Foreign Policy

In 1871 Bismarck imposed on the defeated France a heavy indemnity and annexed Alsace and Lorraine. Nobody thought of asking the inhabitants of those two provinces whether they wanted to become Germans but then nobody had asked them in 1648 whether they wanted to become French and most Alsatians, as well as some Lorrainers, still spoke a German dialect. Bismarck later claimed that it had been his constant endeavour to induce the French to forget their defeat in 1871 as they had forgotten that of 1815 but later kindness could not heal the initial wound; the French leader Gambetta advised his fellow-countrymen to 'think of it always, speak of it never'. Consequently the first aim of German policy needed to be the isolation of France.

This task was complicated by a rather less obvious result of Germany's victories. The successful creation of a new national state gave great encouragement to the other national groups in Eastern Europe which still had no states of their own or (like Serbia and Rumania) had numerous members living outside the frontiers of the national state. Many of these lived in the Habsburg Empire, so that any widespread demand for self-government on a national basis was likely in the long run to prove incompatible with the effective functioning and indeed with the very existence of that venerable organisation. In 1867 the Magyars had secured self-government for themselves in Hungary, though they amounted to less than half of its population; the Empire, in consequence, became known as 'Austria-Hungary'. The question was how long they and the Germans in Austria could keep the upper hand over the Czechs, Poles, Serbs, Croats, Rumanians, Italians and others who made up the rest of Emperor Francis Joseph's multifarious subjects. Moreover the first four of these groups were, as Slavs, susceptible to Russian influence, while Austria-Hungary and Russia had conflicting ambitions in the Balkans. For Germany to choose sides in an Austro-Russian quarrel would incite the country which she did not choose to ally itself with France. Yet if the quarrel developed into war, Germany would have to prevent the weaker side, which was clearly Austria-Hungary, from being beaten, since defeat would probably lead to its break-up and Germany might then be left without any significant ally in the event of a victorious Russia coalescing with France against her.

When in 1875-8 a rising in the Balkan provinces of Turkey almost led to an Austro-Russian war, Bismarck did his utmost to remain the 'honest broker' between the two and in 1878 succeeded in getting a compromise accepted at the Congress of Berlin. But the Tsar's Government resented his impartiality and made what he considered to be threats as to what it might do if on another occasion he were not more co-operative. His reaction was to negotiate a treaty by which Germany and Austria-Hungary promised one another mutual aid if either was attacked by Russia; the existence of the Treaty was known though its exact terms were secret. He then set to work to 'repair the telegraph line to St Petersburg' i.e. to give Russia enough assurance about his sympathy for her other aims as to stop her from seeking French help, a task made all the easier by the ideological gulf between the Tsarist autocracy and the Third Republic. In 1881 he persuaded the Russians to join with Germany and Austria in the 'Three Emperors League' in which each country promised to remain neutral if any were attacked by a fourth.

The League lasted till 1887 when its further renewal was made impossible by a fresh Austro-Russian clash over Bulgaria. To complicate matters, France was in a state of nationalist excitement which at one point seemed capable of leading to war with Germany. Thereupon Bismarck secretly concluded the 'Reinsurance Treaty' (*Rückversicherungsvertrag*, meaning literally Treaty providing security for one's back). This Russo-German agreement provided for the two countries to remain neutral if either was involved in a war with a third, except for an Austro-Russian war begun by Russia or a Franco-German war begun by

Germany. It was thus made clear to the Russians that they could not afford to attack Austria since, if they did, they would find Germany too against them. On the other hand Germany would give no help to an attack on Russia by Austria, which would be suicide without such help. In return Bismarck got a promise that Russia would not join in a French attack on Germany, so that the entire German army could be concentrated in the west; France would hardly dare to move single-handed. There remained the danger that, if Russian actions in the Balkans drove the Austrians into war, Germany might feel compelled to rescue Austria from defeat by joining in, despite the promise of neutrality in the Reinsurance Treaty. But, as a safeguard against this contingency, Bismarck had induced Italy and Britain to give undertakings which meant that any Russian move southwards was likely to be opposed by these two countries as well as Austria; Germany might therefore hope to escape being drawn in. As Bismarck considered Germany to be a 'satisfied Power', his ideal was a situation in which all the other Powers except France would need her and be deprived of the inclination to form coalitions against her by their relations with one another. The British Prime Minister Lord Salisbury called this 'employing one's neighbours to pull out each other's teeth'.

By the time the Reinsurance Treaty came up for renewal in 1890, the German scene had changed fundamentally. For in 1888 the old Emperor William I died at the age of 90. His son Frederick III had often crossed swords with Bismarck, was much under the influence of his wife, Queen Victoria's eldest daughter, and sympathised with liberal ideas. But in 1887 he developed cancer and only reigned for 90 days.

Frederick's son, the Kaiser William II, was not quite 30 when he thus unexpectedly came to the throne. He had been born with a damaged left arm which did not prevent him from making himself a good shot and horseman but put him under constant strain. For the Prussian ideal took much living up to, and a particularly high performance was expected of the ruler. The effort to prevent his disabilities from standing in his way led William to adopt a hearty toughness or an exaggerated idea of importance which was out of keeping with his real character. Thus he was himself prone to that fault of overemphasising the Prussian virtues which has already been mentioned. But to complicate matters, he had held out in front of him in the nursery not only the pattern of the Prussian Junker but also that of the Liberal English gentleman. He reacted, like any young man of spirit, against the attempts of his determined and domineering mother to impose her standards on him, yet to his dying day they exercised a fascination which he could never for long resist.

The desire to be the Englishman, and to win applause from the British, was alternating all the time with the desire to be the Prussian and to win applause from the Germans. The tension between the two, superimposed on his physical defect and on the tensions inherent in German society, is the ultimate key to his character, which was taut, restless and impetuous, lacking the stability brought by integration. From his mother he also inherited a strong constitution, a quick enquiring mind, a keen intelligence often at odds with his emotions, a preoccupation with himself which left him insensible to the views of others, and an inability to judge character. The creation of a new nation state of 50 million people in the centre of Europe had caused a fundamental shift in the balance of power and what Germany needed was a balanced and cautious ruler who would hold his people back from adventures and check their inclination to overestimate their power. They could scarcely have got anyone worse qualified for such a task.

Characters such as William and Bismarck were bound to collide and the constitution of the Chancellor's own devising had given the last word to the Emperor. The decisive clash of personality and method came in the spring of 1890 and found expression in no less than six issues at the same time. The most prominent of these was how to handle the Socialists who, in elections to the Reichstag, had succeeded in winning more votes than any other party (though, owing to the out-of-date way in which constituencies were divided, they did not get a proportionate number of seats). The Kaiser was anxious to gain popularity by propitiating them; Bismarck was contemptuous of people whom he described as 'dizzy with humanitarianism' and wanted to stiffen his earlier legislation. He was ready, if necessary, to defy the Reichstag over this, reckoning that the resulting crisis would make him indispensable to the Kaiser. One thing led to another and Bismarck was driven to offer his resignation. He was 75 and on the various questions at issue, William was as often right as wrong. Indeed posterity might have regarded the removal of the elder statesman as justified if the policies which he had refused to adopt had been consistently followed by his successors. As things were, it probably only antedated nature by a year or two.

Questions of foreign policy hardly figured in the clash. But in the ensuing confusion and before a new State Secretary for Foreign Affairs had been appointed, the decision not to renew the Reinsurance Treaty was taken, rather to the Kaiser's regret. The new men in charge did not properly understand what Bismarck had been aiming at and felt that the intricacies of his policy were beyond them. There was considerable, if superficial, attraction in the argument that Germany needed henceforward to conduct a 'peaceful, clear and loyal' course which would not create the impression of leaving her formal allies in the lurch. Yet within seventeen months of the non-renewal, France and Russia signed a Treaty pledging one another to act together in the event of a threat to peace. The very thing which Bismarck had been most anxious to prevent was thus allowed to come to pass.

Germany Becomes an Industrial Leader

One of the chief purposes of the first chapter was to explain why Germany was late in starting to industrialise. Her development was further delayed by the Napoleonic Wars and by the continuing lack of unity. It was not until the mid-1860s that German output (in terms of real product per person per year) reached the level which Britain had achieved in the 1830s. Britain had for example vastly improved her roads in the late eighteenth century and her industrial development could get under way before she built her railway system. In Germany little was done to the roads before 1815 and railway-building went hand-in-hand with the growth of productive capacity. By 1870 only a third of the railways had been built, compared with two-thirds in Britain. At the same date, 60 per cent of the population of England and Wales lived in towns, whereas the German figure was only 36 per cent. But German growth, once it began, was all the more rapid and it was naturally stimulated by unification. Germany's production of manufactures grew at an average rate of 4.2 per cent per annum from 1883 to 1913; the British rate was only half that.[3] Britain continued to be the richer of the two countries and the one with a bigger national product both absolutely and still more per individual (since the German population was a third higher); but Germany was catching up fast.

When Germany made herself felt on the world's economic stage, the second phase of industrialisation was beginning. In the first, the key industries had been textiles, coal-mining, iron-founding, railways and shipbuilding, and most of the vital inventions had been British (largely because demand for British products grew so fast that manufacture by traditional methods could not keep pace with it). But in the second phase, where the key industries were steel, chemicals, electricity, optical goods and the internal combustion engine, many of the inventions were German, as the names Daimler, Benz, Diesel, Zeiss and Siemens testify; of the relatively few British innovations, the Gilchrist-Thomas and Bessemer processes for steel-making and Perkins' discovery of aniline dyes were mainly developed in Germany.

The explanation of the contrast is complex and still partly in dispute. British manufacturers would seem to have lost something of their old enterprise. Large sums had been laid out on installing plant for the established industries; switching to new ones, or even to new methods of production for the old, was expensive and threatened loss to both owners and workers, at any rate in the short term. The younger generations, who had come up the easy rather than the hard way, may have had less propensity to save and been less willing to incur discomfort. Thanks to Britain's overseas connections and possessions, her industry could still sell its traditional goods, even if the markets were changing from relatively developed to undeveloped countries; British exports doubled between 1880 and 1913, which distracted attention from the fact that German exports more than trebled and that, whereas the British share of world markets for manufactures fell from 38 to 27 per cent, the German share rose from 17 to 22 per cent.

Many of Britain's best brains were not in industry but in politics and administration, both at home and throughout the Empire; education was designed to produce proconsuls rather than technicians (though Victorian interest in science should not be underestimated). Germany not only lacked an empire to staff but many of the more attractive posts in home administration were closed to commoners, Catholics and Jews. Moreover Britain's output of trained manpower was inadequate. In 1863 Prussia alone had over 66,000 pupils receiving secondary education whereas in Britain the comparable figure was 16,000. Germany had 13,500 students at universities, Britain 3,500. Below the top level Germany had a sound system of technical education, Britain virtually none; this defect was all the more serious because the new industries, unlike the old, called for scientific knowledge rather than practical ingenuity.

One result of Britain's managerial inertia was that investment in productive equipment was notably small. Whereas between 1870 and 1913 Britain was devoting some 11 per cent of her gross national product on average to investment, for Germany the figure rose from 13.5 to 16 per cent. Even more striking is the discrepancy in the ways in which the money was laid out. 39 per cent of the British total went abroad (if fluctuations are evened out) whereas the German proportion was only 11 per cent; in the period 1905-14 the figures were 53 per cent against 5.7 per cent! Part of the explanation was that the British financial system (and notably the Stock Exchange) was primarily designed to channel individual savings into government stocks and railways, and into mines and plantations overseas rather than into home industry. The banking system was well adapted to providing industry with short-term funds but did little to provide long-term capital, which manufacturers mainly found from their own profits or those of their friends. German banks by contrast not only acted as the main depositaries for individual savings but regarded it as their job to provide industry with capital by lending out those savings in long-term loans; they took an active interest in the policies of the companies which they favoured, were represented on the boards and preferred ventures close at hand on which they could keep an eye. Continued credit depended on satisfactory performance. The attractiveness of foreign lending was further reduced by the fact that German domestic rates of interest seem to have been nearly twice as high as the British. Britain was bringing down her costs by providing the 'infrastructure' for obtaining foodstuffs and raw materials from places where they could be produced most cheaply rather than by improving the efficiency of her production methods. By contrast the Germans, who still had most of their productive equipment to install, concentrated on providing the most up-to-date. As a result of the British policy, world prices of primary materials fell steadily between 1880 and 1896 (causing some people to worry about a 'Great Depression'), while real wages rose. Yet even though Germany prevented her workers from enjoying the full benefits of this development by keeping out cheap wheat, her industrial wages rose faster than the British.

Inertia and lack of investment are not however final answers. Even if the people in charge of Britain's traditional industries had lost drive, new men, whether native-born or immigrants, could always have started up, yet examples are relatively few. Shortage of manpower was neither a constraint on expansion nor a spur to innovation, since there was far more unemployment in Britain than in Germany, while emigration continued right up to 1914, whereas in Germany it tailed off after 1890. The failure to invest at home was not due to lack of available funds. Investment, and particularly investment in new directions, was insufficiently attractive because it was insufficiently profitable. Britain's costs were clearly too high and her productivity was growing too slowly by comparison with the US and Germany. One reason was the fear of workers that the only result of greater exertion or improved methods of production would be increased unemployment. Because enough capital was not being made available to provide new investment and thus absorb the workers who would be displaced by improved productivity, there was no incentive to labour to co-operate in securing this.

In the short-term Britain's course may well have made sense. Innovating is apt to be risky and expensive. British manufacturers probably made bigger profits by selling traditional goods in new markets (primarily in undeveloped countries) than they would have done by developing new products to sell in industrialised countries. By investing so much abroad, they not only reduced their costs but enabled the primary producers overseas to buy British manufactures and, by earning dividends, reduced Britain's need for visible exports to pay for her primary imports. The weakness of the course was that it aggravated rather than answered the long-term problem. How was Britain, with a population too big to be fed from home farms, to pay for her essential imports once the countries supplying them had started to make their own shirts and kettles and no longer needed steam engines or coal?

Britain has been said to have acquired her Empire 'in a fit of absence of mind', as the result of manifold situations and influences and of innumerable individual decisions rather than of any deliberate plan. This lack of collective effort was reflected in her easy-going institutions and mode of life. Germany by contrast was seeking more articulately to catch up with pioneers who had already established their position. To have any hope of success, she had to make the most of her resources. She applied herself to the task with characteristic vigour, method and attention to detail. Much has been said of the willingness of her salesmen to learn local languages. What is forgotten is that the numerous expatriate Englishmen scattered round the globe provided plenty of agents and interpreters for home-based salesmen.

In their anxiety to find foreign markets for their rising output, the Germans showed some interest in colonies in the somewhat ingenuous belief that, since countries with colonies were wealthy, colonies must bring wealth. In 1884-5 Bismarck's Government, for a variety of reasons in which internal politics predominated, did acquire colonies in Africa and the Pacific four times as large as the home country, only to find them expensive and unrewarding. Indeed, if they had been more attractive, other countries would no doubt have acquired them earlier. The disappointment fostered resentment that the parcelling out of the more valuable parts of the overseas world should have been carried out while German attention was still absorbed at home. Undeniably, for reasons already described, Britain's overseas possessions were of great benefit to her. But the pride which she expressed in them prevented both other countries and herself from appreciating the reverse side of the picture. The development of the Empire absorbed a considerable proportion of limited resources and gave a distinctive pattern to her economy. Whether that precise pattern turned out to be to her advantage in the long run is open to argument. But there would have been little advantage to Germany in acquiring colonies (assuming that there had been plenty to be had) unless she had been prepared also to go some way along the British road and accept the repercussions on the rest of her economy. As it was, her banks and merchants saw little prospect of profits in such colonies as she did acquire and only invested in them out of deference to government pressure. Even in the home market German industrialists preferred regulation to competition; cartels and other agreements to fix prices and share out orders were widespread. Entry into many occupations and trades was strictly regulated. Not only were the railways and most of the gas and electricity companies publicly owned but a certain number of coal-mines and iron-works as well. Thus the balance of social forces in Germany and the tendency towards a managed society meant that the allocation of her economic resources was more the result of deliberate planning than was the case in Britain.

In the end, of course, talk about nations making choices is unhistorical; they take the openings presented to them and seldom have the collective insight to consider whether a better 'mix' may be available. Moreover, if Germany had done less to build up her industrial strength at home, she could not have remained a major military power. As it was, industrialisation made her dependent on certain products from overseas and the failure of her political leaders to keep Britain out of the enemy camp meant that in the end this weakness was fatal.

Internal Affairs under the Kaiser

The major internal problem between 1890 and 1918 was the struggle as to how far the German political system should be adapted to the industrial developments just described. The pace of social change accelerated and increasing numbers of people acquired an occupational status and a real income in advance of that enjoyed by their parents. They looked for this to be reflected in a greater say about the running of the country and until this was accorded to them, inclined to support the parties of the left. The seats won by the Social Democrats in particular rose from 35 in 1890 to 81 in 1903 and 110 in 1912.

But though the Socialist threat to the established order might seem to be increasing, other forces were operating in the reverse direction. German workers had always inclined to the petit bourgeois virtues of industry, frugality, loyalty to the community and moral restraint, which do not as a rule turn men into revolutionaries. The German educational system made it hard for working-class children to pass through the grammar-schools (*Gymnasien*) to the universities but it did help them to acquire technical skills and thus rise up the social ladder, while improved living standards had a similar effect. The various measures of social insurance introduced by Bismarck and extended after his fall were beginning to have a delayed action in reconciling workers to the established order. The leaders of the Social Democrats and still more the functionaries of the trade unions, enjoying a regular salary, had little incentive to put it at risk. They were not only reluctant on general grounds to do anything which might provoke renewed repression but also reluctant to risk the confiscation of the considerable funds which had been built up out of subscriptions. It was from their ranks that Deputies were chosen to represent the Party not only in the Reichstag but still more in the State Parliaments and municipalities (where in some cases there was a Social Democrat majority); the practical experience so gained was as usual a brake on radicalism. Given encouragement from the Government, the success and prosperity achieved by the Second Reich might have induced the workers to follow the example of the Liberals and Centre by becoming integrated into the existing structure of society.

Government encouragement was not, however, forthcoming. Bismarck's successors at first tried to pursue a moderate course in the hope of securing the widest possible support for the regime. But the policy was blocked by the hostility of the right without achieving enough to reconcile the left and in 1897 it was abandoned in favour of one which sought to rally all those who wanted to keep things as they were. The alliance between corn and iron was given a fresh lease of life. The benevolent intentions towards the workers which the Kaiser had professed in dismissing Bismarck were soon dissipated by the reactionary influence of the court and he took openly to describing Socialists by such abusive terms as 'scoundrels without a Fatherland'. To say who ran the country is hard. The Kaiser certainly established his right to have his way if he wanted but his interventions in policy-making were too slapdash, spasmodic and inconsistent to amount to a programme. His officials could not openly disobey him but had to spend much of their time persuading him to allow them their way or dissuading him from insisting on his own. Compliant though the Reichstag was, a regular majority could no longer be found for a policy of unqualified reaction and during the 1890s there was much talk of a *coup d'état* to abolish universal suffrage. But neither the ruler nor his more responsible advisers ever mustered up the courage to embark on such a course and the reactionaries gradually became inured to living with something which they could not alter. But this made them all the more insistent on maintaining the 1870 distribution of constituencies for the Reichstag (which favoured country districts), the three-tier Prussian suffrage, the open voting which went with it and the tariffs on grain which were its economic counterpart. The Government sought a quiet life by proposing as little legislation as possible.

In face of such immobility, the left wing of the Social Democrats continued to argue that nothing short of a revolution would break down the resistance and give the workers due influence in the state. The right wing called for the Marxist revolutionary programme of the Party to be revised so as to allow for the possibility of securing reform by constitutional means. The leadership, torn between the two extremes, concentrated on holding the Party together; this they succeeded in doing by maintaining the letter of the programme and departing from it in practice whenever occasion arose.

As the Conservatives and National Liberals, from 1898 onwards, made up less than a third of the Reichstag, the Government became increasingly dependent on the Centre. An attempt by Bülow between 1907 and 1909 to rely instead on the Progressives came quickly to grief because the right refused to make the concessions needed for its success and could not be forced to do so because of their economic and social power. But the Catholics in Germany no longer consisted predominantly of landowners and peasants; Catholicism had always been strong in the Rhineland and Silesia, which had become major industrial districts. Both priesthood and political leadership realised the need to give some evidence of social enlightenment if they were to keep a hold on their followers. Various incidents from 1895 onwards foreshadowed the emergence of an alternative coalition between Centre, Progressives and Social Democrats. The Social Democratic gains in the 1912 Election gave this grouping a majority in the Reichstag while a government on this basis took office in Baden. For the time being, the threat to the corn-iron alliance was not activated but a political crisis clearly loomed ahead.

The main justification offered by the ruling classes for their obstinacy was that a parliamentary system was too dangerous a thing to introduce into a country surrounded by enemies, since no single party would be strong enough to have an absolute majority and governments would always be unstable coalitions. Popular demands would also threaten the delicate balance between the Reich and state governments and thus create a risk of civil upheaval. Power must stay in the hands of people whose loyalty was unquestioned, while it was unpatriotic to hold discordant opinions and thereby weaken the nation. Germany's internal policy was considered to be dictated by her external position.

But such a view was only half the story. If the attitude of Germany's neighbours towards her was less than friendly, it was mainly because, as will be explained in the next section, they were alarmed about her intentions towards them. And there is evidence to show that the vigorous foreign policy of the Kaiser's Governments was largely adopted in the hope of distracting attention from tensions at home by appealing to national sentiment and calling for unity against threats from outside. External policy was dictated by internal considerations. This was particularly true of the naval expansion from 1897 onwards, inaugurated by the Kaiser out of vanity and a desire to emulate Britain but also developed because of its popular appeal. Its chief advocate and executant, Admiral von Tirpitz, gave in 1895 as the main justification for Germany becoming a World Power the prospect that 'such a great new national task and the economic benefits which went with it would provide a good antidote to sophisticated and unsophisticated Social Democrats'.[4]

This sacrifice of liberal to national values was of doubtful wisdom. Some of the wilder remarks of Socialist leaders may have seemed to justify it but their practice showed them to be just as loyal and considerably more realistic in their appraisal of Germany's position. For the outlook of the ruling classes fostered an overemphasis on power and a disregard of world opinion which led to Germany's capacities being exaggerated. It was a recipe for disaster to risk war by being uncompromising abroad and at the same time, by being uncompromising at home, to alienate people whose support would be essential if war came. The best way to encourage unity was to trust the workers and show consideration for their views. But the half-hearted efforts in this direction of Bethmann Hollweg, Chancellor from 1909 to 1917, only won him hatred and accusations of weakness from the Prussian Conservatives and such bodies as the Pan-German Union, the Navy League and the Defence Union.

The political deadlock made it impossible to do anything effective towards remedying what one of the Kaiser's subjects described as his 'undergraduate impetuosities', leading too often to 'rhetorical derailments'.[5] A particularly bad example of his 'mouth-shooting' occurred in 1908 when he gave to the London *Daily Telegraph* an interview which could hardly have given more offence abroad as well as at home if that had been its deliberate intention. Even the Conservatives joined in demanding that something should be done to check William's 'personal rule'. But as long as the Chancellor and his subordinates were chosen by the Emperor and depended for their tenure of office on his pleasure, he could not easily be denied a voice in their policy. Yet if they were not to be appointed by him, what other source was there except the Reichstag? But the existing impotence of that body was shown when in 1914 military high-handedness in Alsace led it to pass what was virtually a vote of no confidence in the Chancellor. The Government made no appreciable change in policy and, when the Social Democrats proposed rather belatedly to enforce one by refusing to grant money, the Centre took the view that Germany's external situation made such a course impossible.

The Road to War

The conclusion of the Franco-Russian Alliance in 1891 (p. 41) did not cause the alarm in Berlin which might have been expected, in spite of the extent to which Russia thereafter came to depend on French loans. For at this period the chief enemy of both parties to the Treaty was not Germany but Britain who was finding her far-flung dominions involving her in an uncomfortable variety of disputes. In 1898 her traditional antagonism to France reached a head in the Fashoda crisis when the two countries seemed for a moment on the brink of war over the Sudan. Russia's activities in Central Asia were watched with alarm from Whitehall and Delhi for fear that they would spark off a fresh mutiny in India, while Russian ambitions in the Far East were thought capable of starting a scramble to divide up China. The struggle with the Boers in South Africa united almost the whole of Europe against the British, so that the telegram of congratulation which the Kaiser at the prompting of his advisers sent to President Kruger after the Jameson Raid in January 1896 met with general applause on the continent. By contrast Russia's absorption in Asia distracted her attention from the Balkans and until after her defeat by Japan in 1905 her relations with Austria-Hungary were almost cordial.

This situation lulled those responsible for German policy into thinking that the British, and not themselves, were the people in a tight corner. They doubted whether Britain could come to terms with France and were convinced that, if she did, the result would be a breach between France and Russia. British policy was however coming into the hands of men who, themselves disliking and fearing German behaviour, considered their attitude to be widely shared in Europe. The result was that when, on two or three occasions between 1898 and 1901, the officious zeal of subordinates led each of the two Governments to think that the other was seeking an alliance, neither felt any need for urgency. Each side distrusted the other and each thought that, by waiting, it could secure better terms later. The approaches had more results than appeared on the surface. When they ended, there was not a single British minister left inclined to start any further attempt at drawing the links closer. With few people in responsible positions prepared to argue the case for friendship, popular animosity had free rein and the Press and public on both sides saw to it that any act capable of arousing suspicion did so. An underlying divergence of will was becoming steadily more obvious and neither nation was prepared to make the compromises which would have been the pre-essential to co-operation. Britain was coming to feel instinctively that German expansion, political, economic and naval, challenged the system which she had built up and on which she depended to keep her people employed and fed.

Britain's first step to relieve the pressure on her was to conclude an alliance with Japan in 1902. The Germans welcomed this as likely to embroil her with Russia and probably with France; in fact, it held the ring while the Japanese, more to Britain's surprise than Germany's, beat the Russians in 1904-5 and precipitated a revolution in St Petersburg. Before this result was evident, the British had responded to a French suggestion that the two countries clear up the points of difference between them. In April 1904 this was done in a series of agreements known collectively as the *Entente Cordiale*. At this, some of the German leaders took fright and decided that, while internal unrest made Russia incapable of action, the opportunity must be secured for showing the French how dangerous it could be to disregard Germany. Morocco, where the British had promised the French a free hand in return for a similar one themselves in Egypt, was chosen as the stage for this demonstration and the Kaiser was sent in April 1905 to show the flag at Tangier. But confusion of purpose and loss of nerve at the crucial moment led to the affair being mishandled; at the Conference of Algeciras in the following year the Germans found themselves virtually alone and emerged almost empty-handed. Instead of disrupting the *Entente*, they consolidated it and even precipitated military conversations which had the effect of committing Britain morally, though neither legally nor publicly, to come to France's aid in the event of an attack. The coalition against Germany which had been Bismarck's nightmare was steadily taking shape as a reaction to the policy of his successors.

Instead of learning from their mistakes, the Germans repeated them over Russia. An attempt by the Kaiser in 1905 to talk the Tsar into an alliance by personal diplomacy collapsed as soon as the project was referred to their respective Ministers. This should have shown how deeply Russia was committed to the opposite camp, and the commitments increased two years later when Britain copied her procedure with France and made another series of agreements easing her outstanding disputes with Russia. Then in 1908 the Austro-Hungarian Foreign Minister, with little reference to Berlin, outwitted his Russian opposite number in a deal over the Balkans. When the Russians demanded compensation, the Germans tried to be clever and, in the guise of friendly mediators, forced the Russians into a corner, thereby enabling them to attribute to German intimidation the climb-down which they would have had to make in any case. They did not forget their humiliation or forgive the authors of it, while the British and French realised that, to keep Russia's friendship, they must be prepared to offer some support for her interests in the Balkans. Thus the bonds grew tighter on each side and the stock of international willingness to compromise was depleted.

Throughout these years the British were growing slowly but steadily more perturbed about the character and purpose of the German naval programme. In so far as a navy was desired as more than a badge of Great Power status, its expansion was undoubtedly started in order to have an instrument for putting pressure on Britain. But this concept dated from the turn of the century when Britain had many enemies so that a navy considerably smaller than her own could still constitute an inconvenient threat. By 1907 the international situation, as has been described, had completely changed. Yet all suggestions that the Germans should build fewer ships were met by emotional tirades from the Kaiser and his subordinates about constitutional necessities and the right of nations to behave as they wished. The archives make it clear that the German leaders did not believe Britain had the money or the men to sustain a race indefinitely. They refused to recognise the risks involved in challenging the major naval power at sea at the same time as they prepared to impose their will on their neighbours on land. They not only did much to ensure that, when war came, Britain joined in against them; they also spent vast sums of money (and compelled Britain to spend more) on a fleet which in the event proved to be incapable of use in an effective way.

In 1911 the French decided to tighten their hold on Morocco and their Prime Minister, behind the backs, not only of the British but also of his colleagues, tried to insure against German objections by offering compensating concessions. But the German State Secretary decided that negotiations would go better if he got his claim staked out before the other side had realised their gains. He therefore persuaded the Kaiser and Chancellor to send a gunboat to the port of Agadir. The British were (with some justice) afraid of a deal being done behind their backs which might even start off a Franco-German reconciliation. Lloyd George, the Chancellor of the Exchequer, therefore gave a warning in a speech at the Mansion House which the Germans interpreted as a threat to themselves and the French used as a justification for resisting German demands. After four months of negotiations France emerged with exactly what she wanted in Morocco and Germany with some small but strategically useful bits of land in Central Africa. The German public, which had been led to expect bigger things, were indignant and put most of the blame on the British, who in exchange acquired the almost certainly unfounded conviction that only their Government's firm action had stopped Germany from attacking France. British arrangements for sending an expeditionary force to France in the event of war were made more formal, though a binding commitment to do this was still withheld. The whole episode, which provides an object-lesson in how diplomacy should not be conducted, left all countries involved less ready to be conciliatory in future.

Yet during the next two years a series of upheavals in the Balkans was prevented from leading to a war between Austria-Hungary and Russia, largely because Germany was prepared to hold back the former while Britain did the same to the latter. In Germany however the conviction was growing that, unless the Habsburg Empire was before long enabled to achieve some striking success, it would disintegrate in face of subversion among the subordinate nationalities and in particular the Serbs and Croats, who were receiving aid and encouragement from the independent kingdom of Serbia on the other side of the south-eastern frontier. The Serbs in turn were supported by the Russians who, like the Germans, were encouraging national feeling as an antidote to internal upheaval. Even if an Austrian collapse were not enough of itself to start a general war, Germany could not afford to see the Middle Danube basin pass into hostile hands since she would then be left without allies in an unfriendly world. The Government in Berlin reluctantly came to the conclusion that a war with Russia in support of Austria-Hungary was inevitable sooner or later, while the General Staff estimated that the chances of winning would grow worse the longer it was put off.

The murder of the heir to the Habsburg throne, Archduke Franz Ferdinand, by a Serb in Sarajevo on 28 June 1914 was thought by the

German Government to provide Austria-Hungary with an opportunity such as might never recur for disciplining Serbia with the sympathy of the world behind her. Accordingly when the Vienna Government enquired about the German attitude, it was assured that whatever it did would receive full support. The danger of war spreading was realised but the hope was that for a variety of reasons Russia might not choose the occasion for a fight.

The Germans had, however, assumed that the Austrians would strike quickly while the shock caused by the murder was still vivid. Instead they delayed for nearly a month before delivering an ultimatum so stiff that it was obviously intended to be rejected. The Serbian Government disconcertingly agreed to almost all of it within the time-limit of 48 hours so that, when Austria-Hungary none the less broke off relations, declared war and bombarded Belgrade, the sympathies of the world began to change sides. The British Government pressed Germany to join with them in mediating as they had done in the Balkan War but Bethmann Hollweg showed great reluctance to act on the suggestion, possibly because he wanted to allow the Austrians a chance to secure a clear prestige success. By the time he had changed his mind, Russia had mobilised and it was too late.

For General von Schlieffen, the Chief of the German General Staff some twenty years earlier, in planning how to fight France and Russia simultaneously, had decided that Germany could not withstand a long war against both Powers and, since a quick victory was unlikely to be forthcoming on the vast plains of the east, the most hopeful strategy would therefore be to throw as many divisions as possible against France and try to knock her out within six weeks, leaving the Austrians to hold up the Russians until this had been done. But one of the factors which made this course attractive was that Germany could mobilise her army faster than Russia. This advantage would, however, be lost unless both mobilisations began simultaneously and therefore the German generals could not afford to wait and give mediation a longer chance. The military timetable took over.

Nor was that all. The German plan of attacking first in the west assumed that either France would declare war on Germany or that it would not matter if Germany were openly the aggressor. To complete the predicament, the General Staff had decided that the Franco-German frontier proper was too short and well-defended to make practicable the quick breakthrough which was so essential. Instead a strong right-wing was to make an encircling sweep through Belgium, which was to be invited to give passage to German troops; if she refused (as she did)

she was to be overrun, in defiance of a Treaty which Prussia, in common with other European states, had signed in 1839, guaranteeing her
neutrality. Although three German Chancellors, including Bethmann
Hollweg, had known of this plan, nobody had ever challenged it. The
danger of Britain coming to Belgium's help was realised but discounted
on the ground that, in a war which was only going to last for six weeks,
she would not have time to make herself felt. For Germany had 95
divisions to face about 60 French ones; Britain had six to send.

Under the constitution the Chancellor had no control over the military machine. Responsibility for ensuring that the military and civilian
sides of the Government were co-ordinated rested with the Emperor.
Kaiser William had never realised what the job implied, let alone tried
to tackle it. Moreover, by brusquely rebuffing any attempts by civilians
to show interest in military matters, he had stacked the cards against
their questioning the political implications of the generals' plans. The
damage which Germany did to her cause in the eyes of third parties by
the way she began the war sprang directly from the whole character of
her society.

The attention of the world, and particularly the British, French and
American publics, fastened on the fact that it was in all cases Germany
and Austria-Hungary which had taken the initiative in declaring war
and Germany which had on 2 August broken a promise by making an
unprovoked attack on Belgium. The German public, however, were
encouraged to treat this as a technicality. They were led to believe that
it was Russia, France and Britain which were to blame, having allied together out of jealousy to encircle Germany and frustrate her 'legitimate'
growth. They were told that she was inspired by no lust of conquest
but, for the sake of holding what she had, was seizing her sword with a
clean hand and a clear conscience. From this initial discrepancy of view
much recrimination was to follow.

The War of the Three Gambles

At the end of August it appeared that the first great German gamble
was going to succeed and that the campaign of 1914 would be over as
quickly as those of 1866 and 1870. But Moltke, nephew of the victor
of the earlier wars and now himself German leader, had always been
worried about the problem of controlling effectively the much larger
numbers of men who would be under his command. Early in September
the appearance of a gap between two of his formations on the River

Marne led him to lose his nerve and order what he intended to be a purely tactical and temporary retreat. In fact, however, the war of man-oeuvre was not to be resumed in the west for over four years and the two opposing armies settled down to dig trenches all the way from the sea to the Swiss frontier. A couple of brilliant victories by Hindenburg and Ludendorff over the Russians could not conceal the fact that the war was going to be a long one and therefore one for which Germany was ill-prepared, as well as one in which sea-power mattered.

But at sea also things went wrong. The Germans had assumed that the British fleet would institute a blockade close to the eastern shores of the North Sea and planned to attack it piecemeal in the hope of whittling down its superiority until a general action could be under-taken on terms not too unfavourable. But a month before war began the British had decided to take advantage of the accidents of geography and set up a 'distant' blockade at the Straits of Dover and between Norway and John o' Groats. Instead of having the British fleet as a convenient target at the mouth of the Elbe, the Germans found that they could only get at it by themselves making a risky journey across the North Sea. To make matters worse, the British disregarded an International Agreement which they had never ratified and, instead of applying their blockade only to munitions, extended it to all kinds of foodstuffs and materials. A time could therefore be foreseen when, unless the blockade was somehow broken, the people and cannon of Germany would be starved into submission. The British fleet never succeeded in winning a clear victory — but it did not need to win one, merely to avoid getting beaten.

What were the Germans to do? A compromise peace based on a return to the pre-war situation would have been regarded by the Allies as tantamount to defeat since it would have been an open admission that their ten million fighting men were inadequate to bring down the six million of the Central Powers, nor had they any intention of wind-ing up one war and thereby giving the Germans a chance to prepare for the next. On the other hand, the whole reputation of the German ruling classes was at stake in the war which, but for their attitudes, might never have come about. They could not hope to keep their privileges if they returned empty-handed and weakened by casualties.

Moreover, that overestimate of their own strength which had done so much to involve the Germans in the war continued to delude them while they fought it. The majority of people, even in responsible posi-tions, had little idea of the real situation; the public were never told the truth about the opening battles. The belief was general that the country would gain by her struggle which was to bring her the 'break-through to world power'. The outbreak unbridled many unreflecting tongues and ambitious imaginations which had till then been reined in for fear of frightening Germany's neighbours. Although she was represented as only fighting in self-defence there was widespread agreement that, as a compensation for having to do so once as well as a security against having to do so twice, she was entitled to 'guarantees'. German war-aims varied from time to time in accordance with the strategic position, but until late in 1918, control over most or all of Belgium, France's Longwy-Briey basin with its valuable ores, Poland, the Baltic states, extensive indemnities and colonial concessions were constant themes. Behind these demands loomed the wider dream of bringing under German control the whole of 'Middle Europe' from Antwerp to Odessa. Such greed not only removed any inclination to offer terms which the Allies might have considered but prevented Germany from getting neutral opinion on her side by a show of moderation. Yet for long the only people inside Germany to challenge this megalomania were the despised Social Democrats.

If a compromise peace was thus ruled out, the alternative was to resume the original strategy of securing an overwhelming victory on one front so that all available resources could then be concentrated in the hope of doing the same on the other. To this the first three years of fighting were in effect devoted and, in spite of a certain dispersion of effort being caused by differences of view as to which front offered the best chances of a knock-out blow, success came in 1917 with the collapse of Tsarist Russia. Kerensky's liberal regime which gained power in February of that year was in half a mind to keep on fighting. To get them replaced by more compliant people, the German Government gave the Bolsheviks £250,000 and enabled Lenin to return from exile in Switzerland. But before this opportunity of supping with the devil had presented itself, the effects of the blockade had brought Germany close to desperation while Austria-Hungary was in an even worse condition. Something had to be done to escape from Britain's stranglehold and the only course which offered any prospect of doing this was to starve Britain herself out by indiscriminate submarine warfare. Indeed this could have been tried earlier if Germany had formed her navy with light craft and submarines rather than battleships she dared not use.

But by the time enough U-boats had been built to give them a chance of being effective, it had become clear that, if ships were sunk without first making sure that they belonged to the enemy, a number of the victims would be American and that this would bring America into the war on the Allies' side. A dreadful and much resented choice presented itself between risking the loss of the war by failure to press home a sub-marine blockade of Britain and of making such a blockade effective and thus losing the war as a result of American intervention. An attempt to avoid the choice by getting the Americans to act as mediators failed because the Germans refused to say exactly what terms they would accept. The soldiers and sailors, who underestimated the implications of an American entry and the speed with which this would take effect, claimed that they could force Britain to give in before a single American soldier could land in Europe and early in 1917 they got permission to try their luck. This second gamble met the same fate as the first. Britain, though hard-pressed for a time found means of defence against the sub-marines, the United States declared war in April and their first troops reached France in July.

The same month brought a political upheaval inside Germany. At the start of the war the Social Democrats had given the lie to the accusations of the right by voting unanimously for the war credits. But their left wing had never taken kindly to this policy and the example of Russia's revolution now led to their breakaway as Independents. The party leadership, afraid of losing control, felt obliged to adopt as the official policy the demand being made by the Petrograd Council of Workers and Soldiers for 'a peace without annexations or reparations'. Bethmann Hollweg had sought to retain the loyalty of the masses by inducing the Kaiser to make an indefinite promise about reforming the Prussian voting system. To the great indignation of the right, the Social-ists pressed for prompt action and Erzberger, the Centre leader, sup-ported them with a speech which, for the first time, gave the German public some idea of the true war situation. The coalition of Centre, Progressives and Social Democrats again asserted itself to pass through the Reichstag a resolution which, after recalling the 1914 claim that 'Germany had no lust for conquest', demanded a negotiated peace.

The next steps threw a revealing light on German conditions. Hinden-burg and Ludendorff, who since 1916 had held the High Command, declared that Bethmann Hollweg had lost their confidence and that they could no longer work with him. The leaders of the right-wing parties agreed, while those of the new majority wanted him replaced by someone more flexible and open-minded. He therefore decided to resign. But the Reichstag majority still could not bring itself to insist on a Chancellor of its own choosing and indeed would have precipitated a crisis had it done so since the High Command would undoubtedly have refused to accept the kind of man who would have been chosen. After a frantic search for a Chancellor who would be acceptable to both the soldiers and the parties, a nonentity was installed. He made common cause with the High Command and the Reichstag's 'Peace Resolution' was watered down by 'interpretations'. The truth was that the reactionary and nationalist groups in Germany, embodied in Hindenburg and Ludendorff, had taken the management of civilian as well as military affairs into their own hands and nothing short of force was going to get them to relinquish it. Unfortunately for the country, the force had to be applied by their enemies.

For the moment, however, all energies were bent on taking advantage of the Russian decision, after the Communist October Revolution, to stop fighting, and on concentrating all available forces for a final effort in the west before the Americans could fully make themselves felt. Yet to win decisively the Germans had not only to conquer in the field but to break the blockade and for this they had to get all they could in the way of food and raw materials from Russia. Nor could they resist the temptation of exploiting the fact that they appeared to have Slavs at their mercy. In the Peace of Brest-Litovsk they imposed terms so harsh as seriously to impair Germany's title to merciful treatment herself later, and in the process of failing to extract the wheat, oil and ores which they wanted, tied up a million soldiers whom they were to need badly in the west. For although the offensive in March 1918 began by making quick progress and nearly broke the Franco-British line, it gradually ground to a halt without actually achieving this. Later attempts to renew it met the same fate and when in July the Allies counter-attacked with a growing superiority of arms (including tanks) behind them, the fighting morale of the German troops at long last broke. At the end of September the High Command, in a moment of panic, told the Kaiser that they saw no alternative to asking for an armistice on the basis of President Wilson's 'Fourteen Points'. Germany had lost her third gamble.

One of these 'Points' however was 'the destruction of every arbitrary power that can separately, secretly and of its single choice disturb the peace of the world', and the Allies made clear that they included in that description the political system which had hitherto directed the destinies of the German people. On the day on which the Kaiser ordered an armistice to be sought, he announced that 'men who possessed the public confidence' were to take a larger part in the government. The Chancellor was to be made responsible to the Reichstag. Deputies were to be allowed to become Ministers without having to resign their seats and authority over the armed forces was transferred from the Emperor to a Minister of War.

Surprisingly enough the first democratic Chancellor, Max, was a Prince even though Baden from which he came was the most liberal of the German states. But before he took over, consternation had been caused among the party leaders when a spokesman of the High Command revealed the true situation to them. For four long years the German people had held out with remarkable tenacity against unfavourable odds; a great part of the credit was due to the fidelity and competence of their officials, but it was the hope of making their country greater which had kept them going. Once the knowledge spread, with little advance warning, that success was not to be had, they naturally asked why they should go on enduring the hardships of war. The number of people who wanted a radical recasting of society was small. But as long as the only group which offered to bring peace quickly was the extreme left wing, others who did not share their social views would listen to them. Prince Max's Cabinet seemed too implicated in the past and failed to get on quickly enough with the job of liquidating it. At the end of October, Austria-Hungary stopped fighting. Sailors in Kiel mutinied when ordered to sea to fight a last hopeless battle. A Workers' Republic was proclaimed in Munich. On 9 November the Berlin workers went on strike and the garrison fraternised with them. Prince Max handed over power to a government of Social Democrats and Progressives under Friedrich Ebert who had once been a saddler and, in a moment of excitement tinged with panic, one of its members proclaimed a Republic. At his headquarters in Belgium, the Kaiser was with some difficulty persuaded to abdicate and next day sought refuge in Holland. The other German princes followed his example; when the King of Saxony was advised to abdicate by a delegation in top hats and frock coats, he replied in his broad accent 'Eh well, mayke yer mook yerselves' and added, 'Luvly repooblicans you be'!

On 11 November a delegation led by Erzberger signed an armistice whose severe terms were designed to put out of question any attempt at renewing the conflict. But that was the last thing which the majority of the German people wanted to do. The achieving of this result had however cost the lives of at least 13 million people of whom 2.7 million were German.

3 THE FIRST ATTEMPT AT DEMOCRACY, 1918-1933

The Revolution which Lost Its Way

On the night of the Kaiser's flight Ebert sat at the Chancellor's desk in Berlin and contemplated his problems. Germany seemed to be heading for chaos; the system which had been held together for so long by such great efforts threatened to collapse as soon as the motive for making the efforts disappeared. External failure threatened to reverse the internal integration which had been achieved since 1871. There was a danger that separatist movements in the different states would undo Bismarck's work of unification. All over the country the soldiers and workers were forming themselves into Councils (which in Russia were called Soviets) and hoisting red flags. Those in the capital were talking in wild terms and it was natural, if incorrect, to suppose that the same held good everywhere. The Spartakists, as the left-wing Socialists called themselves, clearly intended to follow the Russian example and, by seizing the leadership of the Councils, precipitate a social revolution. But Ebert had no intention of being the German Kerensky. He and his immediate colleagues were Democrats before they were Socialists. Long years spent trying to establish parliamentary government in Germany had accustomed them to think in terms of order and fairness; their first instinct was to let the German people as a whole decide on the future by a free vote. But their chances of putting through their ideas depended on the force at their command. What attitude was the army going to take?

There lay in front of Ebert a telephone giving direct access to General Headquarters. Suddenly its bell rang. Ebert lifted the receiver and heard the voice of Hindenburg's deputy, Groener. The armistice terms which he had just received were such that a strong government would be needed to carry them out. For one thing, they required the German army to withdraw to the east bank of the Rhine within a month. To do this so fast was a major administrative task. Would the Government back the generals or would it seek to undermine their authority? The men at the two ends of the line needed one another and out of their conversation a working alliance was born.

The effect of that alliance however was to put the fate of the Republic into the hands of the military and the term 'military' increasingly

meant men who were imbued with the autocratic traditions of the
Second Reich and unsympathetic to the idea of government by the
people. For the temporary soldiers who had left peacetime jobs in order
to fight hurried back to them, leaving the regular troops — the officers
and the people with no definite civilian occupation. Some of these,
when their units were disbanded in compliance with Allied requirements, were formed into special groups called *Freikorps* and largely
used to protect the eastern frontier. What was true of them went for
much of the administrative hierarchy, the Civil Service, the judicial
system, the universities and the Churches. The people staffing these
institutions found themselves compelled to serve under a changed set
of masters but this did not make them change their views. The landlords
and industrialists were left with their property intact.

True to their Marxist training, the left-wing Socialists, some of whom
in December 1918 founded the German Communist Party, argued that
in these circumstances the political revolution would not endure unless
it was followed up by measures which deprived the old ruling classes of
the economic and social bases of their power and put into all the key
positions new men committed to the new system. The majority of the
Social Democrats however, though aware of the need to safeguard the
constitutional changes which had been achieved, were afraid that extending them outside politics would precipitate violent resistance and
that dispensing with the services of trained administrators in the very
difficult conditions of the time would lead to starvation and chaos.
They were further afraid that, if civil war did break out, they would
either be unable to win it or could only do so at the cost of themselves
setting up a dictatorship. For the forces of reaction in Germany were
more numerous and better organised than they had been in Russia and
there were no land-hungry peasants to back up the workers.

The theory that Germany had to choose between reaction and revolution has in recent years been challenged. It has been argued that the
danger from the left and the strength of the right were both overestimated. The revolutionaries certainly only composed a small proportion of the Councils and Ebert might well have steered control of these
into moderate hands instead of holding them, as he did, at arm's length.
As it was, a Congress of them held in December agreed that a National
Assembly should be convened and decisions about the future left to it.
There was no need for interference with property rights. The vital need
was to put convinced democrats into key posts instead of relying on
experts whose claim to be 'non-political' was only temporarily valid.
Regular soldiers, even officers, with democratic convictions were to be

found who could have been the nucleus of a citizen force; Groener's nervousness suggests a lack of confidence in the army's ability to prevail.

The die was cast, however, in January 1919 when the Army and *Freikorps* were allowed by Ebert's Government to suppress a Spartakist rising in Berlin and murder the leaders Karl Liebknecht and Rosa Luxemburg. Left-wing writers have called this 'German democracy's Battle of the Marne'. The bitter feelings which resulted made it all the harder for the left to present a united front to the right. Gradually, however, the authority of the Government was established although extremists held power in Munich with scarcely a break till May.

The National Assembly elected on 19 January met at Weimar, to mark a breach with Prussian traditions and to escape the influence of events in Berlin. Between February and June it drew up a constitution. A proposal to abolish Prussia was defeated and Germany was divided into nineteen units on traditional lines, which were called 'Lands' rather than 'States'. The black, red and gold flag (the colours of 1848) was adopted in place of the Imperial black, red and white (to the distress of monarchists). The abolition of Prussia's three-tier franchise (p. 27) turned the area from a stronghold of reaction into one of Social Democracy. The powers of the Reich Government were strengthened, particularly in finance and military affairs. The Bundesrat was replaced as Second Chamber by a *Reichsrat*, with limited delaying powers. The Head of State was to be a President, chosen by popular vote for seven years; he was to sign treaties, command the Armed Forces and appoint the Chancellor and other Ministers who had to have the support of (but not necessarily belong to) the Reichstag. The President could also dissolve the Reichstag before its time was up. An article later to become notorious gave him power to take emergency action when public security and order were seriously disrupted or threatened. This, however, could be cancelled in retrospect if the Reichstag so demanded. Ebert became the first President.

The new Reichstag was to be elected every four years by universal suffrage (including votes for women) and proportional representation, so that each party was to obtain one seat for every 60,000 votes that it received. This system meant that people voted for a party rather than an individual. It resulted in a very accurate representation of opinion but encouraged the multiplication of separate parties. Much of the blame for the political situation which subsequently developed in the Republic tended to be placed on it. But in fact all it did was to exaggerate rather than counteract a position which was bound to cause trouble and which had been foreshadowed by the Election to the National Assembly itself.

The Communists boycotted that event and the Independent Socialists only won 22 seats. But the Social Democrats themselves only obtained 163 out of 421. Thus they were unable to get a majority without the support of the Centre (89 seats) or the Democratic Party (as the Progressives, with 74 seats, renamed themselves). Further to the right came the People's Party (the former National Liberals, 42 seats) and the Nationalist Party (the former Conservatives, 22 seats). Thus the group which had formed the opposition under the Empire came to power under the Republic but the formation of each Cabinet was going to involve negotiations between two or three parties before it could be sure of support, while the middle- and working-class representatives who habitually engaged in such negotiations were flanked to the left and right by groups whose loyalty to the regime was questionable. The Republic's chances of success depended on the possibility of strengthening the centre at the expense of the extremes, it would be doomed if affairs so developed as to encourage the reverse process. In 1920 and again in 1922 the Social Democrats went out of office rather than work with the People's Party. This was hardly a good omen.

Moreover the former ruling classes went through an unnerving experience. At the outset and at short notice, they had the bottom knocked out of their view of life and expectation of the future. Then for months they lived in conditions which reminded them (though as it proved, wrongly) of the beginnings of the French and Russian revolutions. A community which traditionally set great store by order and discipline persuaded itself that the foundations of these qualities were being undermined. They refused to accept that Germany could have been beaten in battle but maintained that the army had been betrayed by the civilians. They regarded the new regime as something alien to German traditions and unsuited to German conditions which was being imposed at the behest of their enemies. Much of Germany, as the poet Rilke was later to say, 'wanted to persist and not to alter'.[6]

Peace without Honour

Most Germans considered that they had agreed to make peace on the basis of President Wilson's Fourteen Points. But four of those points did not directly concern Germany at all and five more stated broad principles on such matters as open diplomacy, the freedom of the seas and the removal of economic barriers. Another called for 'a free, open-minded and absolutely impartial adjustment' of all colonial claims. The remaining four required the evacuation of all Russian, French and Belgian territory, the restoration of damage in France and Belgium, the return of Alsace and Lorraine to France and finally the creation of 'an independent Polish state which should include territories inhabited by indisputably Polish populations and be assured a free and secure access to the sea'.

The Treaty presented to a German delegation at Versailles on 7 May 1919 had been arrived at by inter-Allied bargaining behind closed doors and was handed over for comment rather than negotiation. But it cannot be said in its treatment of Germany to have clearly violated any of the actual 'Points'. The refusal to allow the Germans in the new Republic of Austria to join the Reich was inconsistent with the hopes which Wilson had held out about satisfying national aspirations but the matter had not featured in the 'Points'. For all of Germany's colonies to have been taken away from her was hardly an impartial adjustment of her claims and the Germans found much to dispute about the character of the population in many of the territories which were to be handed over to Poland. But these were partly adjusted by plebiscites and in any case details of this kind were only marginally responsible for the storm of indignation which broke out in Germany when the terms became known. Most Germans had in fact failed to read (or at any rate to remember) the small print of the various Allied pre-surrender statements and had based their expectations not so much on the 'Points' as on the spirit in which they thought Wilson would persuade the other countries to approach the peace. The hope had also been that, by adopting a democratic form of government, they would get a milder peace. Germany, however, was required to hand over about 27,000 square miles in Europe and 6 million people, to allow the East Prussian homeland to be cut off from the rest of the country (since otherwise Poland could not be given her free and secure access to the sea) and to pay considerable sums in reparations (in security against which the whole country west of the Rhine was to be occupied for fifteen years). Both reparations and occupation were only extensions of the terms imposed on France in 1871 and in fact represented modifications of what had been originally proposed by the advocates of a 'hard' peace. But this was not remembered by the uninformed German observer, and his leaders did not choose to remind him of it.

On the ground that a legal justification was needed for the imposing of reparations, Article 231 of the Treaty required Germany, along with her Allies, to accept 'responsibility' for 'causing all the loss and damage to which her opponents had been subjected as a consequence of the war imposed on them by German aggression'. This was promptly labelled by the Germans 'the war-guilt clause', in spite of the fact that the word 'guilt' did not occur in it and imparted an element of moral judgment lacking in the original. It had indeed been Germany which had declared war on France and Russia and had invaded Belgium, thus indisputably committing aggression according to the rules of international law. Subsequent research, as summarised on pages 49 to 54 of this book, has tended to the conclusion that Germany did much deliberately to precipitate the war. But a very different picture has been painted for the German people, who as a result bitterly resented the charge of 'war-guilt' and embarked on a campaign to disprove it. Moreover they knew that the Allies had during the war made a great impact on neutral opinion by denouncing them for exalting might above right – but considered that this was precisely what was now being done to them.

For the time being, however, the nation was helpless. Groener reported that armed resistance was out of the question (though not all his subordinates agreed with him). Bitter protests and elaborate arguments only secured marginal changes in the terms, coupled with an ultimatum to sign or take the consequences (which would have included the occupation of the Ruhr and a renewal of the blockade, hitherto only partially lifted). The Social Democrats and Centre reluctantly decided to advocate compliance and obtained a majority in the National Assembly against the votes of all the Parties to the right of them, with the result that the Treaty was signed at Versailles on 28 June 1919 (exactly five years after Sarajevo). Prompting signature was the fear that the Allied penalties for refusal would lead to social breakdown and the dissolution of the Reich. On the other hand it might have been preferable to what inevitably became signature in bad faith, with a widespread if undeclared intention to escape as quickly and as fully as possible from fulfilment of the terms. Defiance might have brought the Allies more quickly up against the permanent realities and, by showing them the limits of their power, have served the world's interests better in the long run. But belief to the contrary did not imply treachery to the nation; the men who took the thankless decision did not merit the attacks which they suffered later and which amounted in the case of Erzberger and the Jewish Foreign Minister Rathenau to assassination. The most serious practical defect of the Treaty was that the superiority of force needed to make it possible did not remain to uphold it. The British and French could never have won a clear victory without US help but in November 1919 the Senate refused to ratify the Treaty and the country relapsed into isolation. The French reacted by demanding that the Treaty be enforced more strictly, the British by favouring its revision.

Large numbers of the German people had been so schooled to believe in their country's superiority as to be unable to reconcile themselves to the fact of its defeat. Some dreamt of repeating the national rising against Napoleon; others set themselves to 'organise sympathy' abroad. The tendency to reject the outcome of the fighting received powerful encouragement when Hindenburg misinterpreted a British newspaper article as endorsing the view that the German armed forces had been 'stabbed in the back' by the inability of the home front to hold out. He also put much of the blame on Allied propaganda, implying that that had been deceptive when it had actually concentrated on publicising Wilson's speeches and the facts of the military situation.

With the example of Prussia's resistance to Napoleon in mind, the Allies had insisted on the German army (henceforward known as the *Reichswehr*) being cut down to a long-service force of 100,000 men, on the General Staff being suppressed and on the possession of tanks, aircraft and certain other weapons being prohibited. They required all troops in excess of this figure to be demobilised and the effort to comply brought the Government into collision with the Freikorps. In March 1920 an Allied order demanding the dissolution of these bands led some of them to advance on Berlin and endeavour to set up a right-wing government under a Pan-German farm inspector called Kapp. General von Seeckt, the officer responsible for organising the Reichswehr, had not been unaware of what was in train but took no steps to prevent it and only allowed his troops to intervene when the action of the trade unions in calling a general strike made it clear that the rising (*Putsch*) was going to fail.

After the rising, the unions presented the Cabinet with a number of demands for a new and more democratic Minister of Defence, for a greater say in policy and for closer democratic control over the Reichswehr. These demands were first watered down by Ministers and then, after the emergency was over, forgotten. Had they been successfully enforced, the subsequent history of the Republic might have been considerably altered. But enforcing them might have precipitated a head-on collision with the Reichswehr, who for their part insisted on the resignation of the Minister of Defence because 'no member of the Government which had supported the general strike could ever regain the confidence of the armed forces'. The effect of the civilian victory was to turn these forces to the right and increase the tension between them and the Social Democrats.

Suspecting that the Reichswehr was trying to get round disarmament and worried by a Treaty of friendship which the Republican Government signed with the Soviet Union at Rapallo in Italy in April 1922, the Allies gave that Government little latitude. Disregarding both the basic principles of economics and Germany's internal problems, they treated requests for postponing the payment of reparations as attempts at evasion (which in part they were). Mounting disagreement on this score led the French and Belgians in January 1923 to occupy the Ruhr and redouble their efforts to get separatist governments set up in the Rhineland. This step, from which the British dissociated themselves and to which the Germans replied by passive resistance, cost its authors more than they gained by it and gave a final blow to the German economy.

Instead of paying for the war by higher taxes, the Imperial Government had met the cost by loans which it intended to make its enemies repay after their defeat. When instead those enemies won (and required Germany to pay for the debts which they themselves had incurred to one another), the result was fundamentally to alter the relationship between money and goods, so that by 1919 the Mark was only worth a third of its pre-war value. Government expenditure rose whereas revenues fell. Although industrial activity recovered a little, reparations upset the balance of payments and by June 1922 the Mark's value had dropped to 1 per cent of its 1914 value. The French suspected the Germans of deliberately facilitating this inflation in the hope of proving that reparations were impossible. The Ruhr occupation naturally made things worse; the currency became practically valueless and output fell to almost half the 1913 level.

At this point reason slowly began to prevail. To secure support for abandoning passive resistance, a 'Great Coalition' Cabinet from Social Democrats to People's Party was formed under Gustav Stresemann, who before the war had been a chauvinistic National Liberal. It was confronted with threats from left and right. In Saxony, always a radical stronghold, the local Socialists defied their leaders by insisting that Communists must be brought into the Cabinet. Much the same happened in Thuringia. In Prussia and Bavaria Nationalists were considering risings to overthrow the Republic and prevent a surrender being made to the French. The Bavarian conspiracy included Ludendorff, now a nationalist crank, and a 34-year-old Austrian agitator called Adolf Hitler whose National Socialist German Workers Party (NSDAP) was beginning to find its feet. Some government officials and the local commander of the Reichswehr were also implicated. Stresemann, on 26 September, proclaimed a state of emergency and gave to the War Minister and Seeckt

many of the arbitrary powers which the latter had been thinking of seizing. The Reichswehr commander in Saxony was authorised to proclaim
a state of siege, depose the Cabinet and install a Reich Commissioner.
Thanks to Social Democrat support, Stresemann was able to get Reichstag endorsement for his actions. These included the discarding not only
of passive resistance but also of the old currency. A new one was substituted based upon the total value of German real property. This change
favoured people who had owned material things rather than money or
government stocks. The new *Rentenmark* worked because the Germans
were ready to believe in it, but the reduction in monetary values dealt a
lasting psychological blow at thrift and confidence.

The conspirators in Munich vacillated and Hitler thought he could
force their hands. But when on 8 November he proclaimed a revolution
in a beer cellar, Ludendorff made him march his followers into the
centre of the city, where they were shot down by the police. He turned
his subsequent trial into an occasion for propaganda and devoted his
six-months imprisonment to writing *Mein Kampf*. The kid gloves with
which the Reich Government handled the Bavarian situation contrasted
so remarkably with their vigorous action in Saxony that the Social
Democrats withdrew their support from Stresemann who resigned the
Chancellorship at the end of November but remained Foreign Minister
in a series of subsequent Cabinets more to the right.

The Republic thus survived the emergency of 1923, though for some
time its continuance and the continued unity of Germany had been a
matter of touch-and-go. The next contribution to consolidation was to
come from the Allies. Before Stresemann resigned, he had already secured their consent to an examination of the reparations problem by a
group of technicians and thus completed the essential steps towards a
long-term settlement.

Precarious Fulfilment

The Dawes Plan (named after the American Chairman of the Committee
which drew it up) proposed an apparently realistic programme for paying reparations, provided for sufficient international control of Germany
to ensure that this programme could be maintained and backed up the
arrangement by an international loan. The Plan was linked with a gradual
French withdrawal from the Ruhr. Even so, its acceptance was bitterly
opposed by the German Nationalists.

In February 1925, President Ebert died, having been to the last the target of bitter and undeserved vituperation. At the first Election for his successor, no candidate got the necessary votes and just before the second, the Nationalist Party talked Hindenburg into standing. The Communists insisted on splitting the left-of-centre vote by putting up their own candidate and as a result the old Field Marshal of 78 won by a short head. For the next seven years he treated his oath to the constitution seriously and listened to his Ministers even when they were Social Democrats.

Stresemann as Foreign Minister maintained that the only practicable policy for Germany was to recover the confidence of the world by scrupulously fulfilling her commitments, in the hope of getting the restrictions imposed on her gradually relaxed. By the autumn of 1925 he had succeeded well enough for a group of treaties to be signed at Locarno in Switzerland. In these France, Belgium and Germany accepted the existing frontiers between them (including a demilitarised zone along the Rhine) and agreed to settle all disputes by arbitration; Britain and Italy promised to come to the help of the victim if this agreement was ever violated. In the east, Germany, Poland and Czechoslovakia promised never to seek to alter their common frontiers by force but the German Government did not dare to defy public opinion to the extent of formally renouncing the areas taken away at Versailles and no guarantees of third-party help against aggression were given. The other countries promised to support German entry into the League of Nations (which followed after tiresome hitches in 1926) and to begin winding up the occupation of the Rhineland. The instruments embodying these Allied concessions were criticised as 'instruments of shame' by the Nationalists but the Reichstag approved them by a five to three majority.

Stresemann's aims were not confined to the west and in 1925 he also concluded a Trade Treaty with the Soviet Union, followed six months later by a Treaty in which each signatory promised to remain neutral if the other were attacked. An even closer liaison with the Russians was being built up by Seeckt, who as early as 1920 said that 'only in firm co-operation with Russia will Germany have a chance of regaining her position as a World Power' and two years later recorded that 'Poland's existence is intolerable — incompatible with the survival of Germany'.[7] Seeckt evaded the disarmament provisions of the Versailles Treaty by building up a force sufficiently highly-trained (and free of Socialists) to act as a cadre for a subsequent rapid expansion, and by getting secret facilities in Russia for trying out prototypes of forbidden weapons. This was known to Stresemann and other Ministers but their somewhat half-hearted attempts at interference were brushed aside.

In the second half of the 1920s the Republic seemed to be on the verge of establishing itself. The Nationalists lost ground and the National Socialists dwindled to insignificance. The Social Democrats, after being out of office at national level since 1923 (though controlling a number of *Länder*, notably Prussia) gained strength in the 1928 elections and joined a 'Great Coalition' Cabinet. But there were still disturbing aspects. Much of the prosperity was based on loans from abroad and indeed Germany's ability to pay reparations depended on the fact that she was being lent a sum three times as great by America. Fourteen parties were represented in the 1928 Reichstag. There were five governments in as many years and the bargaining needed to produce a new Cabinet sometimes lasted a week.

But above all there were the incessant attacks of the right wing on the policy of fulfilment, on the very existence of the Republic and on the characters of the men who were trying to make it successful. The old agrarian-industrial combination was still active and awaiting its chance. The defeat, the peace terms, the Allied occupation, reparations and the inflation had swollen the ranks of those who regarded the entire course of German history since 1870 as a mistake. Such people now longed for a German revolution which would bring into being a new, third, Reich, based upon the application of traditional German principles to the modern situation. On the practical consequences of this application there were considerable differences of view. While many nationally-minded conservatives continued to regard communism (with which they virtually equated Social Democracy) as the main enemy, others had picked up from the left hostility to hereditary privilege, just as they had often picked up from Liberals scepticism about Christian beliefs. Without being against private property as such, they insisted that it must be used for the benefit of the community. The one point on which all were agreed was hostility to Jews.

Paradoxically the Social Democratic gains at the 1928 Elections made matters worse rather than better because they resulted in the leadership of the Nationalists passing into the hands of Hugenberg, an industrialist with large newspaper and film interests; he made it his aim not to join in governing the Republic but to make republican government impossible. In 1929, on American initiative, a new 'Young' Plan for reparations was drawn up, scaling down the amount which Germany was to pay. Although German industrialists and bankers (led by the head of the *Reichsbank* Dr Schacht) had sat on the drafting committee, Hugenberg and his associates demanded that all the concessions made in it by the Allies should be accepted but all further reparations payments refused. In association with Hitler the Nationalists organised a plebiscite against the Plan but they only got 14 per cent of the votes and the Plan was confirmed by the Reichstag in March 1930. Dr Schacht, however, resigned in protest; possibly his acute nose scented a change in the wind.

The Wild Men Get Their Chance

The 'Great Crash' on the New York Stock Exchange on 29 October 1929 led to the undoing of many things, including the Weimar Republic. Injudicious speculators went bankrupt; loans were called in and cancelled in a chain reaction all over the world. International trade and demand for raw materials shrank; prices fell and the total process was thus intensified.

This was the situation which was to give an opening to one of the more remarkable characters of history. Adolf Hitler combined a second-rate intellect with pronounced emotional instability. Born in 1889 in Upper Austria, he only came to Germany in 1913 and only became a citizen of the Republic in 1932. His mind was thus formed, largely by self-education, in Linz and Vienna during the last days of Habsburg rule when among the many and discrepant ideas that were prevalent he seems to have had an unfailing flair for the meretricious. The Germans in Austria were at this time losing out in the political struggle and those who did not relapse into resignation or escape into cultural activities compensated for the failure by adopting the most extreme attitudes of racial nationalism and in particular a vicious disdain for the apparent authors of their humiliation — democrats, Slavs, Jews. Hitler reproduced their situation in microcosm, compensating for an initial lack of worldly success by belief in his mission, coupled with hatred of those who failed to recognise it. Self-centred and sentimental, he was prone to violent gusts of rage, sometimes deliberately staged, and derived great emotional satisfaction from being ruthless in imagination or by proxy.

Such qualities are hardly a recipe for greatness, but to them he joined a gift of intuitively divining the mental processes of others. Moreover his intense belief in his own arguments did not render him incapable of regarding them objectively as weapons for influencing people. These faculties made him a most effective public speaker, entering into his audience's frame of mind, presenting his ideas clearly (thanks to over-simplification) and swaying in the last resort by emotion more than by thought. But the same faculties made him a wily tactician, exploiting each man's weaknesses, playing off one group of supporters against another and postponing as long as possible commitments which might lose him support.

Above all, he was lucky in his epoch. The advance of technology had enabled the orator for the first time in history to speak directly to a mass audience which was not physically present. But at the same time and particularly in Germany, it had cut numbers of people adrift from their inherited environment, leaving them resentful and apprehensive, unable to understand what lay behind their plight or how it could be remedied. A complex economic web had come into existence which often put the livelihood of the individual outside his own control and at the mercy of forces or persons whom he could not precisely identify. Hitler's main audience was at the outset one of men living in a small way who in the professions, trade, industry and agriculture alike found themselves pushed to the wall in favour of larger units and a continent-wide division of labour. They were bewildered in an unfamiliar situation which nobody seemed able to master and for which their self-respect made them unwilling to take the blame. The slump, coming on top of the years 1918-24, eroded the social integration achieved in Germany prior to 1914 and the only remaining banner round which there seemed a chance of rallying was that of the nation. But thanks to the studious assiduity of theorists over many years, the nation had in Germany acquired special associations among which hatred of Jews was prominent.

The potential supporters of a 'German revolution' embraced a wide spectrum of outlooks. Hitler succeeded because he 'mobilised disaffection' by promising, with a complete lack of scruple, all things to all men. On the one hand the events of 1920 and 1923 had shown that no right-wing movement had a chance of success if the masses stood out solidly against it. Yet a mass movement was anathema to those who thought that national revival should bring to power an elite leadership, while the possessing classes, whose subscriptions were essential for victory, were not to be had for anything which smacked of socialism. The National Socialists, like the National Liberals and the Social Democrats (and perhaps today the Christian Democrats) were faced with the problem of keeping a balance between the two elements in their title. The anti-Semitism which distinguished them from most other European Fascist parties was not simply the product of passionate conviction; it was also the best way of keeping the Party together. If Hitler was to be believed, Germany's troubles had not been due to an exaggerated idea of the position to which she was entitled in the world but to those decadent and alien elements in her population, particularly Communists and Jews, which had sapped her people's belief in their destiny and thus enabled her external enemies to overcome her. If she could eliminate such elements and recapture faith, she could regain material and psychological prosperity. It was almost the exact reverse of the truth but in the circumstances it carried conviction.

Even before the American crash, the growth of unemployment in Germany had upset the financing of the relatively new system of unemployment pay and strained relations inside the Great Coalition Government between the Socialists, speaking for the workers, and the People's Party for the employers. The fresh developments brought increased unemployment (to reach 5 million in the winter of 1930-1 and 6 million a year later); government expenditure went up, revenues fell. In the spring of 1930 the tensions inside the Cabinet paralysed its capacity for action and on 27 March its Socialist Chancellor resigned. Some historians regard that date as marking the end of the Republic.

For the President, partly on Reichswehr advice, entrusted the forming of a new government to a Centre Deputy called Heinrich Brüning. He was a devout Catholic, a brave ex-officer, an upright man and an expert in economics. He considered that the only way to solve the problems lay in savagely deflating the economy and cutting expenditure and wages till the Budget was balanced and by slow degrees the cheapness of money revived investment round the world. Even if this had not been at the time the generally accepted orthodoxy, Brüning himself doubted whether a reflationary policy of deficit financing would be feasible in a single country, especially when recent experience had made that country acutely nervous of inflation. Yet a deflationary policy meant a return to the hard living conditions from which Germany had only escaped after 1925 and involved a degree of disillusionment and sacrifice which might well destroy (particularly in the middle classes) the last vestiges of support for a democratic system. Indeed the problem of settling exactly how the sacrifices were to be distributed was clearly beyond the capacity of the parties and the Reichstag. Accordingly there was a tacit understanding between Brüning and those anti-democratic conservatives who helped him to power that, as soon as he encountered difficulty, he would resort to rule by an exploitation of the Article in the Constitution about emergency decrees (p. 62). This meant in effect a return towards the system of the Second Reich where the Chancellor had been responsible, not to the Reichstag, but to the Head of State; as soon as Hindenburg refused his signature to an emergency decree, Brüning's position would become untenable.

Not that the Government ruled in defiance of the Reichstag. The only occasion when a majority of Deputies voted against it occurred in

July 1930 and Brüning thereupon called a general election. Its results showed the difficulty of the situation; the Social Democrats and the middle-class parties (including the Nationalists) lost ground whereas the National Socialists leapt from 12 seats to become the second strongest party with 107 and the Communists rose from 54 to 77. Henceforward the Reichstag was only convened at intervals to pass a few trivial laws; it then agreed to a long adjournment during which the Government ruled by decree.

In the spring of 1931, hoping to offset internal misery by external success, the German and Austrian Governments announced their intention of setting up a common Customs Union. France was determined to prevent this evasion of the post-war ban on a political union between the two countries and caused the collapse of a major Austrian bank by withholding promised loans. Germany came to Austria's rescue but two months later two of the four major German banks had to be given state support. Britain came to Germany's rescue but an immediate crisis led to the resignation of the Labour Government and soon afterwards its successor, the National Government, had to devalue the pound by taking it off the gold standard. These dramatic developments did no good to Germany's public finances or to the confidence of her people. A moratorium on all reparations and war-debt payments reluctantly recognised that American inability to go on making loans left everyone else unable to meet their obligations. But the effect of this concession was weakened by being limited in the first instance to twelve months. During the winter of 1931-2 Brüning sought to have it made permanent but negotiations were not finished quickly enough to help him. A proposal to modify the disarmament clauses of the Treaty of Versailles, made with a view to strengthening his internal position, similarly failed in its effect because it was delayed by French objections. It is however doubtful whether, if action had been quicker, much would have been gained. What the German people wanted was work and prosperity; mere diplomatic successes made little impression.

By the spring of 1932 the sands were beginning to run out. There was no sign of economic improvement. The Nazis were growing in strength and boldness; they were winning support outside the classes and areas to which they had originally appealed, and particularly in North Germany. Some senior Reichswehr officers and more junior ones sympathised with Nazi objectives, while all hoped to gain influence and promotion under a right-wing government. Industrialists, with whom Hugenberg had close connections, expected such a government to cut social benefits and make profits easier to earn. There was considerable, though carefully fostered, nervousness about the Communist gain in votes (which never exceeded 17 per cent of the total). There was widespread demand for 'strong men' who would take 'strong measures' to regain prosperity. There was a belief that, if the Nazis were allowed a subordinate place in such a government, the enthusiasm behind them could be mobilised and their sting drawn. The decision lay with a monarchist aged 85 whose faculties were beginning to weaken.

In April 1932 Hindenburg's seven year term of office expired and the election of a new President became inescapable. The straits to which the Republic had come were illustrated by the fact that no truly democratic candidate could be found who would have had any chance of election against a rival who got the backing of the right, though this was partly due to the insistence of the Communists on putting up a candidate of their own. In the end the Field-Marshal was helped back into office, against the competing candidatures of Hitler, a Nationalist and a Communist, by the votes of the groups which had opposed his original election! But he bore a grudge against the people who had forced on him this separation from his natural soul-mates and who now brought him under violent criticism by insisting that he agree to ban the paramilitary gangs whom the Nazis called 'storm troopers'. Intensive and unscrupulous intrigues developed behind the scenes, in which Hindenburg's son Oscar and General von Schleicher, the *éminence grise* of the Reichswehr, played a large part. At the end of May they finally deterred the President from signing any more decree-laws for Brüning, whose Cabinet thereupon resigned. He has been reproached for not showing more fight. But without Reichswehr support, which was highly uncertain, a fight would have been hard to win. All the same, democracy might have survived if as much vigour and confidence had been shown in defending as in attacking it.

Brüning's successor von Papen was a Catholic aristocrat and ex-cavalry officer of considerable charm but somewhat dubious reputation, little political experience and less judgment. Schleicher joined him as Defence Minister, with five nobles and two commoners in what became known as the 'Cabinet of the Barons'. Papen had sat in the Prussian Landtag for the Centre but that Party refused him its support and he was soon defeated in the Reichstag; a fresh election doubled the strength of the Nazis, slightly increased the Communists and decimated the middle-class Parties but failed to solve the problem of where Papen was to find a majority. The stage had been reached at which the only possible alternative to admitting the Nazis to office would have been an attempt to rally against them all the non-Nationalist groups, but the

Communist attitude made this impossible. An attempt to run Germany
on right-wing lines while excluding the Party with the overwhelming
majority of Nationalist votes made no sense and could not last; the Nazis
however refused the terms which Papen offered. In a further election
in November they for the first time lost ground. Schleicher took over as
Chancellor in the belief that he could persuade a wing of the Party led
by Gregor Strasser, who were inclined to take the 'Socialist' part of their
title seriously, to break with Hitler and join the Centre and trade unions
in supporting the Government. But Strasser lost his nerve and left the
country and Hitler reunited the Party while Schleicher's attempt to
develop a social programme lost him the support of the industrialists
without gaining that of the unions. If this was how Hitler was to be kept
out, Brüning should never have been discarded.

By now it was not a question of whether Hitler should come to power
but on what terms. The upper-class Nationalists were divided into those
who did not trust him and those who trusted in their own capacity to
control him. He reassured the first by promising to use only constitutional methods and thwarted the second by insistence on obtaining the
post of Chancellor, even though his votes and his funds showed serious
signs of dropping. The initiative in the final negotiations was taken
by Papen who felt he had been double-crossed by von Schleicher and
wanted revenge. He induced a group of Rhineland businessmen to re-
plenish the Nazi exchequer. On 30 January 1933 the Field-Marshal was
finally talked into giving the post of Chancellor to the man whom he
described as 'the Bohemian Lance-Corporal' (under the mistaken impression that that was the country in which Hitler had been born).
Papen was made Vice-Chancellor to watch him, Hugenberg became
Minister of Economics and there were six other Nationalists in a Cabinet
of twelve. The plotters failed to realise that with Frick as Nazi Minister
of the Interior, with Göring doubling the newly-created post of Air
Minister and that of Prime Minister of Prussia and with the Reichswehr
under the charge of the crypto-Nazi General von Blomberg, the Nazis
effectively controlled the police and the troops.

There has been much subsequent discussion as to who was to blame
for letting the Nazis into power. Relatively few people were whole-
heartedly in favour of the move, which explains why so many felt able
afterwards to deny ever having been Nazis. But a number of groups had
for various reasons come to believe (often as the result of adroit propaganda) that such a development could be turned to their advantage. On
the other hand there was not really anybody left by 1933 who had both
the will and the resources needed to resist. The workers would not do

it, as had been shown in July 1932 when Papen turned the Social Democratic Government out of power in Prussia; the view was taken that men demoralised by lack of work and food could not be expected to make a general strike in protest succeed. The Allies would not do it, for they neither accelerated concessions to help Brüning nor denied them to his successors. The Communists had been schooled to believe that a Nazi government would precipitate their own accession to power; they talked of the Social Democrats as 'the moderate wing of Fascism'. The Reichstag was so divided as to be impotent. Army, President and civil service were at best fair-weather friends. Once again Germany had sacrificed liberal values to national ones and once again the result was to be an arrogant misjudgment of national strength which led to disaster. But any reasonable observer is bound to admit that the environment under which Germany had made an attempt at democracy was exceptionally unfavourable.

4 THE THIRD REICH, 1933-1945

The Totalitarian State

Part of the Nazi technique lay in never allowing their competitors a let-up or the German people a dull moment. No sooner was Hitler installed as Chancellor than another election was announced – the third in eight months. The propaganda machine, which now had full access to the radio system, was turned on in full strength (subject only to the discovery that Hitler was a poor speaker in the studio). The storm-troopers, 40,000 of whom were taken on as auxiliaries by the Prussian police, were let loose in the streets. We are unlikely ever to know for certain how the Reichstag building was set on fire on the night of 27 February; it is perfectly possible that the half-witted Dutchman found inside really did the job on his own. What is beyond dispute is the energy with which the Nazis exploited the supposed Communist conspiracy. On the following day, Hindenburg was induced to sign an emergency decree suspending many of the vital personal liberties, authorising the Reich Government to interfere in the Länder and making death the penalty for a number of crimes.

But when the Election came on 5 March, the result was far from being the triumph which was represented. 13 million out of 32 million voted for democratic parties and the Communists lost no more than 19 seats; the Nazis only won 43.7 per cent of the poll and were left relying on the Nationalists for a majority in the Reichstag. When it met, the Deputies were presented with an Enabling Bill which would for five years authorise the Chancellor, without reference to the President and irrespective of what might be said in the Constitution, to issue laws on any subject he chose. Only one Deputy (a Social Democrat) spoke against it and only Social Democrats voted against it (the Communists having already been proscribed). Hitler thus made himself dictator by legal methods while the Reichstag abdicated its functions and henceforward only met at intervals to be harangued.

'Co-ordination' (*Gleichschaltung*) now became the catch-phrase of the day and, as its visual symbol, the Swastika flag waved everywhere. (The black, white and red colours recovered their place from the black, red and gold.) The Nazis worked on the principle that all institutions and activities inside the state must be made to serve the purposes of the dominant group; many middle-class professional organisations had been infiltrated already. Germany, long inclined to authoritarian rule, now became totalitarian: sleep was said to be the only thing left private. The Party professed its intention of taking over the state. Reich Commissioners had been put into a number of Länder after the Reichstag fire but on 7 April they were replaced by Reich Governors; the man chosen for this post was usually the Party leader for the area (*Gau*) corresponding most closely to the *Land* in question. Papen found himself replaced by Hitler in Prussia. Germany thus became for the first time a thoroughly centralised state; totalitarianism could not tolerate local freedom.

So it was in almost all aspects of life. On 11 March Goebbels, one of the most talented but unscrupulous publicists who ever lived, was added to the Cabinet as Minister for Public Enlightenment and Propaganda. He proceeded to organise a 'Reich Chamber of Culture' with subsidiaries covering all forms of publicity and the arts. Persons who were not accepted as members were forbidden to engage in any activity within its field. Editors were told what to say, even where to print the news. A number of papers were left in apparent independence, to conciliate people whose opposition might be dangerous and to impress the outside world but in due course they were nearly all acquired secretly by one of several Nazi holding companies. The press as a result acquired a dull uniformity and wits adapted a current slogan to run 'One Reich, one Führer, one Paper!'

The unions were dissolved and replaced by the German Labour Front. Farmers were organised in the Reich Food Estate, schoolmasters in the Teachers League, women in the *Frauenschaft*, youth in the *Hitler Jugend*, sport under the *Reichssportleiter*. University senates were no longer allowed to choose their own Rectors but had to accept the Minister's nominee, while for the first time Germany acquired a single Minister of Education responsible for the whole country. (Of 7,758 university teachers in 1932, 1,145 had been dismissed by 1934.) The police force was also unified by being subordinated to the SS. The German people were thus left with the choice of falling into line by joining the organisation appropriate to their work or endangering their livelihood. But those who had the choice were in one sense fortunate, for it was not open to Communists or other known opponents of the regime, while the supposed superiority of the Aryan race led to all Jews being deprived of public positions and severely limited in their private activities. The ordinary prisons were inadequate to hold the numbers detained for political reasons and 'concentration camps' were established to accommodate them; these, though not yet slaughterhouses, soon earned an ugly reputation.

A number of Nazi leaders were put into official posts, as the simplest way of giving legal authority to their actions, but a system which relied as much as the German one did on the letter of the law could only be run by people trained for the purpose. There were many other positions needing skills which too few Party members possessed. The result was a two-way process of absorption. The abler Nazis were taken into the official machine but at the same time many officials joined the Party — often being required to do so as a condition of holding their jobs. If the Party took over the state and particularly the Police, the state went a long way to taking over the Party. But this meant that the regime was served, as the Republic had been, by a number of people who were only fair-weather friends.

The principle of leadership (*Führerprinzip*) laid down that decisions should come downwards from the top, but the Third Reich was no exception to the rule of all bureaucracies that problems for decision are put up from below. Hitler, however, disliked the desk-work involved in studying issues. Unless he had strong views of his own, he preferred to stand aside until it became clear which point of view would come out on top whereupon he endorsed it. In the end, he had about 42 executive bodies reporting directly to him (though some had little to do). Everyone had a rival against whom he sought to get the Leader's support. Thus although Goebbels was supposed to be in charge of propaganda, Dietrich, Ammann and Rosenberg had independent responsibilities in various parts of the field. The Foreign Office was till 1938 duplicated by the Ribbentrop Bureau. The Ministry of Economics had after 1936 to compete with Göring as Commissioner for the Four Year Plan, which itself went far to supersede the Army Economic Office. Frick, as Minister of the Interior, struggled with Himmler for control of the police. The army's exclusive authority was increasingly challenged by the SS Black Guards. The Cabinet never met after February 1938; its secretary once suggested inviting its members to gather for a drink but the idea was forbidden as too dangerous. The net result has been described as 'calculated chaos'. As time went on, decisions were taken more and more haphazardly, with the help of whoever happened to be around; often they were left to one of Hitler's four secretariats. At first this did not matter too much, since the Nazis never embarked on a serious programme of administrative reform at home and things were much more orderly in the military sphere, but the lack of system proved more of a handicap during the war when the home front came under strain. It is a curious fact that a country which can organise so well lower down should twice over have organised so badly at the top!

In industry the principles of leadership were applied to establish a planned economy much on communist lines, though mainly managed by capitalists. Each concern was told what to produce at what price and issued with the necessary raw materials. Instead of decisions about output being taken in relation to consumer demand as expressed in prices, the demand which was effective was that backed by government order. 'Small businesses were bullied into *Gleichschaltung*, big business was bribed.'[8]

The result was that, after some early months of enthusiasm, few people were wholly content. Old-established but incompetent Party members found themselves with little to do. Instead of small businesses having the economic system reorganised for their benefit, the trends to large-scale industry were reinforced, partly to conciliate the tycoons, partly in preparation for war. All those concerned with institutions and spheres which were being co-ordinated resented the pressure put on them and the loss of autonomy. The great and good disliked the flattery lavished on the small man (to distract his attention from what was not happening) and the need to deal on an equal footing with men of humble origins. The lawyers and all who had been brought up to revere the principles of the *Rechtsstaat* watched with growing concern the tendency of Nazi tribunals and judges to make their own law. The technicians and administrators were increasingly disturbed by the confusion and corruption which Nazi methods encouraged but feared that, if they refused their collaboration, things would only get worse. Those who had looked for an improvement in the Republic's rather libertarian standards of public life were fobbed off with the excuse that they were being unreasonable in expecting this to happen while a revolution was in progress. At the outset many, remembering what had gone before and swayed by insidious arguments dinned into their ears, were anxious to give the regime a fair trial. Later they hesitated to turn against leaders who had had so much success in economic and foreign policy. Time was needed for members of a legalistically-minded society to realise that resistance to the legal order might be justifiable on moral grounds. Thus the Nazi leaders not only succeeded in giving Germany once again the unity needed for effective action but in maintaining this for ten years on what was seldom more than a provisional basis.

In any case an individual who was shocked by the cruelty, the violence and the denial of human rights (as were too few) could not find much positive action to take beyond circulating information discreetly and giving surreptitious aid to victims. Reliable knowledge was hard to come by (though rumours abounded), all organisations were being drawn into the Nazi net, the police were ubiquitous, informers frequent and all channels of communication liable to be watched. Germans did not have to know exactly what went on in concentration camps in order to fight shy of being sent to one. The most that developed was a distinctive type of activity better described by the German word *Widerstand* than as 'Opposition' or 'Resistance'. To any person not directly attacked, the temptation to go along with the regime on account of its redeeming features was strong. Even when it became apparent that Germany had got into the hands of megalomaniac gangsters who would stop at nothing, there seemed tragically little that any ordinary decent person could do about it. Many of Germany's best and most gifted citizens, including Albert Einstein and Thomas Mann, saw no tolerable course other than emigration. Of the scientists who did so, 19 were to win Nobel prizes.

The problem was well illustrated by the Churches. The Party expected to 'co-ordinate' both Catholics and Protestants with no more difficulty than had been experienced in the professions and universities. The Evangelical (Protestant) Churches had always been conservatively inclined and susceptible to both nationalism and anti-semitism. There was a widespread desire to unite the 28 *Land* churches into a single nation-wide institution. Some theologians had flirted with the idea of a 'German Christianity' which would eliminate what were considered to be Semitic elements introduced into Christian beliefs by 'the Rabbi Paul' and others! Consequently elections to a Synod for a new National Church resulted in a majority favouring its foundation. But when the practical implications became evident in the shape of personalities and doctrines, many pastors were driven in revulsion to band together under Martin Niemöller in a defensive 'Confessing Church'.

The struggle between this Church and the regime lasted throughout the Third Reich. Numbers of pastors, including Niemöller, went to prison or concentration camps; not a few were executed. Both sides became increasingly convinced of the impossibility of serving two ultimate masters. The Party abandoned little by little its effort to use the Churches for its own purposes and started instead to drive them to the wall by financial and legal measures. By 1939 these methods had achieved considerable success. Thereafter a tacit truce was observed. The Party judged it inopportune to alienate the many believers among the armed forces by open persecution but used the emergencies of war to justify such steps as the requisitioning of Church property and the Church leaders were anxious not to lose sympathy by appearing unpatriotic.

The story with the Catholics was not radically different. The Papal Secretary of State (from 1939 Pope as Pius XII) had been Nuncio in Germany from 1917 to 1929 and there acquired a profound fear of communism. The traditions of the Church inclined it to sympathise with an authoritarian rather than a liberal regime. Papen soon tempted the Vatican with the offer of a Concordat on a Reich basis, something which had been long desired but hitherto ruled out by Socialist opposition. The price paid for its signature in July 1933 was the abandonment of the Centre Party and withdrawal of the Church from all political activities. The terms, had they been kept, would have assured the Church freedom for worship, education and social activity, as well as the safeguarding of its personnel against molestation. But the Nazis regarded promises as tools to be discarded as soon as their purpose had been served, and a stream of Church protests, culminating in March 1937 in the encyclical *Mit brennender Sorge* (which had to be smuggled into the pulpits) only resulted in tactics of gradual erosion being substituted for more direct methods. The existence of a Concordat made official resistance more difficult for fear of giving the Government a pretext for denouncing it and made unofficial resistance more difficult out of respect for the hierarchy. After 1941 the Catholic dilemma became acute and could only have been resolved by a compromise peace since either a Communist or a Nazi victory seemed bound to be won at the Church's expense.

There was, however, one institution in Germany which did succeed for a long time in retaining its independence. That was the Reichswehr, still Prussian dominated; enrolment in it was once described as 'the aristocratic form of emigration'[9]. For the only hope of security against the Nazis lay in superior and organised force. The navy, which had always been more nationalist, and the air force, which owed its existence to the new regime, proved more susceptible to influence. Envious eyes were indeed cast on the soldiers' independence and not least by the storm-troopers under their leader Röhm. By 1934 these rowdies had largely lost their function. As soon as everything had been co-ordinated, there was little left to bully or break up. But the brown-shirts hankered for something to do, they hankered for a second Socialist revolution, they hankered to turn the aristocrats out of the officer corps and convert the Reichswehr into a people's army. They pressed the Führer to agree to their plans.

They were not Hitler's only difficulty. There was widespread dissatisfaction among his Nationalist allies over the way he had treated them as tools. As early as June 1933 Hugenberg had allowed himself to be provoked into resignation. The Nationalist private army, the *Stahlhelm*, was manoeuvred into impotence about the same time. Even the vestiges of the Freikorps were showered with plaudits but seen off the stage. Papen found himself increasingly on the outside. In a speech at Marburg in June 1934, with the encouragement of Hindenburg, he allowed words to be put into his mouth which criticised the Party's excesses and called for a restoration of the monarchy. When Goebbels suppressed the speech, Papen took the matter to Hindenburg. Hitler got there before him, only to be received by von Blomberg whose demeanour was for once too firm to merit his usual nickname of 'rubber lion'.

What made the situation acute was that Hindenburg's life was running out. The conservatives planned to use his death as the occasion for bringing in one of the Kaiser's grandsons as Emperor. Hitler had no intention of being edged out in this way and planned to succeed the President himself. With the encouragement of Göring and Himmler (who was emerging as the man behind the SS Black Guards), he did a deal by which Reichswehr support for such an arrangement was traded for the virtual liquidation of the Storm Troops. Hitler's side of the bargain was fulfilled on 30 June in 'The Night of the Long Knives' when Röhm and over 100 people were summarily done away with on charges of immorality and plotting. The opportunity was taken to settle old scores and remove men with inconvenient knowledge such as von Schleicher; one innocent music critic was shot by thugs who mistook him for somebody else of the same name. Papen was allowed to escape with his life and go as ambassador to Austria. Hitler told the Reichstag that for an hour of crisis he had become Chief Justice for the German People, thereby shocking all those who expected men only to be executed after having been found guilty by due process of law. But the pay-off came five weeks later when Hindenburg died and all the armed forces obeyed the order to take an oath of personal allegiance to Hitler as Führer and Chancellor (the title of President being allowed to lapse).

The full consequences of this change were only gradually revealed. The generals were progressively disabused of the idea that their independence had been safeguarded. It was true that they were rid of Röhm and the Storm-Troopers, who soon ceased to have any practical purpose at all. But they found that the beneficiaries of this elimination were Himmler and the SS, who constituted much more formidable rivals. To go on with, they had bound themselves (and oaths meant much in German military tradition) to someone who was going to insist on being his own strategist. This connection was drawn closer in February 1938 when von Blomberg inadvertently married a barmaid of dubious reputation. Göring and Himmler, and possibly Hitler, knew of the lady's antecedents before they attended the ceremony, and encouraged Blomberg to dig his own grave in the hope of benefiting themselves, Göring by becoming Minister of Defence. After Blomberg had been forced to resign, the secret police trumped up a charge of homosexuality against his obvious successor General von Fritsch (by persuading a man who had been blackmailing a Major von Frisch that he had got the name wrong). The way was thus clear for Hitler (and not Göring) to annex to himself the job of Commander-in-Chief of the three defence forces, or *Wehrmacht* as they came to be called collectively.

An expansionist solution to Germany's economic ills had been ruled out under the Republic for fear of the effect it would have on public confidence in the Mark and on the balance of payments. But Hitler cared nothing for economic orthodoxy and called back Dr Schacht to provide the expert ingenuity, making him Minister of Economics on Hugenberg's resignation. *Gleichschaltung* was then extended to the monetary system. All payments to and from foreign countries were put under control and a network of clearing agreements negotiated with individual countries. Germany's creditors and those who wanted to sell non-essential goods to her were given the choice between taking most or all of their payment in kind, or in blocked (i.e. unconvertible) Marks, or going without. So keen were foreign producers to find markets that most of them put up with this treatment.

At home the abandonment of deflation enabled the Government to spend or stimulate capital investment on rearmament, industrial expansion and public works, of which the motorways (*Autobahnen*) are the most notable monument. The benefits of this expenditure were felt throughout the economy at a time when natural forces were anyhow coming into play to reverse the depression. By 1937 GNP per head had risen 10 per cent over 1929. Moreover Hitler not only kept more men in a variety of uniforms but created in the Labour Service (*Reichsarbeitsdienst*) (which like the Autobahnen was an idea started on a small scale in the Republic) a system by which all young men between 18 and 25 were required to work for six months on projects of general benefit to the community such as afforestation or land drainage. These various measures explain why unemployment fell to 3.8 million by the end of 1933 and went lower thereafter. Its reduction was a considerable feather in the Nazi cap.

There has been considerable argument as to how much German recovery owed to rearmament. No doubt the 1935 increase in the size of the Reichswehr to 350,000, the manufacture of equipment for 36 divisions, the creation of an air force and the building of plants for making synthetic rubber and oil (to reduce Germany's vulnerability to blockade) all played a part. Göring once told the public that they must choose between guns and butter. But that was largely ulterior decoration. Hitler was then and for long afterwards frightened of alienating the masses by asking them for too heavy sacrifices; in practice they got both guns and butter. There are, however, grounds for thinking that, after the initiation in 1936 of the Four-Year Plan for rearmament, the position got tighter. A year later Schacht resigned on the ground that the demands being made on the economy exceeded its resources. By 1939 supplies of foreign currencies were virtually exhausted. Whether Germany would have become unable to pay for her vital imports is hard to say; the victories of 1939 and 1940 removed the problem. In the last three pre-war years Nazi policy generally took a more radical turn and it may be that one of the reasons for Hitler's aggressive actions in 1938 and 1939 was the need to extricate himself from an awkward corner.

The Bluffs that Succeeded

Hitler had absorbed the ideas of the geopoliticians according to which great states need to command large areas as sources of supply and markets. He intended to find these primarily in the east. But on coming to power he and his colleagues were well aware of Germany's weaknesses. His problem was how to head off other states from intervening to overthrow him while those weaknesses were being remedied. This dilemma was handled with great skill. Human inertia, fear of war, desire for fairness, fear of communism, international jealousies and personal vanities were exploited at appropriate moments. Coups were staged when public attention was otherwise occupied and notably on Saturday mornings. Much was made of the wrongs done to Germany; solemn professions of peaceful intentions alternated with unilateral acts of defiance. The very secrecy surrounding German rearmament was exaggerated to convey the impression that she was already more dangerous than the facts warranted.

For a fair judgment on the reaction of other countries, certain considerations must be remembered. It had long been a principle of international affairs that a country's internal politics were its own concern with which outside states should not meddle. Men were widely afraid of another war, expecting aerial bombardment in particular to be even more devastating than it proved. The course of events since 1918 had disillusioned them about the advantage of winning a war. There was a widespread desire to learn from history and avoid repeating what were taken to have been the mistakes of 1914, 1919 and 1923. Those who most loathed National Socialism were also the people most likely to admit that it was to some extent the product of other countries' actions. Materialist interpretations of history were in vogue and men hoped, by adopting more generous policies, to bring Hitler to a more reasonable frame of mind or, if that was not possible, to induce better Germans to overthrow him. Where they went wrong, of course, was in failing to understand that only superior force could deflect a man so bent on world power, that internal resistance was unlikely to occur except in conjunction with external resistance (if then) and that promises did not mean the same to Nazis as to most of us. Men of good will were gradually driven to the realisation that there was no satisfactory alternative to the use of force. But by the time that happened, the amount of force needed was considerable and the experience underlying the realisation had generated a cold exasperation which boded ill for Germany.

There is little to be gained by lingering over most of the steps on the road. A conciliatory speech by Hitler on 13 May 1933 was followed in October by Germany's withdrawal from the Geneva Disarmament Conference and the League of Nations, which went unpunished. In January 1934 the Poles, whose apprehension had been considerable, were pleasantly surprised by the offer of a non-aggression pact. Not only did they fall for this but they allowed the new intimacy for a time to put into the background their older links with France. Later that year however Hitler made his first mistake. In between the Night of the Long Knives and the death of Hindenburg, the Austrian Nazis were allowed to attempt a rising in Vienna. The job was bungled and the attempt failed. Mussolini massed troops on the Austro-Italian frontier and gave every sign of being prepared to cross it if the Germans moved. Hitler's quick repudiation of any such intention showed that this was language which he understood but he for his part learnt a lesson in the importance of thorough preparation.

In March 1935 Hitler officially admitted that Germany possessed the air force forbidden to her by the Versailles Treaty. When the world showed little excitement over something which it had come to take for granted, he went on to announce plans for an enlarged conscript army. This left open the question of the fleet, which had been forbidden to possess ships of more than 10,000 tons or more than 25,000 men. Britain with considerable distaste began to prepare for a return to naval competition. Her relief can be imagined when she was offered a promise to limit new German building to 35 per cent of her own level and an agreement authorising the Nazis to break the Peace Treaty up to this level was quickly concluded. The price was estrangement from France and Italy (who on Nazi insistence had been left unconsulted) and the gift to Hitler of a propaganda success as great as that involved in the Concordat; of course the document was valueless since, once the Germans felt capable of building beyond its limits, they would have found a pretext for denouncing it (as they did in 1939). All the same, the German navy was not in a position by the time war came to wage it effectively against Britain.

The winter of 1935/6 was occupied by Mussolini's Abyssinian campaign and his dispute with the League of Nations. This suited Hitler excellently for, if Mussolini came out on top, the chances of the League being invoked against Germany later would be reduced, while if the League won, Mussolini would no longer be able to protect Austria; the actual outcome combined both results. The failure to get sanctions made effective led to recriminations inside France and Britain as well as between the two countries. Germany was thus given the opportunity in March 1936 to send her troops into the demilitarised zone along the Rhine. As long as such a zone existed, she could not undertake any action in the east without being vulnerable in the west. The moment was therefore the last at which Britain and France could have intervened to overthrow Nazism with relative ease. Had they marched, the Germans would have withdrawn. But they were taken by surprise and obsessed with uncomfortable memories of the passive resistance which had greeted the French in the Ruhr in 1923. Hitler's bluff, which had caused his generals much anxiety, met with nothing more serious than protests. In the circumstances, it would not have been surprising if, in the plebiscite which he organised, the 99 per cent of the German voters who were said to have expressed approval actually did so.

The Führer had all along recognised that allies would be an asset in the process of achieving predominance. The ally he would have liked was Britain; he considered the Kaiser's biggest mistake to have been challenging Britain and Russia at the same time. But such an alliance would only suit him if Britain were prepared to let Germany become supreme in Europe, and much as Britain shrank from paying the price of preventing such supremacy, the cost of not preventing it would be finding herself at the mercy of a regime which she profoundly mistrusted. She took time over making up her mind and Hitler had to be content instead with exploiting Italy's isolation and the apparent similarity of the two political systems. Mussolini was gratified and in November 1936 described the relationship between the two countries as 'not a diaphragm but an axis'. During the Spanish Civil War of 1936-9 the two dictators, in common with Stalin, treated their signature of non-intervention agreements as scraps of paper. While most of the troops sent were Italian, the Germans used the peninsula as a testing-ground for their new weapons: they must have found the performance of their dive-bombers in devastating the town of Guernica in April 1937 encouraging. But the closer Mussolini drew to Hitler, the harder did it become for him to stand up for his interests in Austria and the Balkans.

On 5 November 1937 Hitler expounded to his Chiefs of Staff and Foreign Minister his plans for the future. The size and density of Germany's population gave her in his view the right to a greater living-space than she possessed. Self-sufficiency was impossible, dependence on imported supplies too dangerous. Her future was therefore conditional on obtaining more space in Europe. The history of all ages proved that expansion could only be carried out by breaking down resistance and taking risks. Two hate-filled enemies, Britain and France, stood in the way. Neither was invincible but must be considered, along with Russia, as 'power factors in our calculations'. Provided he lived long enough, it was his unshakeable determination to solve Germany's space problem by 1943-5 at the latest. In certain circumstances he might move as early as 1938. The process of rearmament was already approaching completion so that soon the position would begin to deteriorate. The first target must be the overthrow of Austria and Czechoslovakia, to prevent an attack from the rear in the event of trouble in the west. Neither Britain nor France would intervene.

The Führer's audience was horrified, not so much at the thought of war as at the thought that the war might be one which Germany could not win. But when they told Hitler this, his reaction was to remove them from their posts; this was the reason behind the fall of Blomberg and Fritsch (p. 85). The French Ambassador described the occasion as 'a dry thirtieth of June'. Within a week of taking over as Commander-in-Chief, Hitler summoned Dr Schuschnigg, the Chancellor of Austria, and browbeat him into taking two Nazis into his Cabinet. Schuschnigg was in a weak position. His predecessor had crushed the Austrian Social Democrats instead of making allies of them. The police and army were so riddled with Nazis as to be unreliable. Mussolini had written Austria off. The British and French publics, unenlightened as to strategic considerations, saw no reason why the Germans in Austria should be prevented from joining their fellow-nationals if they wanted to, and were certainly not prepared to adopt the only course by which this might have been prevented, namely war.

Schuschnigg however declared that he would hold a plebiscite to decide whether the Austrians wanted to give up their independence. The Nazis were not prepared to risk a negative answer; their own answer was to send their troops across the frontier. When the plebiscite was held a month later, 99.7 per cent of the population were said to have voted to join the Reich. Meanwhile the Vienna Nazis expended their prejudices on the city's 180,000 Jews.

It was now the turn of Czechoslovakia. Although the capture of Austria put the head of that country into the tiger's jaws that head was protected all round by fortified mountain barriers and by a well-equipped, well-trained army of 35 divisions. But Czechoslovakia had inherited from Habsburg days — and indeed even earlier — a weakness which was to prove fatal. In the 'Sudetenland', it contained over three million people speaking German, most of whom lived close to the German frontier. These people had not been badly treated since they lost their old predominance to the Czechs in 1919, but they resented being ruled by those on whom they had previously looked down. Hitler had for long been fanning their dissatisfaction and by 1935 the Sudeten German Party, which voiced their claims, had become the strongest in the country. He now set out to exploit their supposed grievances, not with the object of getting those grievances alleviated but of making the world, and particularly the British and French publics, think that the Czechs were in the wrong. In May 1938 he decided to 'smash Czechoslovakia' by military action before October. When he conveyed this decision to the generals, they were once again horrified. Not only did they seriously doubt whether the 36 divisions which they had available could break through the Czech fortifications but they could only obtain the troops which they did propose to use by reducing to 13 divisions those left in the west for keeping out some 56 French ones. If the French moved (and they were bound by Treaty to come to the help of the Czechs) they could not possibly be held up. General Beck, the Army Chief-of-Staff, was so disturbed that he resigned his post in mid-August and worked out with several other generals and diplomats plans to seize Hitler as soon as the order to attack Czechoslovakia was finally given. Information about these plans was conveyed to the British Government which was implored to stand firm.

Hitler welcomed Beck's departure though he did not think fit to make it public. He was convinced that he could bluff the Western Powers out of acting, and by a chain of events culminating in the Munich Conference on 29 September, this was precisely what he achieved. He was deprived for the time being, to his annoyance, of the pleasure of actually marching into Prague but he secured without war the handing-over to Germany of all the Sudeten German areas, with which went the Czech ability to put up a successful fight later. The British Government under Chamberlain was sceptical about the Czech ability to resist and about the will of the German generals to rebel. It suspected that the French would not have their hearts in a war and knew that the rest of the Commonwealth would not. It vastly exaggerated the likelihood of German air raids and the damage which they could do; crucial improvements in the defences against them were due to become available in the next twelve months. Being unsure itself, it could give no clear lead to the public, which was deeply divided. A promise by Hitler that this would be his 'last territorial demand' inclined it to give him the benefit of the doubt. The French agreed with relief and Mussolini provided a way out of a last-minute impasse. The Czechs were compelled by their allies to accept a surrender worked out over their heads.

The Bluff that Was Called

For the first time since the Middle Ages, virtually all the German-speaking people in Central Europe (except for Switzerland) were now united in a state of 80 millions. But what Hitler failed to realise in his self-satisfaction was that, as far as the British people were concerned, he had exhausted his credit and their patience. Events in the following months did nothing to make them better disposed towards Germany. In November the murder of a German diplomat in Paris by a Jew with a grievance was used as an excuse for an attack on Jews throughout Germany, in which some were killed, many arrested and much property destroyed. In the past, anti-Jewish violence had mostly been perpetrated unofficially while police looked the other way; the 'Crystal Night' (so-called because of the broken shop-windows) was the first large-scale operation to be officially engineered and its execution whetted appetites.

The rump of Czechoslovakia had been divided, at Nazi instigation, into three provinces. When in March 1939 two of these tried to break away from the third, Dr Hacha, who had become President after Munich, dismissed their governments and proclaimed martial law. For this, he was ordered to Berlin and there compelled to advise his people not to resist the occupation of their country by German troops. This 'Rape of Czechoslovakia' so shocked the world that the seizure of Memel from

Lithuania five days later went almost unnoticed. But Hitler had taken a more momentous step than he realised, for his action could no longer be justified on the principle of 'national self-determination' while it showed that his remark about having no more 'territorial demands' had been a lie. He thus demonstrated that there was no knowing where he would stop, since nothing he said could be trusted. Britain could not risk letting such a man dominate the Continent, no matter what the cost of stopping him might be.

The British Government's response was to promise all possible support to Poland should that country's independence be threatened. France was already pledged to such a course by treaty. The British promise, of course, made strategic nonsense. The Polish Army was bigger than the Czech but less well-equipped and the Polish frontiers were harder to defend. There was no easy way of getting British or French troops to Poland. The only effective method of protecting Poland against Germany would have been to secure for the Poles the help of the Russians, but the Russian price was permission to annex the Baltic states of Estonia, Latvia and Lithuania, while the Poles refused to let the Russians into their country for fear of having it turned communist.

The British change of policy did not deter Hitler; even if she were on this occasion to live up to her warnings and fight (a contingency about which his expectations fluctuated), she would not have time to make her power felt. On 3 April he ordered his generals to be ready by 1 September to seize Danzig and destroy Polish military strength. On 28 April he made a speech in which he ridiculed President Roosevelt's proposals for preventing war and tore up the Polish-German Treaty of 1934 as well as the Anglo-German Naval Treaty of 1935. In May a formal military Alliance – the 'Pact of Steel' – was signed with Italy. But the Führer had few illusions about the quality of the metal, realising that Italy's pro-German policy was mainly due to Mussolini, who was most unwilling to go to war. Hitler had a much larger fish on the line and finally landed it on 23 August when the conclusion of a non-aggression Pact between Germany and Russia caused a sensation. How could a Party which had always proclaimed Bolshevism to be one of its greatest enemies, which along with Italy and Japan was a signatory to an anti-Comintern Pact, bring itself to make terms with the leader of world communism? Had the Russians lost their senses for them to join hands with people pledged to destroy them?

Hitler of course never intended the Pact to be lasting. But for the time being it secured him against Russian interference while he dealt with Poland. Stalin was unlikely to have been under any delusions about Hitler's good faith. But the Pact contained a secret clause dividing Eastern Europe into spheres of influence and assigning to Russia Finland, Estonia, Latvia, Eastern Poland and Bessarabia. If Russian influence could be established in these countries, the Germans, should they break their word, would have all the more hostile territory to cross before they reached Russia proper. Stalin may also have hoped that the attack on Poland would embroil Hitler with Britain and France, that the resulting war would weaken both sides to Russia's benefit, and that a Nazi attack on the Soviet Union would thus be postponed, perhaps for ever. The Pact cost the Kremlin nothing except the loyalty of a few (but by no means all) European Communists.

With Russia's neutrality in his pocket, Hitler might have been expected to hesitate no longer. Indeed he told his generals on 22 August that his only fear was an attempt to mediate by some *Schweinhund*. Yet the reasoning which made Stalin want Britain to fight made Hitler want her to be neutral and he held up the attack on Poland for a week in the hope of finding her an excuse for remaining so. But the minimum British condition was the abandonment of the attack and they would not even put pressure on the Poles to accept specious proposals of Hitler's about coming to Berlin to negotiate. The date-line of 1 September fixed in the military timetable arrived without anything having been settled and only when the troops were already moving did the Nazis produce a reasonable set of terms which they declared would have been offered to the Poles supposing that negotiations had ever begun. Once the Polish frontier had been violated, the British refused to consider any proposal for mediation unless Germany agreed to withdraw again. This Hitler would not dream of doing and so on 3 September Britain reluctantly declared war, leaving an even more reluctant France with no honourable alternative but to follow suit.

Europe at His Feet

Thanks to the unprecedented way in which the Wehrmacht exploited the internal-combustion engine, the campaign in Poland was over before the French had had time to move (supposing that they had wished to do so) and almost before the Russians had had time to seize their share of the spoils. The German Air Force had never in fact had any plans for bombing Britain and little active fighting took place in the west. On 6 October Hitler, in a victorious speech to the Reichstag, proposed to

Britain and France that they should make peace on the basis of the new frontiers. But before they had had time to consider the proposal (which they rejected), he had ordered his generals to make plans for an attack on France through Luxembourg, Belgium and Holland. When told to be ready by mid-November, the army leaders were so alarmed as once again to consider removing him. Neither party carried out its intentions. The starting date for the operation was postponed fourteen times and the winter was chiefly remarkable for a naval action which led to a German 'pocket battleship' (i.e. one designed to fall under the limit of 10,000 tons) scuttling itself in South America and a bitter northern war which led the Russians to think that they had ensured the subservience of the Finns.

The coming of spring brought a dramatic end to the 'phoney' war. On 9 April German sea-borne forces, with the help of a few parachutists, evaded the watch of the British navy (which was itself on the point of laying mines inside Norwegian waters) and landed without warning or declaration of war in Denmark and Norway. The first country was seized virtually without fighting. Five of Norway's six ports were also taken without difficulty but at Oslo plans miscarried. The King and Cabinet managed to get away and refused all suggestions that they should surrender. For the last ten days of April small British and French forces endeavoured to help in resistance but the Germans had gained too big a start. At the end of the month the effort was abandoned as hopeless, the King and Ministers were evacuated to Britain and Norway left to the traitor Quisling and a German commissar. Only at Narvik, inside the Arctic Circle, did fighting go on for another month until events elsewhere made withdrawal inevitable. The loss not only impaired the British blockade but also facilitated German naval operations.

Then on 10 May the assault on the West was launched. Belgium, Luxembourg and Holland were entered without notice. In addition to the techniques which had overwhelmed Poland, parachutists, gliders and airborne troops were used to create confusion and leap over obstacles like rivers and forts. An air raid on Rotterdam killed some 900 civilians while negotiations for surrender were already under way. Concern for their own neutrality had kept the Belgian and Dutch Governments from having more than the most superficial contacts with the French and British and though the armies of the latter now raced forwards to their aid, the effort was partly responsible for the disaster which followed.

For the Germans had calculated that the enemy would expect them to repeat their 1914 strategy by which the main weight of the attack was concentrated on the right wing and used in a wide encircling movement through the Low Countries. This had indeed been their original intention and plans for such an operation had come into Allied hands in January. But later on Hitler had adopted a new and daring scheme proposed by General von Manstein. Four days after the original invasion, when the British had had time to rush to their left flank, a concentrated force of armoured divisions, supported by motorised infantry, fell upon the French centre, although the hilly nature of the country was supposed to make it unsuited to tanks. The Allies in fact had as many tanks but were not able to deploy them or prevent the Germans from reaching the sea on 20 May. Though the Dutch had to stop fighting on 15 May, the Belgian, British and French forces managed to halt the German right wing east of Brussels but this achievement was rendered futile when they were taken in the rear. The German spearhead moved rapidly north along the coast, took Boulogne, surrounded Calais and by 24 May stood poised outside Dunkirk for the final kill.

At that point it was halted by Hitler, with the approval of its commander General von Rundstedt, for what appear to have been a variety of reasons. One was to keep the tanks intact for later use against the main French army further south. The second was Göring's desire to secure for his air force (*Luftwaffe*) the credit for the final act. The third was the belief that anything left after the air force had finished could be 'mopped up' by ordinary infantry. But finally Hitler was reluctant to bring Britain to her knees. He explained on a number of occasions that all he wanted from her was an acknowledgement (presumably by a new and more friendly government) of Germany's position on the Continent. To destroy the British Empire would in his view benefit 'not Germany but only Japan, the United States and others'. His air force however, in face of bad weather and British fighters, fell down on its assignment and, to the surprise of the High Command accustomed to think in terms of land warfare, the British succeeded in evacuating nearly the whole of their troops, the essential trained nucleus on which a new army was to be built, as well as many of the French. The Germans had to be content with the capture of 40,000 French, quantities of equipment and the surrender on 28 May of the Belgians, on the orders of King Leopold against the advice of his Cabinet.

On 5 June, the morning after the last British troops had left Dunkirk, the Germans launched the final phase of the campaign by attacking the remaining French forces further south. These were demoralised and outclassed and were soon in full retreat. Paris fell on 14 June and three days later Marshal Pétain, the new Prime Minister, asked for an armistice. It was given to his delegates on 20 June on the same spot, and indeed in the same restaurant-car, as the Allied terms had been handed to Erzberger in November 1918. The German terms were now no more merciful. Not only were Alsace and Lorraine taken back but the whole of the north and west of France was to be occupied. Her fleet was to be disarmed to keep it out of British hands. All prisoners were to remain in German custody till the war ended (which proved a more serious stipulation than anyone imagined at the time) and all anti-Nazi refugees were to be handed over. Nothing was said about reparations — the Germans proceeded to take what they wanted. Mussolini, who had waited to declare war until 11 June, had only managed to get hold of a small strip of frontier territory and that was all he was allowed to keep.

Hitler had thus succeeded in less than six weeks in an even greater achievement than the one which had eluded the Hohenzollerns. The whole of Western Europe from the North Cape to the Spanish frontier, from Memel to Trieste, lay at his feet and the lands to the south-west and south-east looked likely to do his bidding. Only Britain stood out and nobody in Europe thought Britain could resist much longer — few even of the British saw how they could ever reverse his success. This he had brought about with the help of German enthusiasm, German efficiency and German resources — but very largely by his own intuition and against expert advice. Even those of his countrymen who still disapproved of him felt unable to withhold respect, while an American who saw him at the French surrender described his face as being 'afire with scorn, anger, hate, revenge and triumph'.[10]

The Long Road Back

Hitler and his generals never seem to have considered that they might have to invade Britain and had made few plans or preparations for doing so. For an invasion to succeed, the attacker had to command two out of the three elements. The Germans were supreme on land and if their troops could be got across the Channel, would have made quick work of the British army. But the British were supreme at sea, particularly as the Germans had suffered heavy losses in the Norwegian campaign. Britain's warships were, however, vulnerable to air-attack, while airborne forces could be used as advance troops provided that they could be quickly reinforced by sea-borne ones. But to use aircraft for either of these purposes would be risky as long as the British had fighters available with which to attack them. Everything therefore turned on the air and here Göring set out to show the Luftwaffe's superiority; although his losses were all along heavier than those of the Royal Air Force, he might have succeeded had he concentrated his attacks on the British fighter aircraft, control centres and radar stations. But not only did the Germans fail to appreciate the extent to which radar and 'Ultra' (intelligence obtained by breaking the codes of intercepted signals) were combining to give the enemy advance knowledge of their movements; at the crucial moment their attention was diverted. One night a dozen German planes lost their way and dropped their bombs blindly on what was in fact the centre of London; the British thought that this bombing was deliberate and retaliated by making two raids on Berlin, in which a certain number of planes found the target. Little physical damage was done but the psychological effect was considerable for, if the German victories were as complete as was being made out, the German capital should have been invulnerable. Hitler called for retaliation and London was heavily bombed by night for a week. Then on 15 September a massive daylight attack was ordered; the RAF had used the interval to recover and shot down 52 planes (some accounts say 60) for the loss of 26. The barges and other boats which the Wehrmacht had collected in Channel ports for use in the invasion had already suffered severely from British bombing; the autumn had arrived and the weather was expected to get worse. On 17 September the operation was postponed indefinitely and on 12 October called off until 1941. Night bombing of Britain throughout the winter (the 'Blitz') had little military effect.

One cannot help wondering what would have happened if Hitler had returned in the following year with all the resources of Europe behind him. But Britain had never been his main objective and when her defeat eluded him, he decided not to let failure hold up his timetable. He had frequently spoken of the Germans as 'a people without living space' (*Volk ohne Raum*). He had said in *Mein Kampf* 'If we speak of soil in Europe today, we can primarily have in mind only Russia and her vassal border states.' And the Germans had been observing with displeasure the way in which during the western campaigns Stalin had been strengthening his hold on those same border states. When Molotov, the Russian Foreign Minister, visited Berlin in November 1940, he was awkward and uncompromising; Russia's requirements were too big for Hitler to concede. He persuaded himself that what was preventing Britain from making peace was her hope of Russian (rather than American) help and at the beginning of December he ordered the Wehrmacht to put itself in a position to attack the Soviet Union at any date from 15 May 1941 onwards.

Russia was not the only direction in which things were going wrong.

The hopes which Britain set on America were justified when in December 1940 Roosevelt proposed his scheme for lending or leasing to her all the war material she wanted, and thus ruled out the danger of her having to stop fighting for lack of money to buy munitions. General Franco refused to bring Spain into the war and so deprive Britain of Gibraltar. Mussolini, although well on the way to being driven out of North Africa by the British, thought fit to retaliate on the German habit of acting without notice by launching in October an unheralded and unsuccessful invasion of Greece. German troops had to be despatched to stiffen up both areas and it was decided that the Balkans must be cleared before the Russian operation began. Despite the complications of a popular revolt in Yugoslavia, the whole area including Crete was conquered ahead of schedule. During the episode Rudolf Hess, the crank who was Hitler's deputy, sought to put himself back in the limelight by flying on his own to Scotland in the hope of inducing the British opposition (a figment of his imagination) to turn Churchill out and make peace before they and their Empire were annihilated; he certainly succeeded in creating a nine-days' wonder, not least among the German leaders, but one that was soon obliterated by other events.

The attack on Russia was not started till 22 June but the lateness of the date did not worry its instigators; they were confident of being able to complete another lightning campaign within six weeks. At first their hopes seemed well-founded. The Russians had had notice of the impending attack from at least five independent sources but may have decided that the warnings were a capitalist plot intended to embroil them with Germany. Their troops were taken by surprise and the Germans got two-thirds of the way to Moscow in three weeks. The remaining third took longer but on 9 October Otto Dietrich was authorised to tell the world that the campaign in the east was decided. But the Russians had more troops than the Germans expected; their heavy tanks were superior and they fought with great stubbornness. The autumn rains set in earlier than usual; the Wehrmacht got bogged down before it reached the capital and was caught unprepared and in the open by the Russian winter. The Germans might have done better if they had set out to win the support of anti-communists in Russia by promising them self-government. But not merely did Hitler scorn the idea of such a grant; it would have been inconsistent with his general views on race to have made such a promise. When news spread of the inhuman way in which captured Russians were being treated, it did not encourage the rank and file of the Red Army to give in.

On 6 December General Zhukov counter-attacked with troops trained and equipped to fight at sub-zero temperatures. The Germans began to give ground; their Führer, adding the job of Army Commander-in-Chief to his other functions and superseding demoralised generals in quantity, forbade them to do so. Thereby, he possibly prevented a headlong retreat but could not prevent operations from coming to a virtual halt for the next four months. Meanwhile Japan's attack at Pearl Harbour on 7 December (which came as a surprise to the Germans) brought the United States into the war. At the stage when Hitler had been confident of beating Russia, he had sought to distract American attention from Europe by inciting Japan to attack Britain in the Pacific. The idea of a Pacific war, but one against America as well as Britain, was received so favourably in Tokyo that later, when Hitler would have welcomed Japanese help against Russia, they could not be persuaded to change targets. Their obstinacy proved disastrous. Sorge, the Soviet secret agent in Tokyo, just had time before being caught to advise Moscow of the Japanese decision to strike south (rather than west) and it was therefore with confidence that the Soviet command could take troops away from East Siberia to turn the tide against the Germans. But Hitler aggravated the situation gratuitously by taking the initiative of himself declaring war on the United States, thereby helping Roosevelt to win acceptance for his strategy of giving the European war priority over the Pacific one.

As their Führer realised, the Germans now faced a different kind of war from the one which they had got used to winning. For, like his predecessors in 1914, Hitler had gambled on his campaigns being short; unlike them, his gambles had come off. The equipment and munitions needed for such speedy operations could be produced at relative leisure beforehand and the losses made good at equal leisure afterwards. Many of the reserve soldiers, called up from the factory benches, got back to them again before civilians had noticed much interruption in normal supplies. Germany had therefore had no need for industrial mobilisation on the scale achieved by Britain after 1940. The failure to knock out Russia in a single summer, along with the entry of America, brought this happy state of affairs to an end. The Germans and their allies were now outnumbered on the scale of 2 to 9, while the biggest productive machine yet known in history was set to work at full stretch against them, so that progressively they were to be the side which found itself at a logistic disadvantage. Their tactical methods had lost the advantage of surprise; the rest of the world was hard at work coping and copying. Belief in the invincibility of the Wehrmacht had been shattered in front of Moscow and there had been over a million casualties in Russia.

In such circumstances Hitler's readiness to take risks, which had been

a major reason for his success, turned into a liability. Strain and un-
healthy seclusion in his headquarters were beginning to tell on him; the
remedial drugs which his doctors prescribed did more harm than good.
Göring was growing lazy and incompetent; Himmler gained more power
than was desirable. Yet the challenge of the new conditions was met
with considerable success. Between February 1942 and July 1944 the
output of German armaments rose threefold, that of tanks sixfold. By
1943 the proportion of GNP devoted to military expenditure roughly
equalled the British figure. Although the American contribution made
it out of the question for Germany to match her enemies in quantity,
the shortfall was until 1944 partly made good by superior design. The
credit for this was due to Fritz Todt and then, after his death in February 1942, to Hitler's favourite architect Albert Speer, who between
them turned the organisation originally created to construct the Autobahnen into a new central body which set over-riding priorities for all
production.

Another reason why the German people escaped serious privation till
a late stage in the war was that the produce and possessions of occupied
Europe were mercilessly requisitioned to ease the life of the master
race. It has been estimated that 15 per cent of Denmark's GNP was
taken to Germany without payment – and Denmark was better treated
than most. France was made to pay reparations at more than four times
the rate against which Germany had protested so vigorously under the
Dawes and Young Plans (pp. 68 and 70). In addition the Germans removed 9 million tons of cereals, three-quarters of the total steel production and large quantities of textiles. Numbers of special machines were
carted out of the country for use in Germany. By the end of September
1944 some seven-and-a-half million civilians from other countries of
Europe were working in Germany as slave labourers under miserable
living conditions. The persons concerned had often been chosen by
hazard; one of the customs of the SS was to round people up as they
came out of church or the cinema! In addition 40 per cent of prisoners-
of-war were employed on making munitions or other war work, in
contravention of international law. Some three million Russian prisoners
– over half the total number – were so badly treated that they died. It
is small wonder that Germany's difficulties on the battlefields were
accompanied by growing difficulties in securing co-operation from the
occupied populations.

German brutality was not confined to exploiting subjects and cap-
tives. Slavs and Jews were murdered on a mass scale for the simple
crime of having belonged to what were regarded as inferior races. By

1940 over a million Poles had been uprooted from their homes in the provinces nearest to Germany (where they were replaced by Germans expelled from Russia or the Baltic states) and driven eastwards across the Vistula where they were left to maintain their existence on starvation rations. In all some six million Poles are believed to have died violently during the war (though some of these were killed by the Russians). In 1939 there are thought to have been ten million Jews living in the lands which came under Hitler's control. When the war ended, between four-and-a-half and six million had been exterminated, some by firing-squads, others (because firing-squads were too slow) in the gas-chambers of concentration camps. Paradoxically the scale of extermination grew as defeat came closer since the Nazi leaders were determined to satisfy their hate while they still had power.

This is not the place to make a full catalogue of the crimes against humanity which were committed by Germans on the orders of Germans during the five-and-a-half years of war. But there are two reasons why the whole subject should not be glossed over, like a bad dream. One is that the memory inevitably infected the attitude of other peoples towards Germany and Germans after 1945 – and especially that of the nations which received the worst treatment, and the second consists in the need to remember the Nazi record when considering the claim that the German nation, in battling against communism, was performing a heroic role in the cause of civilisation and that the Atlantic Powers, in allowing it to be defeated, were guilty of a fatal miscalculation. To be sure, Nazism had no monopoly of cruelty and crudity, but to have allowed it to take the place of communism would hardly have contributed to the greater happiness of mankind.

Although from the beginning of 1942 onwards the balance of material resources was heavily against Germany, time was needed for the superiority of her opponents to be deployed and the events of the first nine months of that year, with sweeping Japanese victories in the Pacific, were such as to conceal the real state of affairs. In the summer German armies swept over the frontiers of Egypt and up to the summits of the Caucasus. But in order to have the troops needed to get there, Hitler had to fill the centre of his Russian front with Hungarian, Rumanian and Italian divisions; even so, his generals were held before they could cross the Volga or reach either the Nile or the oilfields of Baku. Indeed the advances which he did make proved the high water-mark of his success. For in the autumn Montgomery defeated the *Afrika Korps* at Alamein, Eisenhower landed with an Anglo-American force at the other end of North Africa and the Russians, breaking through the second-rate satellite divisions, surrounded the Sixth German Army of 285,000 men at Stalingrad. Hitler refused to consider withdrawing them, ordering them to die rather than give in. Their desperate position was for long concealed from the German people while attempts were made to supply them from the air. These failed and at the end of January 1943 the 91,000 still alive surrendered; German morale received a blow from which it never fully recovered. The turning-point of the war had arrived; henceforward it was not a question of whether Germany could win but of whether she could avoid total defeat.

A week before the Stalingrad surrender, at a conference at Casablanca, Roosevelt, backed by Churchill, had announced that 'peace can come to the world only by the total elimination of German, Japanese and Italian war power . . . [which] means the unconditional surrender of Germany, Italy and Japan'. Churchill a year later pointed out to Parliament that the Allies would not in consequence be bound to the German people after their surrender by any pact or obligation.

> No such arguments will be admitted by us as were used by Germany after the last war, saying that they had surrendered in consequence of President Wilson's 'Fourteen Points' [p. 58]. If we are bound, we are bound by our consciences to civilisation. We are not bound . . . as the result of a bargain struck.[11]

This attempt to learn from history has been criticised on the ground that it prolonged the war, since the prospect of a relatively mild peace might have induced the German generals and administrators, who were becoming increasingly critical of Hitler and concerned about his consequences for the country, to overthrow him and negotiate conditions of surrender.

Roosevelt and Churchill, however, headed a strong school of thought in Britain and America which held that the aim of the war was not just to overthrow Hitler and the Nazis but to eliminate from German life the authoritarian nationalist influences (labelled loosely by Churchill as 'Prussian militarism') which were held to be responsible for the five wars started by Germany during the previous 80 years. What was needed to this end was a clear demonstration that militarism did not pay, in the shape of complete defeat in the field (making impossible another 'stab-in the-back' legend), the occupation of the whole country (so as to ensure a thoroughgoing reconstruction of society such as the Germans had failed to carry through for themselves after 1918) and the disbandment (rather than mere reduction) of the German armed forces. But such a drastic settlement would mean the elimination of Germany as a power factor in Europe for at least a generation and this was the very thing which the generals, by training and temperament, were chiefly anxious to avoid. Consequently any attempt to negotiate conditions of surrender would quickly have reached deadlock.

For the British and Americans by themselves to have imposed on Germany the terms which their leaders thought necessary would have been a costly and perhaps impossible task. Nor did those leaders have any intention of attempting it. Another of their main concerns was to keep Russia in the war until complete victory had been won. In this, 'unconditional surrender' had a part to play since it reduced the risk of inter-allied disagreement about terms leading Russia to make a separate peace and provided the Russians with some reassurance against the fear that the British and American Governments were themselves prepared to make a separate peace with a non-Nazi but conservative German regime.

But this is the aspect of 'unconditional surrender' which has most led to post-war criticism of the doctrine. For by eliminating German power in Central Europe and helping Russia to advance to the Elbe, it brought the dividing-line between the free and communist worlds several hundred miles further west than might otherwise have been the case. One of the major reasons underlying the desire of the German generals to keep their power intact was precisely their belief in the need for a strong barrier to keep the Russians out. Moreover it can be argued that the German state which the Western Allies brought about did not in the end differ much from the one which the generals might have established (except that it only covered two-thirds of the area) so that nothing was gained and a good deal lost by refusing to compromise. Yet speculation on what might have been is a pursuit of questionable value. For not only were the forces opposed to a compromise peace in a majority in Britain and America. Roosevelt, and to a lesser extent Churchill, would have had to be different men before they could have taken a totally different line. And if they had been different men, the whole course of history would have been altered in many other incalculable ways and not simply in this momentous but particular respect.

The problem might have been avoided if a democratic non-militarist movement had developed in Germany to overthrow the Nazis and seize the government. But this was never an available option, not so much because of the lack of suitable people as because of the impossibility of organising resistance privately. As long as such resistance remained un-obtrusive, its effects were limited and as soon as they began to become serious, they would also have become obtrusive enough to get sternly suppressed. The army was the only body with the security needed to plan and with the formations of armed men needed to overcome rulers who were in no mood to relinquish power voluntarily. Indeed it is not certain that the army would have prevailed against the SS: an attempted coup might have precipitated civil war, which was another reason why generals hesitated about attempting one. The military would no doubt have called in civilians to form a government, presumably from much the same circles as had held office during the Weimar Republic. But the dependence of that Republic on the military was widely regarded in the West as an object-lesson which must not be repeated.

If the first nine months of 1942 had been dismal for the Atlantic Powers, the same months in 1943 brought a series of disasters to the Axis. In May North Africa was lost, with the surrender of over 100,000 German and Italian troops, and in July Eisenhower's forces landed in Sicily. Mussolini was overthrown in favour of a government under Marshal Badoglio which began secret negotiations for surrender. An armistice was proclaimed in September at the same time as Anglo-American forces landed south of Naples, but the Germans managed to withdraw their troops intact and establish a front south of Rome. Mussolini was rescued and put back on his pedestal but his image had been permanently dented and the dent did not go unnoticed in Germany. If Fascism could fall so easily, how secure was Nazism? The offensive at Kursk which was designed to rescue the situation for the Germans in Russia was not ready for launching until July and then proved a failure; the enemy, by a counter-attack, turned it into a steady retreat towards the frontiers of Poland and Rumania. In the Atlantic the British cracked the codes which the German submarines were using so that the losses of food and munitions on their way from America were drastically reduced.

By this time the British bombing attacks, which had been growing steadily in weight since 1940, were making life very uncomfortable for the inhabitants of most German cities; a series of raids on Hamburg from 24 July to 3 August caused particular damage and loss of life. As bombing by day had led to unacceptable losses and as precision bombing at night had proved impossible, the attacks had to be directed at central urban areas rather than strictly military targets. This strategy has been criticised in that its weight fell on civilians but had relatively little effect on the German war effort, as the figures for arms production (p. 100) show. When initiated it of course represented one of the few ways in which Britain could strike back at Germany and the spirit which prevented surrender from being seriously considered was also the spirit which insisted on using whatever weapons were available. The RAF's existence as an independent force had always been justified on the theory that future wars would be won by air power and that, since 'the bomber would always get through', the only satisfactory defence was retaliatory attack. Too many material and psychological resources had been invested in putting this doctrine into practice for an admission that it was mistaken to be easily made, especially as long as 'the fog of war' complicated the collection of evidence and led to its military effects being considerably overestimated. Moreover, until the autumn of 1943 its advocates would have argued that it had not been used on a large enough scale for its results to be fairly judged. In the spring of that year Goebbels and other leaders of the German home front had been seriously afraid of civilian morale collapsing. All in all, it is easy to see in retrospect why the strategy should have been adhered to for so long.

From all points of view the prospects which any level-headed German could see for his country from the autumn of 1943 onwards were such as to make urgent the question of removing Hitler, even if the Allies would not commit themselves over what would happen thereafter. But as no general in command of troops was prepared to start a revolt, the conspirators at the next lower level of the army began to see in assassination the only hope of forcing their superiors to move. The Führer was however so closely guarded as to render an attempt on his life extremely difficult; those who had access to him were not prepared to act while those ready to act had no access. An attempt in March 1943 which might have changed the course of history failed because a bomb smuggled onto his aircraft failed to detonate. From October 1943 onwards the chief organiser of the conspiracy was Colonel Claus Count von Stauffenberg, a staff officer of the Reserve Army Headquarters in Berlin. In the following June he took up a new post which required him to report periodically to Hitler in East Prussia and on 20 July he managed to plant a bomb which, after his departure, exploded at Hitler's feet. The coup however failed, partly because Hitler was not killed but partly also because nobody but Stauffenberg was in a position to give the necessary orders from Berlin and by the time he got back there to do so, the news that Hitler was still alive prevented them from being obeyed. As a result of the summary trials which followed, a Field Marshal, eight generals and some two hundred other eminent Germans were hanged. Thereafter nobody dared any further attempts. If the opposition had never attempted a rising but left the task of removing the Nazis to the

Allies, many valuable lives would have been saved to help in building up a new society after defeat. But a lasting blot would have been left on the German record if no risks had ever been run to get rid of the gangster regime. That the attempt should be made mattered more than that it should succeed.

It was indeed hastened forward because the June invasion of Normandy by British and American armies under Eisenhower was threatening to bring the war in the west to a speedy end. Hitler's much-advertised V-weapons gave south-east England an inkling of what future conflicts might be like but came too late to affect the course of the present one. In fact the Allied advance ran out of steam in September along Germany's western frontier and an attempt to get round the flank by seizing a bridgehead over the Rhine at Arnhem failed. But it was clear, especially after the repulse of a German winter offensive in the Ardennes, that Allied progress would be resumed irresistibly in the spring. In August the Russians had reached Warsaw but halted there for two months while the Germans annihilated the non-communist Polish insurgents who had risen in the hope of helping the Allied cause. Stalin felt strong enough to dispense with the assistance of people who were not committed to Communism, thus condemning 200,000 to death, and the British and Americans were too far away to help.

The Russians resumed their offensive in mid-winter. By now they were reaching districts like East Prussia and Silesia which had long been German and the civilian population faced a choice between flight through the snows and the hazards of capture. Goebbels increased his efforts to arouse in his audience strength through fear:

> If the German people were to lay down their arms . . . the Soviets would occupy the whole of Eastern and South-eastern Europe, plus the largest piece of the Reich. In front of these territories . . . an iron curtain would come down behind which the mass slaughter of the people would take place.[12]

But the material prerequisites for resistance were vanishing. For one thing, the Wehrmacht, weakened by all the casualties it had suffered and fighting on two fronts, was numerically outnumbered. Secondly Western air superiority had become such that precision bombing by day was at last practicable and was directed with particular effect at oil installations. As a result the Luftwaffe was all but grounded for lack of spirit while Speer's production efforts led to more tanks being turned out than could be fuelled. The shortage was aggravated by a Russian thrust into Rumania so that the Germans lost the use of its oil wells. Germany's ultimate defeat was due above all to lack of men and lack of oil.

Realising that all was lost, Hitler tried to increase rather than lessen the damage to the country. On 19 March he gave orders for the German earth to be 'scorched' in face of the invader. When Speer protested against denying the nation the possibility of future reconstruction, the Führer burst out:

If the war is lost, the nation also will perish. This fate is inevitable. There is no necessity to take into consideration the basis on which the people will need to continue a most primitive existence. On the contrary it will be better to destroy these things ourselves because this nation will have proved to be the weaker one and the future will belong solely to the stronger eastern nation.[13]

Fortunately Speer had not lost his ability to disobey and, with his staff and Wehrmacht support, showed almost as much ingenuity in frustrating his master's wishes as he had previously done in facilitating them.

By now it was merely a question whose troops would reach Berlin first. The German commanders would have gladly helped the Anglo-Americans to do so by surrendering to them, while continuing to resist in the east. But fear of provoking the Russians was still strong enough in the west for the proposition to be firmly rejected and for the Anglo-American armies, which were anyhow outrunning their supply lines, to be halted. Hitler, by this time a nervous wreck, retreated into his underground shelter (*Bunker*) in the centre of Berlin and it was there on 30 April at the age of 56 that he died; the most plausible interpretation of the evidence suggests that he was shot at his own request by his long-time mistress and recent bride Eva Braun who then took poison herself.[14] Five days previously, American and Russian forces had met near Leipzig. Seven days later Jodl, the Chief of the Wehrmacht Directing Staff, signed at Eisenhower's headquarters a document of unconditional surrender for all such troops as were still fighting. This time, unlike 1918, the generals were not allowed to evade responsibility for the outcome of the appeal to arms.

The war in Europe was over and the Third Reich at an end. To say how many people's lives they had cost is difficult since many extermination agencies kept no records. But the figure now given in the leading German encyclopaedia is 55 million. About 8 million of those were German.

THE POST-WAR SETTLEMENT, 1943-1945

Plans Prior to Surrender

For over two years before the Germans unconditionally surrendered, the Allies had been trying to settle what was to happen afterwards. Some things had been agreed without too much difficulty. Americans, British and Russians, for example, all took the view that the whole country must be occupied. An Allied Control Council in Berlin was, for the time being, to replace a German government and each of the three Powers was to be responsible for maintaining order and for seeing that the Council's decisions were carried out in a 'Zone' approximating to one-third of the country. A western boundary to the Soviet Zone, running roughly south-east from Lübeck, had been proposed by the British and accepted by the others; a belated American scheme for a line much further east, which would have resulted in three zones converging on Berlin, was never discussed internationally. A prolonged argument between Americans and British as to who should have the north-west was settled in September 1944 in favour of the latter, though the former were given Bremen as their port. At the same time it was agreed that Berlin should constitute a special area, occupied and administered by all three Allies, each of whom would be assigned a 'Sector' of the city. Then at the Yalta Conference in February 1945 Stalin was persuaded to allow the French a seat on the Control Council and a Zone of occupation, which was formed out of the south-west corners of both British and American Zones and as a result shaped like an hour-glass.

For any decisions of the Control Council to be valid, all four members had to consent to them. This put a premium on inter-governmental agreement about the instructions each gave to its representative. The Allies saw eye-to-eye about how to impose their will. But unless they also reached accord about what will to impose, they would be in danger of setting up not one new Germany but four. No great difficulty was found in agreeing that National Socialism must be eliminated, its representatives removed from positions of influence and its laws annulled. Nor did any of the victors object to the disbandment of the German armed forces and the destruction of all military material. There was even unanimity that the future Germany should be 'democratic', though events were to prove that East and West attached discrepant meanings to that elastic word. Where agreement ceased was over frontiers and reparations, both of them subjects crucial not only for the future life of Germany but also for the answer to the question 'How can Germany be prevented from disturbing the world again?'

From the outset of discussions, the Russians had insisted on hanging on to virtually all those parts of Poland which they had annexed in 1939, along what was known as 'the Curzon Line' (after the British Foreign Secretary who had proposed it in 1920 in an unsuccessful attempt to stop the fighting then in progress between the Russians and Poles and in the belief that it was the ethnic frontier). This obstinacy had secured for the Russians the agreement first of the British, then of the Americans and finally of the pro-communist government set up in Poland after the Germans were driven out. But if the Curzon Line was taken as the frontier, Poland would be 180,000 sq km smaller than she had been before 1939 and would lose 11.6m people (many of them admittedly more Russian than Polish). Consequently, there was general agreement that Poland must be compensated by annexations in the north and west at the expense of Germany; these were to go 'up to the line of the Oder', a river which, after flowing south from the Baltic, turns south-east through the centre of Silesia. It thus involved the transfer of half that province to Poland. But at Yalta the Russians proposed that, where the Oder turns, the frontier should continue due south along the Western Neisse river to the Czech border, thus giving Poland the *whole* of Silesia.

This alteration was resisted by the Americans and British, Churchill in particular protesting against 'stuffing the Polish goose so full of German food that it gets indigestion'. The Conference agreed that 'the final delimitation of the western frontier of Poland should await the Peace Conference'. This procrastination did not, however, stop the Russians from handing over to the Poles the whole area up to the Neisse soon after they had wrested it from the Germans. By such largesse (which even then only amounted to four-sevenths of what they were taking from the Poles) the Russians not only increased the distance which any future German army would have to march over non-German land before reaching Moscow, but they ensured for the Poles the enmity of many Germans and thus reckoned to safeguard themselves against any later risk of a Polish-German deal at their expense. (What the German nationalists were even more likely to resent was the loss of East Prussia with all its memories; this the Russians and the Poles divided between them, without any attempt being made by either Americans or British to object.)

A question which had produced uncertainty rather than disagreement was the disposal of the rest of Germany. At various times the Allied leaders had shown an inclination to carve the area up into two or three separate states. At Yalta dismemberment was agreed on in principle and a committee set up to work out the details. By the time this committee met, all three Governments were beginning to have second thoughts. The Western Allies realised that there might be advantages in having a united Germany as a barrier against Russia, and feared that a divided Germany would be an impoverished one needing help from outside; the Russians seem to have hoped that one Germany would be easier to turn communist than several, while they were also anxious to get reparations from the Ruhr and Rhineland. No plan of division was prepared and on 9 May Stalin in a proclamation denied that the Soviet Union intended either to dismember or destroy Germany. The idea of putting the Ruhr under some sort of international control was, however, taken almost for granted.

But what was the post-war Ruhr to be like? Here one touches on the most deep-seated problem of all, where the conflict between East and West overlapped with that between 'doves' and 'hawks'. For the West was divided between those who believed that the only way to stop Germany from aggression was by depriving her of the tools essential for war and others who argued that, since the prosperity of Europe was bound up with that of Germany and since she must therefore be left with some industries capable of being used for war, the aim must be to see that the country got into the hands of people who were not aggressive. The leader of the hawks was the US Secretary of the Treasury, Henry Morgenthau, who threw all Western post-surrender planning into confusion by getting, for a few weeks during the late summer of 1944, the support of Roosevelt and Churchill for his ideas. These were based upon the ease with which modern industry can beat ploughshares into swords and so involved depriving Germany of almost all her heavy industry. While the 'doves' quickly succeeded in recovering ground, the episode weakened their position during the next few crucial months in which the Allied armies were moving into Germany and starting to put ideas into practice. Roosevelt was not only inclined to treat Germany harshly but during the closing months of his life discouraged the taking of decisions about the future so that Western policy-making was in many respects paralysed.

The Russian approach was different, for in their Marxist eyes, Germany's aggressive tendencies were the inevitable result of her capitalist structure. The appropriate remedy therefore was not to worry about the control of the political government but about ownership of the means of production. Their less ideological if more immediate interests included, besides keeping a German eastern frontier as far removed as possible from their own western one, as much compensation as possible for the damage which Germany had inflicted on them. Taught by the experience of reparations after 1919, they proposed to extract this in kind rather than money. Factories and equipment were to be removed from Germany and taken to the victor countries; factories left in Germany were to be used to produce goods for the Allies while prisoners-of-war and Nazis captured on defeat were to be kept for ten years to work on reconstruction. What is not clear is whether they realised how much more difficult such treatment would make it for them to win Germany for communism. There were already many reasons for Germans and Russians to dislike one another. If a harsh peace were added, the chances of Germany adopting communism voluntarily would be minimal. Yet if the Russians were not prepared to meet the wishes of the Anglo-Americans and preferred to run the risk of a quarrel, they would find themselves wanting to win the friendship of the Germans against the West.

At Yalta the Soviet Government proposed that the total value of reparations should be set at $20,000,000,000, of which their own share would be half. Neither the British nor the Americans opposed the idea in principle and the Conference's communiqué said that Germany was to be obliged to 'make compensation in kind to the greatest extent possible'. But who was to say what was possible? Churchill and Eden maintained that the collection of the sum suggested by the Russians would render Germany destitute, that the United States and Britain would then have to provide the means for Germans to live and that they would thus in effect end up paying much of the Soviet bill themselves. It was decided to leave the working-out of the sum to a Reparations Commission.

The postponement of the question was not adroit enough to prevent the Russians from starting exactions immediately they got into Germany. Over and above the official removal of things as various as railway-lines and atomic scientists, individual soldiers were for some time allowed great licence to do as they chose with people and property. Germany was full of stories of the excesses of Soviet troops, many of whom were no more Russian than Gurkhas are English. For, as one Russian officer is said to have remarked 'The Red Army perished on the battlefields of 1941 and 1942. These are the hordes of Asia whom we have whipped to war so that we might roll back the German onslaught.'

A Summer of Make-do and Mend

Thus Germany in May 1945, fell into the hands of four Governments which had not yet reached either agreement or final disagreement about certain vital points concerning the way she was to be treated. Further discussions of these questions at top level was accordingly urgent. A variety of reasons however prevented it from taking place for two months and in the 'deadly hiatus' the proposed Control Commission was unable to start work; the commanders of the four armies, meeting in Berlin on 5 June, could do no more than proclaim its establishment, the division of Germany into Zones and the assumption of supreme authority with respect to the country by their four Governments. The precise basis of their power, along with the question of what happened to German sovereignty after unconditional surrender, was for some time regarded as a merely academic question; it later proved to have political implications.

The gap in the joint handling of Germany, though probably inevitable, was unfortunate, occurring as it did at a time when every day called for decisions to be taken. Since there was no machinery for reaching decisions applicable to Germany as a whole, they were inevitably made by each army at various points down its chain of command, and thus four patterns grew up which did nothing to ease future harmonisation.

The policies followed in the American and British Zones had been largely worked out by the joint Anglo-American staff at Eisenhower's Headquarters before these were dissolved in July. Accordingly they bore some relation to one another, though the Americans (who were bending their energies to the defeat of the Japanese) were in more of a hurry than the British to get on with decentralisation, denazification and democratisation. The French and Russians had their own ideas of how to go about things; these were followed with rather more ruthlessness and a good deal less attention to fairness and uniformity. (A German said later: 'The British like us but don't always notice that we're there; the Americans like us but treat us like badly-behaved children; the French hate us on equal terms.')

To have ruled Germany on a uniform basis during those months would anyhow have been difficult, for the havoc played with the transport system during the final stages of the fighting, along with the inertia accompanying defeat, had removed the previous German drive to keep wheels turning. The territory was fragmented into small districts and the established channels of supply and exchange could no longer function. The Nazi Government had financed the second war much as the

Imperial Government had financed the first. Taxes were raised to a smaller extent than in Britain or America and over two-thirds of the war's cost was met by borrowing; the volume of money in circulation increased about five times. The inflation which would naturally have resulted was held in check by rigid controls over prices and wages. Defeat then destroyed the confidence of the public in the currency. The Americans had provided all the Allies with plates for printing Mark notes in case too few German notes were available; the Russians used these without inhibition, distributing them to their troops, many of whom had not been paid for weeks. Those like farmers who were lucky enough to have surplus supplies of essential commodities sought and found ways of holding onto them or exchanging them for things other than cash.

Not that Germany was as seriously harmed by the war as her outward appearance suggested. The bombing and fighting had done great social damage, particularly to private houses and public buildings, but underneath the rubble of factories, much of the machinery was intact or capable of fairly easy repair. The amount of irretrievable damage to plant was estimated at 15 to 20 per cent, while thanks to wartime expansion Germany's productive capacity in 1944 was 20 per cent higher than it had been in 1936. The obstacle to recovery lay more in dislocation than in destruction.

The dislocation involved supplies, accommodation, transport, finance and ideas. But above all in the early days it involved people. Travel was unusually difficult but an unusually large number of people were nevertheless travelling. Some seven million members of the German armed forces surrendered to the British and Americans; they had to be rounded up, disarmed and either held for trial or dispersed to their homes. A number of Allied prisoners-of-war and just over half the six million foreign workers had to be repatriated. For the remainder, mainly Poles, Balts and Ukrainians, homes which were under Communist rule had lost their attraction. Nevertheless an agreement with the Russians for the mutual exchange of one another's citizens led to those who were or had become Soviet citizens being sent back, often against their will, often to a cruel fate which was often undeserved.

Some ten million Germans who had evacuated the bombed cities sought to return, if only to discover what had happened to their relatives and property. A considerable number more had fled westwards in face of the Russian advance. And no sooner had the Poles, Czechs and Magyars thrown off German control than, remembering the way in which the Nazis had exploited the German colonies in their midst, they began to expel the members of those colonies and send them back to Germany proper. The most notable of these groups were the 3 million Sudeten Germans who now had to take the consequences of having in 1938 put loyalty to Germany above loyalty to the state in which they lived; the refusal of the restored Czech Government to risk the same thing happening again may have been drastic but was certainly intelligible. What was more, the Poles administering the parts of Germany east of the Oder-Neisse line started turning out the inhabitants (8.8 million in 1939) since they needed the land to provide fresh homes for their own people who were being expelled by the Russians east of the Curzon Line. There was every prospect of the population of Germany (which, in spite of war losses, had risen between 1939 and 1945) being swollen by over 10 million extra people. How in these circumstances the country could be deprived of most of its industry was a question which began increasingly to be asked.

The immediate task was seen, in the West at any rate, as consisting in getting everyone provided with a sufficient minimum of shelter and food to prevent revolution, starvation and disease. To do this, communications had to be patched up and essential transport made possible; above all, the harvest had to be got in. But the German administrative system was in collapse. The Nazi leaders had made themselves scarce and, although a remarkable number of officials remembered having sufficient doubts about the Third Reich to justify an assurance that they had never been Nazis, it was a tricky question as to what reliance should be placed on them. If a literal interpretation were given to all that the Allied leaders had said about rooting out Nazism, practically nobody who had held a public post during the previous twelve years (including lawyers and teachers) could be allowed to keep it — though how the country would then be run was obscure. In these early days however the question of whom to use had to be settled off-the-cuff, locally, by men with a jaundiced view of German history and a rudimentary command of the German language. For the time being, there were narrow limits to the amount which Germans on their own could do. The Allies might proclaim that their aim was to control rather than to govern, but they alone possessed the organisation, the authority and above all the power to dispose of internal resources and gain access to external ones. For anything to happen, the officials of the military governments had to have a large hand in it.

The number of practical tasks pressing to be done and the obscurity about the form to be taken by the new state provided the British with a welcome excuse for giving politics a rest, whereas the Americans set up a government in Bavaria as early as May. Things were different in the Russian Zone where a trained group of ten German communists led by Walther Ulbricht were brought from Moscow at the beginning of May and set to work. To the surprise of everybody, including some of themselves, they did not immediately establish a communist regime but made great play with 'anti-Fascist' committees in which anyone who could claim to have opposed the Nazis was encouraged to join. When it came to choosing the new local officials, account was taken of the character of each district as well as of technical considerations; only the first deputy mayor, the personnel officer and the education officer had to be communists. 'The result must look democratic but the reins must really be in our own hands.'[15] In keeping with this policy, the registration of the Communist Party on 25 June was quickly followed by those of the Social Democrats, Christian Democrats and Liberal Democrats. Why the Russians should have preferred 'People's Democracies' of this kind is not altogether clear. They probably realised that there was no immediate hope of setting up a communist government throughout the country and calculated that the best way of spreading their influence was to adopt a system which stood some chance of being accepted in the other Zones as well. For them to tolerate bourgeois parties would justify them in demanding toleration of the Communist Party elsewhere.

Although the division of Germany into Zones of occupation was announced on 5 June, it did not come fully into effect for another month. Until that time, the troops of the three main Allies remained where they had been when fighting stopped. The western boundary of the Russian area thus ran along the Elbe instead of at a distance varying (except in the extreme north) between 50 and 150 miles west of that river, while on the other hand the whole of Berlin was under Soviet control. Churchill, who had regretted the halting of the Western armies before they reached Berlin, was reluctant to give up the extra territory until it became clear how much attention the Russians were going to pay to Anglo-American wishes on frontiers, reparations, the supply of foodstuffs from East to West Germany and various other matters at issue in Austria, Poland and the Balkans. But the Americans considered, and before long were able to quote the Russian commander Marshal Zhukov in confirmation, that the Russians would insist on previous agreements about zonal boundaries being honoured before they would allow the West access to Berlin, or Vienna, let the Control Council start working or indeed come to the conference table at all. Moreover both Russian help and American troops from Europe were wanted to polish off the war against Japan and neither would be available if a show-down was precipitated at that juncture. Accordingly on 12 June President Truman agreed to withdraw his forces and Churchill reluctantly concurred. The move, which took place on 1 July, has sometimes been considered a mistake. But if it had not been made, the many difficulties which were to follow with the Russians and which certainly would not have been lessened by the breach of faith, would have been widely blamed on Western intransigence. There are times when a policy must be followed to its logical end in order to demonstrate to the public that its results are unsatisfactory and so obtain the general consensus needed for a change of course.

As an integral part of the bargain, American and British troops moved to take over the Sectors allotted to them in Berlin, where the royal suburb of Potsdam was to be the scene of a Summit meeting between the Americans, British and Russians on 16 July. The whole idea of a jointly-occupied city two-thirds of the way across the Russian Zone was unprecedented. Its adoption reflected not only the wartime assumption of the Americans that co-operation with the Russians would be as easy as with the British but also the belief that, in a Germany which was to be treated as a unity, boundaries between Zones would only be significant for the stationing of troops and not for government. In the negotiations which led to the agreements on occupation plans signed in the autumn of 1944, the Soviet representatives had insisted that the presence of British and American troops as an integral part of the occupation and administration of the city carried with it all necessary facilities of access. But the Civil Affairs Division of the US War Department had prevented this principle from being spelt out on paper in advance, for fear of being committed to arrangements which might in the event prove inconvenient. The task was therefore left for the military commanders to perform when the time came, though nothing was done to brief those commanders in advance.

When they met on 29 June, Zhukov refused to grant his Western colleagues two out of the three railways, one out of the two highways and one out of the three airfields for which they asked. Moreover he made clear that what they did receive would come as a privilege rather than a right, while he passed over in silence their request that all traffic be free from customs control and military (but not police) search. Faced with the need for an immediate decision and reluctant to hold up the Allied arrival in Berlin, not to mention the Summit Conference, by haggling, the British and American generals contented themselves with what they could get, merely reserving the right to reopen the matter in the Control Council (unaware that in it the Russians would have a veto).

Partly to save time, partly to leave elbow-room for future discussions, they did not even obtain written confirmation of what had been agreed. They imagined that they had only to consider the rights and interests of their own troops. Only when they met again ten days later to settle how the city should be ruled were they faced with a Russian demand that supplies of food and coal for the Western Sectors must be obtained and brought from the Western Zones; only later still did the question arise of how far and under what conditions German persons and goods possessed rights of movement between the city and the West.

Much subsequent argument flowed from the failure to get the Western rights of access to Berlin clearly defined at the outset. The Civil Affairs Department certainly has a good deal to answer for. Against the generals the case is less clear. The cost of being intransigent might have been considerable and the existence of an agreed document would only have impeded and not prevented Russian inclinations to make trouble. In the last resort, the Western presence in Berlin rests not on written texts but on the power which is deployed in its support.

The Potsdam Conference

In the meeting which took place at Potsdam between 17 July and 2 August 1945, the British and Americans were at a certain disadvantage. It was barely three months since the inexperienced Truman had succeeded Roosevelt. He naturally hesitated to break away from his predecessor's determination to work with the Russians and refused Churchill's suggestion of preliminary Anglo-American discussions for fear of thereby antagonising Stalin. Moreover the British General Election was so timed that the Conference had to be interrupted as it neared its climax while the British delegates went home for the poll to be declared and when they came back, the leaders were Attlee and Bevin rather than Churchill and Eden. Attlee had admittedly attended the Conference from the start while both he and Bevin had belonged to the War Cabinet but according to Churchill this did not prevent them from taking their places 'without any serious preparation' and 'unacquainted with the ideas and plans' which their predecessors had in view.[16] Although the French were to join in the Control Council and Occupation, a deaf ear was turned to General de Gaulle's persistent demand for a seat at the conference table, largely because at the crucial moment he chose to make himself difficult in south-west Germany, north-west Italy and Syria.

The meeting was not a peace conference and was in no position to dictate a Treaty to the leading enemy state, since there was no German government to sign such a document. Instead the conclusions were given to the world in a 'Protocol of Proceedings' drawn up somewhat hastily in the closing hours; it was not considered to need ratification by either Congress or Parliament. Thirteen of its 21 sections, amounting to about two-fifths of its total space, did not concern Germany. Those which did, dealt with Political and Economic Principles to govern Germany's treatment; Reparations; Disposal of the German Navy and Merchant Marine; East Prussia; Poland's Western Frontier; War Criminals; the Orderly Transfer of German Populations. Of these it was again Reparations and Frontiers which caused most dispute.

The Political Principles, based upon an American draft, were agreed to without much argument. Germany was to be completely disarmed and kept indefinitely in that condition. The National Socialist Party and everything connected with it was to be dissolved: all Nazi laws which provided the basis of the regime or established discrimination on grounds of race, creed or political opinion (though not necessarily other legislation passed since 1933) were to be cancelled. All members of the Party who had been 'more than nominal participants in its activities' were to be removed from office, while leaders and high officials were to be interned and war criminals were to be brought to judgment. A significant clause laid down that 'so far as practicable' the German population throughout the country was to be treated uniformly. Preparations were to be made for the eventual reconstruction of German political life on a democratic basis, particularly by the encouragement of democratic political parties and the introduction of self-government from local councils upwards. Freedom of speech, press and religion were (subject to considerations of security) to be permitted. Although no central government was to be established for the time being, five or more central administrative departments were to be set up, which were intended to issue to lower levels the orders needed to get the policies of the Control Council put into execution. One of the objects of the Occupation was declared to be the convincing of the German people that they had suffered a total military defeat and could not escape responsibility for the inevitable distress and chaos which they had brought on themselves.

The Economic Principles, again based on an American draft, were more contentious but principally in relation to reparations. Of Morgenthau's ideas little was left beyond an injunction to restrict to Germany's peacetime needs the production of metals, chemicals and other items essential to a war economy, whereas 'primary emphasis' was to be given to the development of agriculture and peaceful domestic industries. The economy was to be decentralised but Germany was to be treated as a single economic unit, common economic policies were to be established and essential commodities equitably distributed between the Zones so as to produce a balanced economy and reduce the need for imports. To the fullest extent practicable, Germans were to be made to administer their own controls.

Productive capacity, even if for peaceful purposes, could be removed as reparations. But a separate clause laid down that sufficient goods and services were to be produced and maintained as, after meeting the needs of the occupying forces and (non-German) 'displaced persons', 'were essential to maintain in Germany average living standards not exceeding the average of . . . European countries'. Much subsequent discussion started from the assumption that Germany was here promised a floor rather than a ceiling and it is hard to see what other effect the words 'essential to maintain' could have been intended to have. But the inclusion of the words 'not exceeding' is out of line with this interpretation and virtually deprives the statement of any meaning at all. To complicate matters, yet another clause laid down that payment of reparations was to leave enough resources for the German people to be able to subsist without external aid i.e. to be able to pay with exports for essential imports.

Here lay the seeds of future arguments. There was general agreement that reparations were to be obtained by 'removals', presumably of plant. No reference was made in the Protocol to the requisitioning of future production (which had been mentioned at Yalta) and the Americans were under the impression that the Russians had agreed to abandon this source. If however they had not, the question would arise of the relative priority of reparations and exports. For production taken away as reparations clearly could not be sold as exports and if exports failed to reach a level high enough to pay for all essential imports, then the bill for those imports would have to be paid from some other source, which could hardly be anything other than the Governments of the Powers occupying the Zones in question. The Russian answer was that imports which could not be paid for, no matter how essential, were not to be made. The Western Powers wanted in the long run to have a prosperous Germany because they believed it to be necessary for a prosperous Europe and they wanted Europe to be prosperous so that it could make its due contribution to a prosperous international trade. The Russians did not mind if Europe became destitute because they calculated that it was then all the more likely to turn communist.

The crucial issues were the size of reparations and the amount of plant which might be removed. Stalin and Molotov fought hard to secure acceptance of the $20 billion which they had proposed at Yalta. But the Americans and British made clear that they would break off negotiations rather than name any figure at all. Instead they proposed that the Control Council be left to work out how much productive capacity Germany could spare in the light of the other economic terms. The Russian action in taking equipment out of their Zone without waiting for Four-Power approval then led to an American proposal that each occupying Power should draw reparations from its own Zone. But the Russians had been promised half the total whereas it was estimated that only 40 per cent of German productive capacity came from their Zone. Accordingly, to honour the pledge, they were offered in supplement one-sixth of the amount agreed to be surplus in the Western Zones.

This solution was then traded against a virtual Western climb-down over frontiers. As has been said, the Poles were occupying the whole area up to the Oder-Neisse line. When the West complained about being confronted with an accomplished fact and about the way in which the German inhabitants had been driven out, they were met by a half-true assurance that the Germans had all fled of their own accord, so that the area would remain an uncultivated desert unless the Poles were allowed to settle in it. Possession proved nine-tenths of the law but the West's face was saved by a proviso that a final decision on the frontier should not be taken till the Peace Conference (then expected to occur quite soon). The meeting thus ended in a compromise, with each side imposing its will where it had power to do so.

Even so, the agreement proved to have several flaws. For one thing, the French were not a party to it nor was their acceptance of its terms made a pre-condition of their admission to the Control Council. This put them in a position to veto any aspects they disliked; these included the establishment of political parties and trade unions on a nation-wide basis and the creation of the central administrative departments. Their obstruction, which the Americans for reasons not altogether clear refused to over-ride, meant that there was no German channel by which the decisions of the Control Council could be transmitted to such lower-level German administrations as did exist or were formed. The gap had to be filled by the Military Governors who took to dealing directly with hand-picked Land Governments set up in the various Zones and even to establishing Advisory Councils for each Zone as a whole. Consequently the Zone boundaries acquired a political significance which they were not originally intended to have. On the other hand the failure to create a central German administration may have saved the Western Powers from having to cope with one which was Communist-dominated.

Secondly a number of the terms used in the Protocol, such as 'democratic basis', 'so far as practicable', 'essential to maintain' and 'removals' were inadequately defined and their interpretation left to the Control Council. But where the Council could not agree, and action was nevertheless urgent, individual Zone commanders were free to go their own way; further scope for diversity of interpretation was given by a clause allowing account to be taken 'where appropriate, of varying local conditions'. In such matters as denazification and education, the most that the Council ever succeeded in doing was to bless and throw an appearance of harmony over measures already being taken in the various Zones. The only denazification action of any importance carried through on a quadripartite basis resulted from US insistence that the chief available Nazis should be dealt with by judicial process rather than disposed of in a summary way or left for judgment to the Germans. This led to the trial by an International Military Tribunal in Nuremberg of Göring and 22 other members of the Nazi hierarchy who had fallen into Allied hands. After ten months of hearings in which much highly illuminating evidence was brought to light, eleven were condemned to death, seven imprisoned and three acquitted.

Early in the morning of the day on which the Potsdam Conference was due to open, a flash of blinding intensity lit up the desert of New Mexico. The news of the first successful explosion of a new weapon was 'casually mentioned' by Truman to Stalin eight days later. 'The Generalissimo seemed pleased but not inquisitive.'[17] His agents had undoubtedly told him of what was afoot and the scientific principles involved were fairly common knowledge; what the explosion showed was that the engineering problems about putting them into practice could be overcome. Any effect on the Conference is hard to detect; the Americans did not become noticeably more uncompromising nor the Russians more conciliatory. Undoubtedly however the event made itself felt during the following months. The Russians neither asked nor were invited to share in the secret and a proposal to vest control of all atomic development in the United Nations came to nothing. But the task of rebuilding Russia must have looked more formidable than ever to her leaders when they realised that, to remain a Great Power, she must forthwith set aside the extensive resources needed to give her a bomb of her own.

For Germany also the explosion had implications which were more profound than appreciated. Even if quadripartite control were to prove temporary, the loss of territory and wealth imposed at Potsdam must have seemed to render the manufacture of a German bomb out of the question for a long time and thus put a further bar in the way of breaking through to become a World Power. But the bomb decisively underlined the effect of modern weapons in making war so lethal as to cause all participants more loss than gain and thus to become unthinkable except as an act of desperation. But with war ruled out, any attempt to reverse the Potsdam settlement, except by mutual consent, had also to be ruled out. Yet paradoxically the fear of such an attempt being made by a Germany in control of nuclear arms was to complicate subsequent efforts at relaxing European tension.

6 TOWARDS TWO GERMANIES, 1945-1948

The Economic Tangle

Throughout the winter of 1945/6 the Economic Directorate of the Control Commission, putting the horse after the cart, laboured to spell out what the broad conclusions of the Potsdam Conference would mean in concrete terms. By the end of March they had managed to agree on the shape which German industry should henceforward assume. Fourteen of its branches were to be prohibited altogether, twelve more to be limited to a percentage of pre-war output varying from 11 to 80. The steel industry was to be allowed an output only slightly larger than pre-war Germany had needed for miscellaneous uses in light industry. Such plant in these branches as was surplus to requirements was to be made available for reparations or dismantled. In all, 1,636 factories were to be closed down in the UK and US Zones. In spite of the confiscation as reparations of Germany's merchant marine and overseas assets, and so of the cessation of the invisible income flowing from them, the balance of trade was to show a surplus by 1949. But this assumed that the money earned before the war from the exports of heavy industry would be replaced by sales of coal and consumer goods, although the total output of these was still expected to be below the 1938 level. No allowance was made for the loss of output caused by the shift of resources, by the amputation of territory in the east or the need to sustain a population swollen by refugees. The German standard of living was to be reduced to 74 per cent of the pre-war average, which happened to be the figure reached in 1932, the slump year paving Hitler's way to power.

The publication of this plan served to bring home forcibly to the British and American publics the implications of the policy to which their leaders had committed them and the reactions were not surprisingly emphatic. Growing difficulties in the Balkans, Iran and elsewhere made the Americans ask whether they were not sacrificing too much for Russian co-operation and getting too little in return. The Russians for their part were finding that the system of removing equipment for use at home left a lot to be desired and were turning more and more to keeping factories in Germany and removing the output instead. They took the line that such a practice had been envisaged at Yalta and not forbidden at Potsdam, while repeating their argument that reparations should receive top priority. The West argued that, as the Potsdam Protocol had made no provision for the use of output as reparations, all such output as was not indispensable inside Germany must be used for exports. None of the foodstuffs which had been wont to flow from the East (and particularly from East Prussia and the areas occupied by the Poles) were reaching the Western Zones; in the chaos of the time there was little surplus to come though there might have been more if the Russian authorities, to undermine the economic position of the land-owners, had not increased the confusion by introducing in August 1945 a programme of land redistribution. Consequently the population of the US and UK Zones, far from self-sufficient at the best of times, were being kept alive on a subsistence diet by 1.5 million tons of food imports paid for by the British and American taxpayers. British Ministers as well as people began to ask indignantly why they should sacrifice scarce foreign exchange and forego increases in their own rations in order to help out the people who had caused all the trouble. What they were in reality doing, of course, was indirectly helping out the Russian people who had done so much to win the war, but this was neither appreciated nor explained. The situation would have been eased if the Americans had made the loan which up to the summer of 1945 they had encouraged the Russians to expect from them but for various reasons the negotiation of this was postponed until a period at which the terms insisted on by Washington were such as Moscow was unprepared to accept. Instead Lend-Lease was cut off abruptly when Japan surrendered without any substitute having been arranged.

Hardly had the Control Council agreed on its Economic Plan than General Clay, the American Military Governor, suspended deliveries of plants from the US Zone which had been allocated to the Russians and French as reparations. The step, intended as a protest against the use of output for reparations, was largely symbolic because at that stage few plants had been so allocated. It enabled the Russians to argue that it was the Americans rather than themselves who had broken the Potsdam Agreements, and neither it nor anything else was effective in stopping them from continuing over the next seven years to take away up to a quarter of the gross national product of their Zone. Nor did it do anything substantial to resolve the economic problems of the Western Zones.

In point of fact, reparations from those Zones only reached 5 per cent of industrial capacity, fell chiefly on industries which in terms of 1938 requirements (though not, as it proved, 1958 ones) were over-equipped and cleared the ground for the later installation (with government subsidy) of fresh and more modern equipment. As the plants taken away were not often of any use to the new owners, the policy was productive of neither serious damage nor benefit. But considerable faith in human incompetence would have been required to foresee this and during the time when the precise effect of the policy was in doubt (and this was much prolonged by the endeavours of the administrators to be methodical and fair all round) great alarm and acrimony were caused. Nobody was going to put much effort into stepping up the output of a factory as long as there was still a possibility that it might be picked on for dismantling.

Yet for more factories to have been functioning would have aggravated the situation rather than eased it. For manufacturing requires the steady consumption of materials and once the stocks available in Germany at the end of the war had been used up, there was nothing to replace them. The modern economic system has come to take for granted the existence of innumerable 'pipelines' through which goods in various stages of elaboration are continuously moving from the primary source to the consumer. Germany had been depending on pipelines which sucked supplies out of occupied Europe with little regard to local needs. These needs, however, recovered top priority the moment that German power was withdrawn. Consequently there would have been few supplies available to flow to Germany even if communications had remained intact. The only continents with substantial resources to spare lay overseas, primarily in the Americas, and to these not only did new channels of supply have to be organised but the problem of payment had to be overcome. Germany could not pay because her currency was worthless and she could not produce. But before she could produce, she must be able to pay for the wherewithal. About the turn of the year 1945/6 Clay's economic chief told him that 'we must have $100m to finance essential imports other than food if we are to succeed'.[18] And not only did Germany need gifts or credits enabling her to buy abroad and thus get her machines restarted, but somebody in a position of authority had to do the buying for her. For all European countries were queuing up to restock themselves and the defeated enemy, if on her own, would have been likely to come last.

Coal vividly illustrated the difficulties. All Europe was short and Britain, a traditional source of supply, had none to spare. The countries which Germany had occupied, and particularly France, insistently demanded that her output should be used to alleviate their needs. As coal exports would earn valuable exchange, there was good reason in Germany's own interest for making them and some were in fact made — though at cut prices. But as German production was down to about a quarter of the pre-war level, these exports left little for German industry, transport and public utilities, and virtually nothing for domestic use. Owing to lack of coal, the steel industry could not achieve even the output allowed under the Allied Plan and without steel other industries, including coal, found it hard to raise their production, while crop yields were held down by lack of basic slag as fertiliser. The occupation authorities, particularly in the British Zone where most of the collieries were situated, were taken to task by the liberated countries on the one hand for not exporting more coal and on the other by the Germans for exporting too much. The Germans further complained that if the coal had been kept in their country and used by their industries to make goods, these would earn much more as exports than coal by itself. But this would have meant restoring employment in Germany rather than among her victims and was therefore out of the question.

German Attitudes

The people of Germany were too much obsessed with their own plight to absorb information about conditions outside their frontiers. This did not mean that their outlook remained unchanged by defeat. During the closing stages of the war (and probably over a longer period) the proportion of 'hard core' Nazis and active anti-Nazis would seem to have been roughly balanced at about 10 per cent, with the former slightly preponderating; 25 per cent had been 'believers with reservations', 40 per cent unpolitical opportunists and 15 per cent passive opponents. The hard core was now in internment or concealment, aware for the most part that their only hope was to lie low and trust to time bringing a reaction. The reservations of the erstwhile believers had swollen to preclude admissions about what they had once approved and some indeed may have become genuinely convinced that ideas which could lead to such disaster must have been mistaken. In common with the conformists, they were ready to go along with the new order even if they were more inclined to criticise its shortcomings than to appreciate the reasons for them. They showed great reluctance to absorb the version of the past and the picture of the present which the British and Americans pressed upon them as if out of a subconscious fear of having to admit that, as the Potsdam Protocol put it, 'the German people cannot escape responsibility for what they have brought upon themselves'.

The anti-Nazis, both active and passive, were in a more difficult position. The perpetual fear of arrest and the self-control needed to avoid trouble had in many cases been replaced by profound searchings of heart about the validity of German values, an obsession with the problem of guilt and a conflict between remorse and patriotism. To admit to mistakes and make recompense might be regarded as surrendering the national case and justifying Allied policy, while nobody could be sure that in a few years 'collaboration' with the victors might not prove as much a cause for reproach as it had just become in liberated Europe. Many of the most positive minds emerged scarred by their experience in the Third Reich. To their resentment of the Allied wartime refusal to make resistance easier by modifying the demand for unconditional surrender, there was now added disappointment that so much responsibility was kept in Allied hands, so little preference shown to those who had proved by their record that they were worthy of confidence. In the long run this Allied caution, born largely of uncertainty, paid dividends, since it postponed the danger of a reaction and saved many valuable democrats from damaging their usefulness by an over-eager association with the victors. In any case those who wanted to assume responsibility were for the first few months in a minority. Most Germans wanted nothing better than to collect their thoughts and their belongings – indeed, much of their time was absorbed in securing the essentials of life. Once again, the integrating processes in Germany had been put into reverse by failure.

Such circumstances hardly encouraged a revival of political life. But parties had been given leave to organise themselves in the Western Zones by September 1945 though they did so at first under close supervision and on a local basis. The most notable innovation was the foundation, as in several other Western countries, of a party designed to rally all the forces which were both anti-communist and anti-Nazi under the positive slogans of religion and democracy. The Christian Democratic Union (which in Bavaria called itself the Christian Social Union) combined Protestants with Catholics (thereby differing markedly from the old Centre) and heirs of the National Liberal tradition with a pronounced radical wing. The Liberal or Free Democratic Party sought to inherit the anti-clerical *laissez-faire* tradition of the middle classes; it also accommodated a number of persons compromised by their association with Nazism. The Social Democrats and Communists both based themselves on organisations which had maintained a precarious underground existence during the Third Reich. The Lower Saxony Land Party, originally founded to reactivate Hanover's past independence, gradually extended the range of what it sought to resurrect.

Two arguments were prevalent in favour of the left-wing parties working together. One was that if such a front had existed in 1933, National Socialism might have been kept from power. The other lay in the general agreement that the essential step towards eradicating the aggressive authoritarian influences in German society lay in bringing the means of production and main sources of wealth under communal control. The chance which had been allowed to slip in 1919 must this time be seized; land reform and nationalisation of the basic industries must not be confined to the Soviet Zone. One of the main reasons why the Social Democrats were impatient with the Anglo-American refusal to put power immediately into German hands was that the accomplishment of this process was thereby delayed. But to the Americans nationalisation was a dirty word and, although the British Labour Government was engaged in just such a programme at home and did take under government control the coal and steel industries in its Zone, in the end the precarious state of the UK economy made it too dependent on American help for it to be able to go its own way in Germany. The British had to agree to the whole issue being shelved until the Germans were in a position to decide for themselves, while in a parallel shelving of a nationalisation clause in the Germans' own constitution for Land Hesse made clear that the decision was to be taken above Land level.

This compromise solution may appear to be justified by subsequent events, since, when the West Germans did come to decide, their verdict was unmistakably adverse. It would therefore seem that, as in 1919, a thorough-going programme of socialisation could not have been carried out and maintained without political dictatorship. What is more, the US administration would have had much greater difficulty in getting Congressional approval for help to Germany if that country could have been represented as being well on the road to socialism. On the other hand there is no doubt that the political climate of Germany immediately after 1945 was more radical than it subsequently became. An early election would almost certainly have produced a majority favouring socialisation and experience elsewhere suggests that there are limits to the extent to which this, once carried through, can be reversed. What must however be doubted is whether co-operation between Social Democrats and Communists would have lasted long. For soon the animosities which had weakened the German left all through its history began to reassert themselves.

The policy of the Russian Government towards Germany and the behaviour of the Soviet troops in that country were proving a serious obstacle to the popularity of the Communist Party and in all Zones the workers looked increasingly towards the Social Democrats. Ulbricht and the other Communist leaders in the Russian Zone sought to turn this awkward development to their advantage by launching the idea of a single anti-capitalist party and in February 1946 induced the executive of the Berlin SPD, led by Otto Grotewohl, to vote for the fusion of their party with the Communists in a new Socialist Unity Party (SED). Two days later, however, a mass meeting of Berlin SPD refused to confirm the executive's decision and at the end of March Social Democrats in the three Western Sectors of the city were encouraged by SPD leaders from West Germany to poll a vote of 82 per cent against the merger (though not against more limited co-operation). What the Social Democrats in the Russian Sector may have thought remains uncertain since the authorities there refused to let opinion be tested and forced the fusion through. When, six months later, elections were held throughout Berlin under quadripartite supervision, the SPD led in all twenty of the city's boroughs, whereas the SED got less than half as many votes, trailing behind the CDU.

Thus began a process in which the SED received steady favouritism in the areas under Russian control, where increasing difficulties were put in the way not only of the SPD but of the other two middle-class parties as well. Since the SED won little support in the Western Sectors of the city and did not exist in the Western Zone, the development created a major distinction between the two parts of Germany. The division between radical and moderate which had existed between the Marxist and Lassallean wings when the Socialist Workers Party was founded in 1875, which had given rise to the gap between revolutionary theory and revisionist practice before 1914, which had led to the breakaway of the Independent Social Democrats in 1917, and which had produced the rivalry between SPD and KPD throughout the Weimar Republic, now took on a geographical form. One part of Germany, under Russian direction, was made to put socialism before democracy; the other, under Western influence, reversed the priorities.

Western Germany was also witnessing the gradual evolution of a federal structure as a means of achieving the aim of decentralisation which had replaced that of dismemberment. The Americans as early as the summer of 1945 confirmed the right of Bavaria to remain a distinct political unit and brought into being a new Land of Greater Hesse. The need to provide the French with a Zone, combined with American communications requirements, led to the northern parts of Baden and Württemberg being divided from the south, though, whereas the French kept their pieces distinct, the Americans combined theirs to form a composite Land. The enclave of Bremen formed a fourth Land. Elections for Land

Parliaments (*Landtäge*) were held in June 1946. In Bavaria they led to a
majority for the CSU, in Hesse and Bremen to ones for the Socialists
and in Württemberg-Baden to an indecisive result.
    In the British Zone four Länder were set up, chiefly on the strength
of German advice. Hamburg and Schleswig-Holstein formed natural
units and Lower Saxony a convenient combination of what had been
several smaller ones. In July 1946 two Prussian provinces were merged
to form the Land of North Rhine-Westphalia, with a population as large
as the Netherlands. This move was variously attributed to a desire to
head off French designs on the Rhineland and Russian demands for a
share in international control of the Ruhr; to a wish to join the industrial complex of the Ruhr with its agricultural hinterland; and to anxiety
to deprive the Socialists or Communists of an almost certain majority in
the main towns by bringing in more conservative rural areas. Indeed
North Rhine-Westphalia was the only Land in the British Zone in which
the Socialists did not emerge as the strongest party when elections were
held in April 1947, though even there the CDU came a good deal short
of an absolute majority.
    The French Zone consisted of South Baden, South Württemberg-
Hohenzollern, the Rhineland-Palatinate and the Saar; its occupiers
dreamt of incorporating the latter, which provided much of their coal,
into France proper (p. 174). Elections throughout the Zone in May
1947 showed a CDU majority in all four Länder. Meanwhile the Soviet
Zone was divided into five Länder (though this was to prove a temporary arrangement). As a net result Germany (including Berlin) became
organised into 18 units which, while still varying in population from the
11.8 million of North Rhine-Westphalia to the 226,000 of Bremen,
were on the whole better balanced than ever before. The vast prepon-
derance of Prussia (p. 29) had been eliminated even before the Control
Council in February 1947 passed a law bringing that state's existence
formally to an end. The responsibilities assigned to the Land Governments and subordinate authorities did much to determine the way in
which powers were to be divided between the federal and Land Governments under the Federal Republic.

Bizonia

By the time that Land Governments had been elected however a considerable change had come over the whole administrative structure of
the Western Zones. For the problem of repriming the German economic

pump could not be indefinitely deferred, yet could not be solved within
the boundaries of a single Zone. Apart from the difficulty of treating as
a separate unit something never designed for that purpose, the Americans, who alone were in a position to provide the wherewithal, were only
prepared to risk their money in a unit which had a prospect of proving
viable. The British, themselves dependent on American support, could
not for much longer afford to go on spending $80 million a year in
support of an area with a population half their own total. Consequently
in July 1946 the American Secretary of State, James F. Byrnes, offered
to merge the US Zone for economic purposes with that of any other
Power willing to join and before the end of the month the British had
accepted. The Russians and French tried to make conditions and found
themselves left in the cold. A complicated organisation was set up to
run the merged Zones, with six boards in four different places, each
supervised by a committee of German Ministers from the British and
US Länder. Machinery was set up to make sure that all available goods
were exported, that the proceeds were used to buy imports and that the
necessary imports were made available. As Byrnes said at Stuttgart on
6 September, 'Germany is part of Europe and recovery in Europe, and
particularly in the states adjoining Germany, will be slow indeed if
Germany with her great resources of iron and coal is turned into a poor-
house.'

It had been fundamental to Morgenthau's arguments that Germany
was *not* necessary to Europe and to Russian arguments that reparations
must have priority over the German standard of living. The Byrnes
speech was a landmark because it explicitly rejected both points of view.
Whereas hitherto an early American withdrawal from Europe had been
taken for granted, Byrnes announced his country's intention to remain
as long as the Occupation lasted. Thanks to their insistence on taking
reparations from current production, the Russians found themselves
denied any influence over developments in West Germany while, if the
American policy succeeded, the prospects of German communists gaining control there would vanish away. But through Soviet spectacles, this
change was seen as the result of international capitalism rehabilitating
the economic system which had produced Nazism and recreating the
danger of another German onslaught on the communist world. A feeling
of betrayal and alarm combined with an awareness of weakness to make
them hold more firmly than ever onto what they had and refuse concessions. A meeting of Foreign Ministers in Moscow in March 1947
coincided with Truman's announcement that America would give active
support to all free people resisting subjugation by armed minorities or

outside aggression. Molotov combined a renewed bid for $10 billion reparations with a demand that the fusion of the Zones be cancelled. As he offered little in return, he convinced Byrne's successor General Marshall that the Russians were stalling in the hope that time would be on their side and that all Western Europe would soon go communist.

The attempt to carry over into peace the wartime alliance with Russia had cost a year's delay in the reconstruction of Europe. The effects of the delay became painfully prominent when the winter of 1946/7 proved exceptionally cold. The waterways which play so large a part in German transport froze over; the roads and railways were still in too precarious a state to carry the displaced traffic. Supplies had for so long been short that everything was distributed as soon as it arrived; when it failed to arrive there were no stocks to fall back on. Rations could not be honoured, power stations ran out of coal, factories closed. But the crisis was not peculiar to Germany. All over Western Europe countries were running out of not merely supplies but of the foreign exchange needed to buy them. In France, the Low Countries and Italy production, which by a great effort had been brought within sight of pre-war levels, stopped expanding. In August 1947 the British attempt to make the pound convertible in accordance with the terms of the laboriously negotiated US loan had to be abandoned after seven-tenths of the $5 billion loan had been exhausted. Also in August the French Government suspended all dollar imports except coal, cereals and other essentials; in September the Italian Government stopped purchases even of coal and oil.

Such was the impending prospect when General Marshall made his Harvard speech on 5 June announcing that if the countries of Europe could agree on a combined plan for recovery, the American Government would finance it. The task of reconstruction had proved much bigger than anyone had foreseen; now at least there was a prospect of it being tackled on an adequate scale. Bevin for Britain grasped at the offer, and Bidault for France followed suit. But at a conference in Paris at the end of the month, Molotov insisted that the money must be given to individual countries to dispose of as they thought fit. To this the Americans were not disposed to agree and it was clear that, to win their agreement, any joint schemes must be aimed at the restoration of free trading conditions incompatible with the operation of a centrally-controlled economy. The Russians accordingly walked out of the discussions and compelled Poland and Czechoslovakia to do the same. Sixteen Western countries then proceeded to draft a four-year programme which was accepted by Congress during the winter and began to operate in mid-1948. In this programme the provision of aid to the Western Zones of Germany formed an integral part, whereas the Soviet Zone was excluded by the Russian reaction. It was therefore an important further step towards the division of the country.

But before the Western Zones could be fully set on the path of recovery, two further steps were needed and for neither was Russian agreement likely to be forthcoming. First of all the totally artificial position of the currency had to be altered. The occupation authorities had kept in existence the controls which the Nazis had imposed (p. 81) but did little towards reducing the volume of currency beyond imposing drastic nominal taxation and thereby discouraging initiative. Money ceased to be of any importance and the legal channels of trade were less and less used; goods were exchanged either in barter or at exorbitant sums on the black market. Cigarettes in particular proved a form of payment which was both convenient and utilitarian. Evasion of regulations became respectable while bribery and other demoralising practices flourished. The widespread realisation that a reform must come increased the reluctance to hold currency and much of what was manufactured got hidden away until the reform should be announced. The volume of money available had to be brought into line with the volume of goods available, either by raising the prices of the goods or by reducing the value of the money. But the Russians insisted on being issued with some of the plates for the new notes and being left to do their own printing; in view of what had happened with the occupation currency, the other Allies would not agree. The introduction of the reform was virtually impracticable without a central bank of issue and there was little prospect of such a bank being able to function on a quadripartite basis when one of the participants held economic views diametrically opposed to those of the others. Moreover communist and free enterprise ideas of who should be the main sufferers in a monetary reform were inevitably at variance. Discussions in the Control Council got nowhere. An ugly choice grew inevitable between jeopardising the success of the other recovery measures and deepening the breach between the two parts of Germany.

Though there could only be one answer to this question, the giving of it was eased by developments in another direction. For some time, and particularly since the 'Great Freeze' of 1947, it had been growing apparent that, if the Germans were to make anything of their country, they must be allowed more say in its control. They had recovered much of their interest in life since 'Hour 0' (*Stunde Null*) in 1945 and lost much of their deference towards their masters, to whose misjudgments, rather than to the complexities of the world situation, they attributed the fact that conditions seemed to be getting worse instead of better. But political responsibility meant setting up a central government and when the Council of Foreign Ministers met in London in December 1947, it became clearer than ever that the minimum Russian price for such a step would be a free hand over reparations and the cancellation of the measures so far taken to unite the Western Zones. After the Council had adjourned indefinitely, the American and British decided to shut another of the doors hitherto left open and give to the economic machinery of 'Bizonia' the political character which they had so far carefully withheld from it. The French had been led by their opposition to a central German government to turn down the original fusion offer but they were induced to think again by the warning that, if they insisted on running their Zone independently, it would receive no Marshall Aid. They accordingly came to a London conference in the spring of 1948 and there somewhat reluctantly agreed to merge their Zone with the other two, bring the Western Zones as a unit into the Organisation for European Economic Co-operation (OEEC, the body set up to run the Marshall Plan) and allow the Germans to begin drafting a constitution. The Russians were not long in replying. On 10 March Marshal Sokolovsky walked out of the Control Council in Berlin and from 1 April increasing restrictions began to be placed on personal travel between the Western and the Soviet Zones. The episode of Four-Power control was in effect at an end, though its formal winding-up was to take a further fourteen months.

A Balance-sheet of Occupation

Many mistakes were undoubtedly made by the Western Powers during the Occupation of Germany, since the period was one in which the world situation made satisfactory solutions of common problems even more difficult to attain than usual. The positive achievements of the episode are too often lost to sight. Amid conditions which could easily have led to civil war or epidemic disease, both were avoided, and when all the world was hungry, the number of Germans whose deaths could be directly attributed to starvation was insignificant (though weakness due to lack of food certainly increased susceptibility to other diseases). This result was not due to luck but to hard work and generosity. The Americans had given $11,300 million to Europe before the Marshall Plan so much as came into operation, while US relief agencies spent

$29 million from private sources between 1946 and 1948. Owing to the need to divert food to Europe, rations were as short in Great Britain in 1947 as at any time during the war. The Germans were wont to say that the demand for total surrender carried with it the assumption of total responsibility; the principle is open to argument but it is one on which the Anglo-American record can stand up to examination.

But what of the attempt to change Germany and provide the world with some guarantee against renewed aggression? Did not this depend on the Anglo-Americans and Russians being able to agree on the ways in which Germany was to be changed? Once the West began to quarrel with the East, could it afford to quarrel with the Germans by insisting on changes which the Germans did not want? And even assuming that East and West had agreed on what will to impose, is not the very attempt to impose outlooks and change minds misconceived? Not only does the overt attempt provoke a natural resistance. Ideas and institutions are so clearly interconnected and so largely influenced by the total character of a culture as to make isolated changes inadequate and wholesale ones impossible. Transplantation of practices evolved in other surroundings seldom proves successful and often produces quite unexpected results. It is tempting to condemn as a waste of effort the whole policy labelled 're-education' (a term likely to arouse prejudice against it) and to condemn along with it the entire process of 'denazification'.

Any such judgment would however be unhistorical and excessive. Unhistorical because it is absurd to suppose that after a war such as that of 1939-45, when success had been won after great effort and sacrifice, the victor peoples would have given power to leaders who said 'There is nothing we can do to prevent this happening again.' To have argued in the middle of the war that Nazism and German nationalism could not be 'rooted out' would have played straight into the hands of those demanding a vindictive peace. The idea of helping Germans to change themselves deserves to be judged as an attempt at providing an alternative to a purely penal solution. In view of the inadequacy and impermanence of the attempts to change after 1919, the process could not be left entirely to the Germans; there were certainly a number who wished to change but it could not be safely assumed that they would be numerous and determined enough to get their way without aid. Moreover, once it had been decided to insist on 'Unconditional Surrender', the Allies were bound to march into Germany and, once there, almost bound to stay until the elements of order had been restored. If the Nazi downfall had led to civil war inside Germany, the Allies would in all likelihood have been drawn in, no matter whether they intended to occupy the whole country or not. This inevitably made the views of the conquerors influential, even decisive, in settling what was to replace the Third Reich.

If ever a country was crying out for a clean slate and a fresh start, it was Germany in 1945. One does not have to be a sociologist to realise that no slate can ever be completely clean and no start completely fresh. But complete and undeniable defeat did make conscientious and intelligent Germans (of whom the veteran historian Meinecke is an outstanding example) reconsider, as nothing else would have done, the role and values of their country — here is perhaps the final justification for insisting on unconditional surrender. And in the vacuum thus created, it was healthy that Western alternatives should be presented to them and that they should have been given active help in rebuilding their links with Western culture after twelve years of isolation. For this was how 're-education' was most effectively practised — a parallel process to the re-establishment in the economic field of channels of trade destroyed by twelve years of autarky. It is true that a number of ideas and institutions were pressed upon German attention without due regard being paid to the difference of circumstances in which they had succeeded elsewhere and that this produced a reaction in the 1950s. But the wiser practitioners tried to forestall such a reaction by relying on reasoning and collaboration rather than compulsion.

Certainly people's minds cannot be changed to order and the possibility of leading the Germans to a new view of the world depended for any chance of success on securing the co-operation of Germans who could not be accused of lacking patriotism. But there were numbers who welcomed the opportunity of access to new ideas. There were also many who were as worried as their enemies by the excesses of their nation and, without necessarily accepting an outsider's diagnosis, were concerned to find a remedy. A good deal was done to help such persons into positions of influence; to have done more might have been counter-productive. Not all those to whom responsibility was given were successful but many have been. Changes were certainly effected in the outlooks of all Germans. This was partly the work of circumstances, partly that of Germans, partly that of the occupiers. What exact share should be assigned to each is impossible to define.

The opposite process of trying to drive out of public life all who had participated 'except nominally' in the fallen regime may also have been carried too far and conducted too slowly, but to conclude that nothing of the sort should ever have been attempted is again unhistorical. To have expected that at the end of a war which was professedly directed 'against the evil things', a war which ended by the uncovering of the extermination camps, public opinion would have allowed bygones to be bygones is to ignore human nature. To have concentrated exclusively on crimes done by individuals to individuals (as some have advocated) would have meant letting many of the accused off lightly, since their influence had often been indirect. Among the people who would have been most critical if the Allies had made no attempt at punishment would have been the very Germans whose opinions were most important for the future.

If more imagination and zeal had been used in working out the practical implications of pledges made indignantly during the war, the scale of the operation would have been reduced; the Nazi Party had some 8 million members, with another 4 million in associated organisations, and to drive out of public life a fifth of the population is not a practicable proposition. There would have been great advantages in a procedure which gave those moderately compromised a quick chance to work their passage back by payment in money, kind or labour to a fund for reconstruction and compensation rather than by detention, but a major difficulty was the need for the Anglo-Americans to be seen to be acting with some attempt at justice, since this called for the collection of evidence and the application of judicial procedures, all of which takes time. Until each individual had been tried, a procedure which sacrificed justice to simplicity and speed threatened to allow too many of the guilty to get off too lightly. But as this happened in any case, there would have been much to be said for any solution which enabled Germans to work off their feelings of shame (and often of guilt) which many felt even when inhibited by patriotic loyalty from openly admitting as much. (The Allies are often said to have adopted and acted on the view that the German people were collectively guilty. Undoubtedly such a view was on occasion expressed, especially after the concentration camps came into Allied hands in the closing weeks of the war. But most of those who were responsible for settling policy towards Germany in Britain and America saw the objections to 'drawing up an indictment against a whole people' and preferred to stress the collective 'responsibility' of Germans in the sense that they had been unable to prevent what had happened from happening so that, even where this failure had not been due to a lack of will but to a lack of power, they must collectively bear the consequences in the shape of defeat's aftermath. The individual could not disassociate himself from the nation's fate.)

At the start of the Occupation, many people were heard saying that, to be effective, it would need to continue for twenty or even fifty years, and indeed, if the function of force is to 'give ideas time to take root', it may have to go on being exerted over a period of that length. From this standpoint the experiment was condemned to futility before it was fully under way as a result of the need to secure German co-operation against the Russians. But even supposing that the Russians had not become a menace, the Control Commission could not have gone on governing Germany for much longer than it did. There are narrow limits to the possibility of ruling a developed industrial country as though it were a colony, especially in an epoch when colonies all over the world were demanding and being granted the right to self-determination. Once the Germans had recovered the will to control their own destinies, the only alternative to letting them do so and avoiding a wave of sabotage and recrimination would have been a descent into iron repression. Indeed the only reason why more unrest and resistance did not develop in the Western Zones may have been the stimulus to co-operation which both rulers and ruled found in the Russians. The Occupation was bound to be an interlude and might have been better used if this had been recognised from the outset.

Above all, the interval of external control afforded the Germans time to sort themselves out. The Weimar Republic had been handicapped from birth by the conditions under which it had to start work. A new German regime after 1945 could not wholly avoid the association with failure which had been one of the chronic handicaps of the democracy in Germany. But, by postponing the assumption of responsibility for four years, so that the first post-war West German Government took over when things were beginning to improve and when the alternative to it was a matter of experience rather than conjecture, the chances of it fairly soon achieving a reasonably creditable record were much increased. The cards were stacked so heavily against the Occupation being successful that the new system only needed moderate success in order to seem an improvement on its predecessor!

7 CRISIS AND MIRACLE, 1948-1949

Currency Reform and Its Consequences

The withdrawal of the Russians from quadripartite discussions and the decision of the French to conform removed the obstacles to a reform of the currency. On 20 June 1948, according to a plan decided on by the Allies with German advice, the old *Reichsmark* was made valueless in the three Western Zones and replaced by the *Deutschemark*. Everyone was immediately allowed to exchange 40 of the old Marks for 40 of the new ones but before they could get any more, they had to disclose how much money they had in cash or at the bank. The original intention had been to issue them with only a tenth of this amount in the new currency but experience showed that this would not reduce the volume of money sufficiently and the rate was therefore lowered to 100:6.5. All debts however had to be paid off at the 10:1 rate so that creditors came out well. Existing securities of the government, municipalities and public corporations were replaced on a much smaller scale by new government bonds with the object of bringing the assets of the banks nearer to their (greatly diminished) liabilities. Thus Germans once again saw their intangible assets reduced in value to almost nothing. Banks were also given new, but scaled down, reserves in the form of deposits with a new central bank of issue, the *Bank Deutscher Länder* (which in 1957 became the *Bundesbank*). The note circulation was fixed at DM 10 billion, a ceiling which the Occupation authorities pledged themselves to observe in order to give the population faith in the new currency. The degree of devaluation gave Germany a level of costs which was relatively low by comparison with other industrial countries and therefore favoured German exports.

As in 1923 the reform bore harshly on those who held their savings in money rather than in goods, though to some extent this was made up for by the relatively light taxation with which they had been let off during the war. The original intention had been to make a 'levelling of burdens' (*Lastenausgleich*) an integral part of the reform so that those who came off best would be forced to help those less lucky. But the Americans insisted that the devising of such a readjustment must be left to the Germans and four years of argument were needed before a final measure could be agreed on (p. 189). But whatever the social effects may have been, economically the reform came at exactly the right time

139

and, after several nervous moments, proved highly successful. A sufficient volume of goods was beginning to emerge from the factories for there to be something to buy and the capacity to produce more was available. The initial issue of the new currency was small enough to leave everyone short of money and therefore reversed the previous situation by making cash more sought after than material objects. As a result, goods which had been hoarded were unloaded, the shops filled up and the black market disappeared overnight. For some time the German people had been ready to exert their habitual industry but had lacked any incentive to do so; they now set to work with a will.

The Western Allies had not intended to extend the Currency Reform to their Sectors of Berlin and on 18 June wrote to the Russians expressing the hope that a single currency could be agreed for the city as a whole. Their only condition was that it must be handled as a completely quadripartite measure. But the Russians, who had just dealt another blow to co-operation by walking out of the quadripartite *Kommandatura* governing the city, turned the offer down. Marshal Sokolovsky announced that banknotes issued in the Western Zones would not be allowed to circulate in the Soviet Zone nor in Berlin which, in contradiction to the 1944 agreements (p. 108), he described as being 'part of the Soviet Occupation Zone'. The Western move had obviously caught the Russians unprepared since they had no new currency notes ready. But they could not tolerate for long a situation in which a unit was worth ten times more on the east side of the zonal boundary than it was on the west side. Consequently, on 22 June they improvised a somewhat less drastic measure of their own, sticking stamps on to the old notes to show the new values. These they then made valid throughout Berlin. But the Western authorities feared that if the currency in their Sectors was to be the same as in the Eastern yet different from that in West Germany, the trend of trade would soon go in a communist direction. Accordingly on 25 June they declared that both Eastern and Western Marks would be valid in the Western Sectors. The ratio between the two established itself in free exchange as 1 to 2 but quickly altered to 1 to 4.

There were cogent reasons why a reform of the currency could not be postponed much longer but its introduction on a tripartite basis only provided the Russians with too clear a challenge for them to let pass. Declaring that the Western action was illegal, the Soviet authorities on 24 June extended to freight movements between Berlin and the Western Zones the restrictions which had already been applied to movements of people (p. 134). They reckoned correctly that this step would catch the

West at its most vulnerable point. As has been seen (p. 117), the circumstances of the American and British entry into Berlin had left them without any written definition or even confirmation of their rights of access. This precarious position had been aggravated by the acceptance in July 1945 of the Russian demand that the supplies of food ànd coal for the Western Sectors must come from the Western Zones (though it is arguable that the Russians would have been in a stronger position in the long run if they had made the Western Sectors depend on the East for both supplies and markets). Although the possibility of an interruption to communications had been at intervals the subject of speculation, no attempt at preparing for the contingency had been thought worthwhile; stocks in the city were limited and in some public services such as electricity the Western Sectors still depended on the Eastern. The Russians therefore had some justification for thinking that they had the Western Allies in a corner, facing a choice between four courses, all unpleasant. One was to withdraw immediately, a second to stay until starved out and a third was to negotiate an agreement for continued access, in exchange for abandoning their plans to rebuild West Germany. Any of these courses would have suggested to the world that the West could not or would not get its way and protect its friends. There was of course the fourth option, to force a way in, despite the Russian superiority in conventional forces, and this General Clay wanted to do. A column of troops would have been more likely to be met by demolitions rather than by arms and might have ended up by having to garrison the entire route so as to keep it open, but the matter was never put to the test because the three Governments preferred to explore a fifth solution.

For in the twentieth century land and water were no longer the only ways into the city; there was also the air. Three air corridors to the city were authorised in a quadripartite document and the Russians could only close them by being the first to use force. Nobody imagined at the outset that a city of 2.25 million people could be kept supplied indefinitely by air but no other expedient was available and even if surrender to the Russians could be postponed for a few weeks, the delay might give time for a settlement to be worked out. But the Russians thought that they held winning cards and in negotiations during the early autumn of 1948 showed themselves intransigent. By then the 'Air Lift' was getting under way and functioning well enough to suggest that, provided enough planes could be made available, it would afford the West a means of escape from the corner in which they found themselves. The question was whether the necessary rate of one plane every two minutes could be kept going through the winter.

The credit for answering that question successfully belongs not only to Western technology but also to the population of West Berlin, under their Mayor Ernst Reuter, who showed themselves ready to bear considerable privations, notably in the lack of heating, light and work, so as to avoid falling under communist rule. Fortunately the weather was relatively mild; had it been such as to make flying impossible for many days on end, things might have become desperate. In three ways also the Russians refrained from pushing their advantages home. After one of their fighters had at the outset caused the crash of a British airliner, they did not persevere in harassing Western planes, whereas by slowing down the timetable they could have materially reduced the amount brought in. They never withdrew their representative in the quadripartite Air Control Centre regulating traffic to and from the city, and although one of the radio beacons used in guiding aircraft was situated in the Soviet Sector, it was allowed to go on functioning unimpaired. What may well have prompted this caution was the knowledge that, although they had atom bombs in the making, the first one would not be exploded till August 1949, four months after the blockade ended. They had probably felt compelled to make their attempt to force the Western hand earlier than they would ideally have chosen.

By the spring of 1949 the attempt had clearly failed and a counter-blockade instituted by the West on the movement of goods to the Soviet Zone was starting to pinch. Feelers were secretly put out through the Russian representative at the United Nations, and on 4 May 1949 the world learnt with some surprise that the blockade was to be lifted. Eleven days later the four Foreign Ministers met in Paris to find a permanent settlement for Berlin, but after arguing without result for nearly a month, decided to leave the future legal position of the city as ill-defined as it had been before the blockade began.

Certain vital changes had however taken place, some of which were irrevocable. In August and September 1948 the Communists organised spontaneous demonstrations in front of Berlin's Town Hall in the Soviet Sector, and councillors from the Western Sectors were thereby prevented from reaching meetings; when a meeting did finally take place, it was invaded by the crowd and forced to stop. As the police for the area refused to intervene, the majority of the City Council decided to transfer meetings to the British Sector. In accordance with the constitution of the city (which had received quadripartite blessing), they called new elections for December. In the Western Sectors, where the SED was forbidden by its own leaders to take part, these resulted in almost a two-thirds majority for the SPD. In the Soviet Sector, however, the

Communists declared the former mayor and executive committee deposed, replaced them with their own people and saw to it that the elections resulted in an SED victory. The divided city thus obtained two governments, neither of which recognised the other.

But the consequences of the blockade were not confined to Berlin. In July 1948 the Labour Government agreed to make British airfields available for squadrons of American B29 bombers, along with the atomic bombs which these machines carried. The West thereby acquired the capacity to deliver nuclear weapons behind the Iron Curtain, whereas the Russians, lacking corresponding advantages on the western side of the Atlantic, were unable to reach America. By November 90 such aircraft were stationed in Britain and after the blockade ended, they were not withdrawn. For Russian policy had led the West to take a fresh look at its arrangements for mutual defence, with the result that a Canadian suggestion made in April 1948 was a year later realised and the North Atlantic Treaty Organisation created. By the NATO Treaty the US Government, with the approval of Congress, joined the Alliance which Britain, France and Benelux had concluded in 1948. The Truman doctrine of that year was expanded into the first American commitment ever made in peacetime for taking military action in the event of an attack on any part of Western Europe; the size of US resources, and the immense superiority in nuclear ones, meant that the accession transformed the Alliance, even though it may only have formalised a situation which already existed in practice. The Russians could no longer have any excuse for not realising that Western Europe was under the American nuclear shield. Germany, it is true, was still outside the Alliance but the feeling of common fate which had been engendered during the blockade between the people of West Germany and their nominal masters created a psychological situation which was bound before long to be given formal expression. The Russians had achieved the opposite of their intentions and had brought into being a bloc which was once described, with a backward look at the war, as 'The Allies and their Associated Enemies'.

Economic Reconstruction

On the Sunday on which the Currency Reform was introduced, the German Director of the Economic Administration Office for Bizonia went to the microphone and promised to the West German people the removal of all but a bare minimum of the multifarious controls existing on prices, wages and supplies. The name of the man responsible for this bold step was Ludwig Erhard. He was not being quite as rash as might appear, for the sectors kept under control included such things as bread, meat, milk, rents, electricity, oil, coal and steel which influenced much of the rest of the economy, while wage control was retained until the autumn. But to cut in this manner through the complex of restrictions which the Occupying Powers had inherited from the Nazis was enough to unnerve many of the Control staff, and great strength of mind was needed to push the change through. But the Americans had a soft spot for anyone who, not content with arguing in favour of free enterprise, was actually prepared to practise it, while the idea commended itself to the Germans because it would reduce the opportunities for Allied inter-ference. It also, of course, increased the differences between the two parts of Germany.

In the second half of 1948 industrial production rose by 50 per cent and in the following year by a further 25 per cent. By 1953 average living standards were higher than in 1938, while in the fourteen years following 1950 the Gross National Product trebled. In 1958 West Ger-many passed Britain to become the world's second largest exporter and by 1961 was the third largest industrial producer. What is perhaps more surprising is that Germany's net balance of foreign trade on current account showed from 1951 to 1964 (and again from 1966 to 1978) an uninterrupted surplus, occasionally of high proportions. No wonder that people talked of an 'economic miracle' and that the prestige of Dr Erhard rose to great heights. In reality however the phenomenon was due to the happy coincidence of a large number of factors, not all of them likely to last. In the euphoria of the hour, this fact tended to be overlooked and the assumption was too easily made that, because the policy of a 'Social Market Economy' had proved brilliantly successful in a particular situation, it would continue to bring equally good results indefinitely. For this reason an analysis of the main features in the West German economy after 1948 is important for an understanding of sub-sequent developments:

(a) The European Recovery Programme (to give 'Marshall Aid' its official title) came into full operation within a month of the Currency Reform and in the course of the next four crucial years West Germany was the fourth largest beneficiary, receiving in all $1,389 million (about a tenth of the total). Without these dollars to draw on for vital pur-chases, the German balance of payments over the period 1948-51 would have caused even more anxiety than it did. Moreover Marshall Aid meant that West Germany was recovering in the middle of a half-continent doing the same; each stimulated the other.

(b) As has been said (pp. 113 and 124), German industrial equipment was less seriously affected by the war and the reparations programme than was popularly supposed, while both processes literally cleared the ground for re-equipment, often with the help of a government subsidy which in other circumstances would have been considered illicit. Some firms which might not otherwise have modernised their plant and products were forced to do so.

(c) The loss of the lands beyond the Oder-Neisse as a source of food has often been considered a great disadvantage for Germany. But in fact these areas were relatively uneconomic producers by comparison with extra-European sources and had only been saved from drastic readjustment by tariffs. As soon as West Germany could find the exports to pay for substitute imports, she stood to gain by the switch (though the position was later complicated by the expensive Common Agricultural Policy of the EEC).

(d) In the years following 1945 many people had been unable to see how West Germany could ever support the vast addition to her population caused by the influx of refugees from the East. And indeed, as soon as many nominal jobs were made uneconomic by the Currency Reform, unemployment rose to 2 million and did not fall below half a million till 1955, while the provision of houses for the newcomers (coming on top of the need to replace the destroyed and damaged homes of the pre-war population) did prove a major burden on the economy. On the other hand the presence of a plentiful supply of labour (and one which was being continually replenished) removed what was to prove a major hindrance to growth in other, more stable countries. Moreover the additional labour, having left its roots behind, could easily be moved to where it was needed (though in practice many new firms established themselves in country districts where refugees happened to have congregated). One estimate has put the value of this labour to West Germany at ten times the benefit derived from Marshall Aid![19]

(e) West Germany is often considered to have gained because her economy was not burdened until the mid-1950s by any defence expenditure of her own but only by the costs of her occupiers (which until 1952 were fixed without reference to her). These did not include any expenditure falling outside the country but for some time they took up a proportion of her resources comparable to the defence outlays of many other countries; in 1950 they amounted to 37.5 per cent of her budget and 4.6 per cent of her GNP, while in 1951 the figures rose to

42.6 per cent and 6.4 per cent respectively. It was only after the expansion of the economy got under way that they fell, to 27 per cent and 3.5 per cent in 1953. This burden was however counterbalanced by the considerable amount of military expenditure made directly or indirectly in West Germany by foreign Governments which was *not* charged to the Occupation costs. Between 1955 and 1964 the country's net balance on government invisibles (mostly military) was favourable to the extent of £2,600 million.

(f) The German people as a whole are industrious and methodical by tradition and training. Their standard of education has long been high so that they make an admirable labour force for an industrial country. Supplies of skilled management talent were ample, not least from highly trained General Staff officers forced to seek fresh jobs as a result of disarmament.

(g) Patriotism, extensive unemployment, lack of funds (as a result of the Currency Reform) and the fact that in Germany membership had never been anything like complete all combined to keep the trade unions from making exorbitant demands. Union structure had been reorganised after the war (partly at British prompting) by the concentration of all workers into twelve unions, with the result that inter-union rivalry and demarcation disputes were much reduced, while German labour has never been able to establish the principle of the closed shop (which would now be illegal under the Basic Law). In 1947, on German initiative, tolerated by the British,[20] workers had received a considerable say in the management of the coal and steel industries ('Co-determination' or *Mitbestimmung*); the extension of this principle to the rest of industry was under discussion and might have been prejudiced if the unions had made themselves awkward. For all these reasons, demands for wage increases remained moderate, while production was not disrupted by strikes. The failure of a 24-hour general strike in November 1948 reinforced this trend which was one of the most important elements in the whole situation.

(h) Nearly everyone in Germany had suffered some material loss or come down in the world. Consequently almost everybody was prepared to work hard and anxious to make money in order to rebuild their capital and provide themselves with fresh security. Hard work was also a way of diverting minds from worrying about who was to blame for the past. West German society, like West Germany itself, was starting again from zero and could use all its resources to build up instead of facing the British problem of how to make greatly reduced resources stretch to maintain an established position. Sacred cows were comparatively rare and vested interests on the defensive.

(i) Thanks to the restraint of the unions, wages remained at a relatively low level and salaries did the same, amounting (1950-60) to only 47 per cent of GNP as compared with 58 per cent in Britain. Although both showed a steady rise over the years, the rates were, for a long time, slower than the growth in output. Thanks to the general desire to rebuild personal positions, the propensity to consume was the lowest in Western Europe. The rate of saving was high while the profits of firms were ploughed back in fresh investment instead of being distributed in wages and dividends. Private consumption only accounted for 59 per cent of GNP as against 65 per cent in Britain (1950-60). The demand for consumer goods, being to begin with limited, could be largely met by home production and by the hoarded stocks which Currency Reform brought on to the market. Imports of such things remained relatively restricted.

(j) The Government exempted overtime from tax and gave considerable premiums to savers. Taxes on the higher income brackets were relatively unprogressive. Considerable inequalities in income were thus tolerated and even encouraged, while the ability of the successful to save was increased. Firms were allowed to write off investments against tax unusually fast.

(k) As will be seen in the next two chapters, the new political system quickly established itself on a firm basis and the growing prosperity combined with the relative stability of prices to create confidence in the future in spite of the communist threat on the very boundary of the country. The general mood was to encourage investment.

(l) The role of German banks in providing capital for industrial investment, which has already been noticed (p. 43), became even more pronounced after 1949 owing to the high demand for capital. Two particular aspects deserve mention. First, the banks and other credit institutions were borrowing short and lending long, thereby approximately quadrupling the amount of medium- and long-term loans available. This practice is often regarded as a recipe for disaster but the truth seems to be that, while it is apt to intensify depressions, it enhances booms. Secondly a far smaller proportion of household savings than in the UK or US was being reloaned to households in the form of house mortgages or hire-purchase loans. As a result about eight times the UK-US proportion was available for lending to industry.

(m) Thanks to all the factors mentioned, the rate of investment was high. Gross domestic capital formation rose between 1950 and 1960 by 157 per cent in real terms, as compared with 46 per cent in Britain.

Total fixed investment at home during the same period absorbed 21.9 per cent of GNP as compared with a British figure of 16.6 per cent. Marshall Aid funds were used to remove particular bottlenecks identified as holding back expansion. But as saving was also high, this rate of investment did not lead to serious inflation or price rises.

(n) A frequent result of high investment is an increase in demand for imports so that the national trade figures are thrown into deficit as Britain knows to her cost. Why did this not occur in West Germany? One answer is that in the early years it did. Until March 1951 Germany was in serious deficit, especially in the European Payments Union (the financial side of Marshall Aid) where she exhausted her credit quota by December 1950 and had to be granted a further $120 million of which she used three-quarters in the next two months. The situation was aggravated by the rapid rise in world prices resulting from the Korean war and the action of German importers in buying unusually large quantities in order to avoid having to pay higher prices later. It was also aggravated by the cuts in import quotas ('liberalisation') which all members of the Organisation for European Economic Co-operation had agreed to make. The West German position led for a time to considerable criticism in OEEC, where it was argued that the West Germans were making other people pay their way for them in order to avoid damaging their long-term interests. Great pressure was put on Erhard to reimpose import quotas and tighten credit. His view was that such measures would merely hold back production just as it was getting under way and invite retaliation against German exports. He also argued that at a time of rising prices it was better to hold goods than money. At the end of February 1951 he was driven to suspend liberalisation and tighten credit but just at that moment West Germany's balance of payments took a turn for the better. By the end of May she had repaid all her special credit and some of her previous debts. From that time forward she moved steadily into a stronger credit position and Erhard's reputation soared higher than ever. The explanation seems to have been threefold:

i. The heavy purchases of raw materials at the start of the Korean boom led to stocks being built up, after which imports could be reduced. Moreover, once the peak of the boom was passed, prices fell as quickly as they had risen so that the bill for subsequent imports was lowered. West Germany's buying policy, though initially expensive, in the long run paid off.

ii. In spite of the large amount of replacement needed inside Germany, factors already described kept consumer demand within limits and consequently also limited the imports to which such demand gave rise. The extensive efforts made by the Nazis during the 1930s to render Germany self-sufficient seem to have had some permanent effect in reducing the need for imports.

iii. The rearmament programme set going throughout the Western world by the Korean war called above all for finished manufactures, and particularly for modern types of machinery. As these were just the types of machinery which West Germany's reconstructed industry was well equipped to supply, external demand for its goods soared. Even apart from Korea, the world's need for goods to replace those which would normally have been disposed of between 1939 and 1945 was still unsatisfied, while the steady liberalisation of trade, the pursuit by governments of policies of full employment and the requirements of backward areas for equipment for development all combined to keep demand for manufactures high. The resources which Germany had devoted before 1914, as well as between 1933 and 1945, to armaments now went to producing engineering goods for export.

In an economy such as West Germany's where foreign trade absorbs a relatively high proportion of output, buoyant exports are of particular importance since it is their course which principally gives manufacturers confidence about the long-term prospects of demand. But the view taken about the future course of demand is the chief factor in influencing the readiness of manufacturers to invest and an economy's growth rate depends above all on investment in productive equipment. With output expanding rapidly, productivity is also likely to rise, thanks to economies of scale and generally improved organisation, thereby reducing costs and increasing still further competitiveness on foreign markets. In addition the return obtainable on investment is likely to rise, making it more attractive in comparison with other uses of money and hence stimulating it.

The essence of the German 'miracle' was that at a time when world demand was high, German industry found itself with spare capacity, the right products and relatively low costs, so that exporting was easy and profitable, and hence popular. Once this export-led expansion got under way, the prospect of making profits attracted investment into export industries whose growing earnings made it easy to pay for all the imports which increasing manufacturing for export involved. The pool of unemployed, continually refilled until 1961 by migrants from East Germany, for a long time prevented shortage of labour from constricting output. Thanks to the high rate of investment, production grew at a rate which allowed for ample increases in prices and wages without inflation.

The exchange rate remained favourable (in spite of being devalued less than most other European currencies in 1949 and being up-valued in 1961 and 1969) and the costs of West Germany's competitors mostly rose faster than hers did, (to say nothing of the fact that she sold on quality and servicing as much as on price) so that she could afford increases without pricing herself out of the market. All in all, she was in the exceptional and fortunate position of a 'virtuous spiral' (such as Britain enjoyed between 1750 and 1850).

(o) Neither the old Reichsmark nor the new Deutschemark was a 'reserve currency' and West Germany was not under any obligation to provide other countries with capital. Indeed the authorities put up interest rates to check home demand with the result that, in spite of a big export surplus, money flowed *into* rather than *out* of the country. Owing to the lack of institutions needed to make foreign investment easy, not to mention the caution engendered by having had her holdings abroad twice confiscated for reparations, West Germany was to be slow in burdening her balance of payments with heavy capital movements abroad. Even in 1966 her total overseas investments, at DM 8.5 billion, were about one-twentieth the size of Britain's – and her income from them of course proportionately lower. A relatively generous agreement made by her creditors in 1953, before the full extent of her prosperity became evident, enabled her to pay off by moderate instalments the debts inherited from the Weimar Republic and those incurred since 1945.

(p) In times of slump, governments are blamed for much that is not their fault; in times of prosperity, the reverse occurs. For this reason the part played by official policy in producing West Germany's success story has been left to the end so as to emphasise the number of other factors involved. But undoubtedly government action contributed in many ways to the total result. Some have already been mentioned, such as the provision of subsidies to help replace bombed or dismantled equipment and the exemption of overtime earnings from tax. Between 1950 and 1955 exports were stimulated, in defiance of international agreements, by certain taxes being refunded in respect of them. (There was for long a widespread belief among British industrialists that the success of their German competitors was due to 'improper' and secret government aid. Not only did extensive enquiries in 1966 fail to reveal anything beyond the aids mentioned here, and other schemes parallel to those available in Britain such as ECGD, they showed that German industry for long believed exactly the same thing about 'secret aid' to British industry!) Measures taken to stimulate internal competition may have contributed to improvements in product design. The abolition of import quotas was originally imposed on West Germany by OEEC but in the mid-1950s the Government went further and deliberately made unilateral cuts in a number of tariffs with the double object of encouraging exports and depriving inefficient domestic manufacturers of a sheltered life in the home market.

These, however, are not the government actions commonly given credit for the West German achievement. Many, particularly in circles where official interference with industry is disliked, have attributed this achievement first and foremost to Erhard's courage in removing controls and using State power to enforce free competition. Though the extent of the freedom has been exaggerated, it did serve a useful purpose. Thanks to cartels and other restrictive agreements, as well as the chronic itch of an authoritarian government to regulate, Germany even before 1933 had never known an economy in which market forces were really allowed free play, and by 1948 the controlled economy had got into a straight-jacket which distorted its natural shape. Initiative was being held back and resources used unprofitably. Their more rational allocation was unlikely ever to have been achieved by central government direction. Nobody knew in what way the horse would naturally choose to go and, in order to discover the answer, it had for a time to be given its head, particularly as regards consumption. But without the incentives to save and invest which have been described, the results of freedom might have been very different.

The second government policy for which much credit has been claimed is the deflationary policy of the Finance Ministry and *Bank Deutscher Länder* in restricting credit and holding down the monetary supply in a world where desire for full employment was producing a steady trend to inflation. Undoubtedly these policies did help to check home demand and encourage exports. A tendency for consumer prices to rise in the early months was also nipped in the bud. But when so many other powerful factors were working in the same direction, a contribution from monetary policy was probably superfluous. During the earlier years however the West German leaders may well be excused for lacking confidence that non-monetary forces by themselves would do the trick; the importance of the country earning its way in the world was great enough to justify their wanting to make assurance doubly sure.

Whether they were wise to go on depressing demand for as long as they did is more questionable. Once a country has paid for all the imports it needs, the only virtue in continuing to expand exports lies in the hope of living more easily later on or in having sufficient reserves to draw on if things go wrong. But there is a limit to the extent to which monetary reserves can be built up without causing grave trouble to the other countries from which the money is drawn. Hence a country which wishes to be a persistent creditor must in the long run be prepared to become a persistent investor abroad as well. This in due course West Germany did but various obstacles had accumulated to make the development a slow one. There would therefore seem to have been all the less reason why the West German people should not have been allowed to become prosperous faster than they did, even at the cost of some inflation. But whereas memories of the 1919-39 period caused British and American policies to be dominated by the fear of unemployment, the same and even more recent memories caused West German policy to be dominated by the fear of the currency losing its value.

Note

The following books and articles have provided valuable material for this section:

W. Beckerman: *The British Economy in 1975* (Cambridge 1965), Ch. 2.
J.C. Carrington and G.T. Edwards: *Financing Industrial Investment* (London 1979), Chs 4 and 5.
A. Maddison: 'How Fast can Britain Grow?', *Lloyds Bank Review*, January 1966.
R.G. Opie: 'West Germany's Economic Miracle', *Three Banks Review*, March 1962.

8 THE GERMAN REPUBLICS ARE FOUNDED, 1948-1949

The Western Parties Jockey for Position

The first time that Kurt Schumacher, the Social Democrat, ever encountered Konrad Adenauer, the Christian Democrat, was at a meeting of the German Advisory Council for the British Zone in March 1946. The one is believed to have said to the other 'Every objective observer will admit that the SPD is the largest party with the greatest future and will remain so.' At the time the prognostication was made, most people in West Germany (though not Adenauer) would have agreed with it. Yet within four years Adenauer was to enter on a tenure of the Chancellorship lasting fourteen years, whereas Schumacher's party was destined to wait twenty years before taking office and only do so after he himself had been dead for fourteen.

The outstanding reason why expectations were thus falsified is of course the quarrel between the Atlantic Powers and the Soviet Union. This cut Germany in two and completed the process by which the north-east and centre of the country, including nearly all the lands which Prussia had held before 1815, was lost by the West. At the end of 1937, Germany had covered 470,000 sq km. Of this 118,000 sq km had been taken in 1945 by the Russians and Poles and 104,000 sq km constituted the Soviet Zone. The area lost was not only predominantly Protestant but under the Weimar Republic had included many Socialist strongholds. Although the remaining 248,000 sq km (about the same area as Great Britain and Northern Ireland) still contained as many Protestants as Catholics, it was almost bound to find its centre of gravity in the Rhineland and south where Catholicism predominated and social antagonisms were on the whole less keen.

The division of the country was of course not merely geographical but ideological as well, and the increasing imposition of a communist system in the east produced in the west a reaction to the disadvantage of the left wing generally. Many Americans regarded 'pinks' as no more than a sub-species of 'reds' and although the Socialists had the sympathy of Britain's Labour Government, Britain's difficulties at home limited her ability to push her views abroad. In proportion as order and prosperity returned to West Germany, the more conservatively-minded of her citizens, recovering their nerve, advanced the line of the last ditch in which they were prepared to die and proposals for which they would have been glad to settle in 1945 became out of the question four years later. All these influences caused the Socialist tide to ebb in the west before power had been put back into German hands.

Personal factors also affected the result. Kurt Schumacher was a Prussian from the eastern borderlands who had dedicated his life to the Socialist cause without ever occupying a position which gave him practical experience in government. Having lost an arm in the first war, he had disdained in 1933 to seek safety in exile and had as a result spent ten years in concentration camps. Though the iron certainly entered into his soul, he was never one to sit on the fence. Such was his faith in his creed that as a subordinate he was inevitably a rebel and as a leader inevitably an autocrat. Before political parties had been authorised to operate above local levels, he managed to convene a meeting of Socialist leaders in Hanover and assert his authority. He was the moving spirit in preventing the Berlin SPD from accepting Ulbricht's proposals for fusion, thereby saving the Party in the Western Zones from communist infiltration, but wrecking the chances of left-wing unity. By a great effort of will-power he overcame the physical damage which had been done to his body but what he could not remedy was the rigidity which had been imposed on his mind. He tried to apply to the Germany of 1950 the outlook which he had acquired in the Germany of 1930. He persisted in believing that a proletarian revolution was imminent and showed great bitterness towards the Americans (though circumstances made him work most of it off on the British) for preventing it from taking place (as he considered, out of capitalist prejudice). Believing that the Socialists' reputation for lack of patriotism had damaged them in the Weimar Republic, he set out to voice German claims to the US and British Occupation authorities regardless of what they were already doing and of the reasons why they found it hard to do more. This lack of support and understanding from one whom they expected in his own interests to take their side reduced their willingness to help the objectives which he had at heart. He regarded the CDU as a refuge for anti-democratic reactionaries and refused to consider co-operation except on his own terms. In particular he demanded neutrality in politics from the clergy and once described the Vatican as 'the fifth occupying power'. Thus he ended by alienating all the people whose aid he needed and damaging a cause for which there was more to be said than he allowed to appear.

Prominent among his mistakes was the underestimation of his CDU antagonist. Konrad Adenauer was a seventy-year-old veteran of the

Centre who during the Weimar period had distinguished himself as Lord Mayor of his birthplace Cologne, had become a member of the Prussian State Council and had once been considered for the post of Chancellor. So downright a personality and so convinced a Catholic was incapable of getting on with the Nazis; he was dismissed from his post and retired to cultivate his roses and his taste for wine. In 1945 he emerged and was reinstated by the Americans as Lord Mayor, only to be dismissed by the British six months later and forbidden to take part in politics. The nominal reason was alleged dilatoriness in reconstruction; the real cause is likely to have been obstinacy in dealing with the military authorities, coming on top of agitation against his 'reactionary' views by Socialist *émigrés*. Though there was some truth in the latter charge, it could have been made equally against a number of other people who were being admitted to posts of responsibility. If, in addition to ex-Nazis and Communists, 'reactionaries' were to be barred from office, there would not have been enough people left to run the country.

The long-term effects of the dismissal were considerable, not so much because it prejudiced Adenauer against the British (the episode left on the whole lack of enthusiasm rather than ill-will) but because it removed him from the ranks of Allied-appointed administrators at a crucial moment and, as the ban on his political activity was soon lifted, enabled him to devote his time to precisely such activity. Before little more than a month was up, CDU executives from all parts of the British Zone were called in January 1946 to. a meeting to decide who should represent the Party on the Zonal Advisory Council. While the rest of those present were hesitating how to begin, Adenauer characteristically sat down and said 'As I am the senior person present, you will no doubt wish me to take the chair.' (He also arranged for the meeting to be held in a monastery where the food was, for those days, unusually good, so that everyone was feeling benevolent!) Nobody saw fit to challenge this assumption of authority, which he promptly used to rule that, as the meeting had been called to choose representatives for the British Zone, only those officially invited to attend in that capacity (many of them picked by Adenauer himself) could participate in the discussion. Hermes from Berlin was forced to leave the room while the other main aspirant to the chair was a refugee from Pomerania who lacked supporters in north-west Germany. Adenauer thus had no difficulty in getting himself confirmed as chairman – a position which he lost no time in exploiting. The various Land parties in the Zone were forbidden to correspond with outside bodies except through his Zonal Party Headquarters. His main rivals were the groups in Berlin (which he seldom or never visited) and south Germany. To hold them off until he was ready, he procrastinated over the formation of a federal party organisation and in fact no such organisation came into existence until over a year after he became Chancellor. The Russians played into his hands by denying authority in the areas under their control first to Hermes and then, at the end of 1947, to Kaiser and Lemmer, the Berlin CDU leaders, thus making it less and less possible to claim that the Party must be centred on the old capital. The southerners were kept at arm's length until the moment was ripe for a deal. But most remarkable was the way in which the wily old man contrived to neutralise Karl Arnold, who throughout this period was CDU Minister-President of North Rhine-Westphalia, the Land in which Adenauer lived.

There was more to these manoeuvrings than a personal struggle for power. The same climate of thought which encouraged the expectation of Social Democratic predominance had encouraged the more socialist wing of the CDU with which Kaiser, Lemmer and Arnold were particularly associated. The community of the future was generally assumed to involve widespread socialisation, and favour to the small man. A planned economy was expected to remain essential if Europe was to make the best use of her scanty resources. The 'Ahlen Programme' of the Party, adopted in February 1947, centred round the idea of a 'semi-public economy'. 'The new structure of the German economy must start from the realisation that the period of uncurtailed rule by private capitalism is over. The mere replacement of private capitalism must, however, also be avoided.'

Adenauer had agreed to the Ahlen programme (which at the time of its formulation possessed considerable electoral appeal) but had no love for it. He was biding his time until a good word for private enterprise might become fashionable again. Kaiser in December 1946 supported Bevin's scheme for bringing the coal and steel industries of the Ruhr into public ownership (p. 128), but Adenauer insisted that a decision on this must be postponed until the German economy was free. Here he saw eye to eye with Clay who in October 1947 wrote that, if only the Americans could succeed in deferring the issue of socialising industry until free enterprise had had time to bring economic improvement, it might cease to be a live political issue. When in the summer of 1948 the *Landtag* for North Rhine-Westphalia passed, against the advice of Adenauer and the votes of the CDU, a bill nationalising the coal mines, it was American pressure which made the British Military Government insist that the issue be held over until it could be considered at national level.

In this situation the Bizonal Economic Administration acquired key significance. In June 1947 this institution (p. 131) was reorganised and an Economic Council set up to control it. On this Council both the CDU and the SPD possessed an equal number of representatives; thus neither party could dominate it in isolation. The CDU would at first have been ready to work with the SPD but Schumacher, who controlled the SPD delegation without belonging to it, refused to co-operate except as a dominant partner. He not only insisted on the directorship of the economic branch being given to a Social Democrat but refused into the bargain to 'buy' this appointment by relinquishing to the CDU three of the eight Economic Ministries which his Party monopolised in the Länder of the British and American Zones. The result was that the CDU joined forces with the Free Democrats and the German Party (as the Lower Saxon Land Party had rechristened itself) and so excluded Social Democrats from the administrative board altogether. Moreover in March 1948 the man originally appointed as the Director of Economics resigned and was replaced after long discussions by a professor whom the Social Democrats and the Americans had eighteen months earlier sacked from the job of Bavarian Minister of Economics. His name was Ludwig Erhard and, although as yet he belonged to no particular party, his appointment and the success of the policy to which he committed himself were of critical importance for the more conservative wing of the CDU.

Like Schumacher, Adenauer kept clear of the Economic Council but many of the CDU delegates to it were his friends. He could be just as pertinacious as Schumacher but was far more adroit. Possessing some of Bismarck's flair for distinguishing the possible from the desirable and anticipating how people would react, he would never have overplayed his hand in the way Schumacher did. For an old man, he could be remarkably quick-witted and these gifts combined with a not inconsiderable intelligence to make him more than a match for his rivals and opponents. As a Catholic Rhinelander he had grown up under a Prussian administration in the full flush of enthusiasm for a Germany at last unified. As a result his local loyalties were tempered by awareness of the advantages of belonging to a large centralised state, while his genuine national patriotism was widened by recognising a European tradition. Nationalism in its more radical form repelled him as brash, unintelligent and uncivilised, but he could understand its appeal to people concerned for the welfare of their country. By temperament and training an autocrat who preferred 'yes-men' to colleagues with ideas of their own, he knew that effective leadership depends upon men being managed rather than intimidated. An unrepentant individualist, he had a lively sense of responsibility for the welfare of others while submission to an authoritarian Church had taught him that individual ends must be sought in and through social organisation. This mix of qualities explains why he became a rallying-point for post-war Germany. Aided considerably by luck he gave West Germany 17 years of prosperity and order in which, for the first time in the country's history, democracy became associated with success.

The Drafting of the Basic Law

The Anglo-American-French Conference in London in the spring of 1948 (p. 134) finally agreed on four documents. The first called for the convening of

> [a] Constituent Assembly [to] draw up a democratic constitution which will establish for the participating states a governmental structure of federal type which is best adapted to the eventual re-establishment of German unity at present disrupted and which will protect the rights of participating states, provide adequate central authority and contain guarantees of individual rights and freedom.

The second called for a re-examination of Land boundaries. The third set out in general terms the powers which the Allies proposed to reserve for themselves after the creation of a German government. The fourth (withheld from the Germans for the time being) set out the criteria by which the Military Governors were to decide whether the constitution produced by the Assembly was acceptable.

The body to which these documents were directed was not the Economic Council but the Ministers-President of the eleven Länder in the Western Zones. They consisted at this time of five Social Democrats, five Christian Democrats (one being Arnold) and one Free Democrat. But when they met at Koblenz from 8 to 10 July 1948, a fortnight after the beginning of the Berlin blockade, they rejected the idea of calling a Constituent Assembly to draft a constitution as prejudicial to the chance of re-establishing German unity. This attitude owed much to the influence of Schumacher who, in his anxiety to secure the reunification so important for his Party, still hoped to persuade the Communists to co-operate on his own terms. The Military Governors were highly surprised to find their gift horse looked in the mouth; Clay described the attitude as a 'catastrophic disregard of the total European situation'. In the end however a more constructive outlook prevailed and the Ministers-President consented to convene a 'Parliamentary Council' to draft a 'Basic Law' (*Grundgesetz*); the Allied proposal to confirm this law by a referendum was dropped in favour of ratification by Landtäge.

The party leaders had not been consulted over this decision but it was from the Parties rather than from the Länder Cabinets or the Bizonal Administration that were drawn the members of the Parliamentary Council which met at Bonn on 1 September. Each Landtag elected one representative for every 750,000 of population, an arrangement which gave the CDU/CSU and SPD 27 members each, the FDP five and the German Party, Centre and Communists two each. As the votes of the last three were seldom all cast on the same side, the FDP often found itself able to exert decisive influence. Schumacher was laid up with serious illness from March 1948 to April 1949 and could only direct the SPD delegation from his sick-bed, whereas Adenauer was chosen as President of the Council and set promptly to work at reducing the influence of the Ministers-President over its proceedings; they were not invited to take any part and not much attention was paid to a draft constitution which they had prepared. A first draft of the Council's own document was ready by the year-end and, after further discussion, was presented to the Military Governors on 13 February 1949. On 2 March they replied, objecting to certain compromises laboriously achieved by the Germans as regards centralisation, and the whole matter went back into the melting pot.

Early in April the three Foreign Ministers authorised the Military Governors to make concessions but on American insistence the knowledge of this was held back from the Germans. Schumacher refused to consider the modifications for which the Governors were calling whereas the Christian Democrats were reluctantly reconciling themselves to giving way. At that juncture the Foreign Ministers' message was published; a final compromise was reached; the text of the Basic Law was agreed by the Parliamentary Council against a minority of eight on 8 May (simultaneously with the lifting of the Berlin blockade), approved by the Allies four days later and brought into force on 23 May 1949. Only the Bavarian Landtag refused to accept the Law, arguing that it gave too much power to the central government but, as they agreed to accept it as valid if the other Länder did so, they were considered to have shouted 'No' but whispered 'Yes'. An election was held on 14 August and the Federal Parliament first met on 7 September.

During the various discussions there were three main questions at issue. The first and biggest concerned the respective powers to be allotted to the Federal and Land governments, especially in matters of finance. American pressure, the first document provided by the Allies and the reluctance of the Länder to lose influence made considerable decentralisation inevitable, but the SPD and FDP were in favour of making the centre as strong as possible, while the Bavarians, the Ministers-President and the Military Governors wanted it to be weak. The CDU/CSU was split, with its left wing inclining to the Social Democratic position, and Adenauer had to fight for a compromise; he bitterly resented the fact that the SPD got the credit for standing up to the Occupying Powers, and attributed this to backstairs influence with the British Labour Government.

The second and related issue concerned the Second Chamber. The SPD and the CDU in the British Zone (including Adenauer) favoured a Senate elected by the Landtäge in relation to party strength and proportional to Land population: the southern CDU/CSU, the Centre and German Party fought vigorously for a Federal Council (*Bundesrat*) made up, as in the past, of delegates from the Land Governments. At the crucial moment a bargain was struck by which the SPD withdrew their opposition to the Council form in return for a reduction in the powers which it was to have over legislation, only to find at a later date that a provision giving the Bundesrat power to veto any legislation which affected the Länder made it much stronger than anyone had allowed for. Today nearly half the laws that are proposed fall into this category.

Voting procedure in Federal elections was not laid down in the Basic Law but in a separate document prepared by the Parliamentary Council. The widespread belief that proportional representation had been to blame for the Weimar Republic's failure led many to favour a British system of election by simple majority in single-member constituencies. Objection had, however, been raised against this on the ground that, in the conditions of Germany, it would lead to one party sweeping the board most of the time. As a result a compromise was evolved which the Parliamentary Council adopted. The 402 seats (now 496) in the lower Chamber were to be divided into two parts and each elector given two votes. The first votes would be used to elect 201 candidates in single-member constituencies; the second votes would be collected Land by Land and each party allocated as many seats as it was entitled to by its proportion of the votes as counted by a special procedure. The total number of seats to which a party was entitled was to be decided by the second method, those of its candidates who had been elected by the first method would be counted first and the total number made up by drawing names off a list compiled by the party before the election. Thus the constituency voting was to some extent window-dressing, though it did connect each constituency with an individual; the strength of each party was decided by proportional representation as in Weimar.

The Military Governors were worried by this scheme and tried to insist on modifications, but only succeeded in securing two. By the first, the proportion of seats to be directly elected was raised to 60 per cent – which did not really affect the issue and only lasted till 1953. By the second, seats were to be denied altogether to any party which could neither win three constituencies nor obtain at least 5 per cent of the votes cast in any one Land; this has materially helped to produce that absence of small splinter parties which distinguishes Bonn from Weimar. The Law as thus amended was then promulgated by the Governors.

The Parliamentary Council had included representatives of West Berlin and the Council's intention was to make West Berlin into a twelfth Land of the new Republic. The news of this intention produced a protest from the Russians; the Western Powers, anxious to do nothing which might give the East a pretext for further assaults on the city's freedom, insisted on the proposal in its original form being dropped. Instead representatives of West Berlin were allowed to sit, but not to vote, in the Federal Parliament. In 1950 it was agreed that West Berlin should have a constitution of its own, with a House of Deputies and Senate, but the House of Deputies was allowed to adopt such laws of the Republic as it thought fit, subject always to reserved powers of control by the Allied Commandants in the city. Most West German laws have been adopted for Berlin but there are some exceptions, notably for laws imposing conscription.

The Basic Law

The Basic Law (*Grundgesetz*) for the Federal Republic of Germany (*Bundesrepublik Deutschland* – BRD) opens with a preamble saying that it has been decided on by the German people in eleven named Länder (i.e. excluding the East and Berlin), inspired by the wish to preserve their unity as a nation and a state and to serve the peace of the world as a fully qualified member of a united Europe, in virtue of their power to make a constitution with the object of giving their political life a fresh form for a transitional period. Nothing is said about either the Occupying Powers or the Land Governments authorising the German people to take this step which is thus tacitly claimed to rest upon an inalienable right inherent in the people. Such a claim corresponds to Adenauer's thesis that the Allies were wrong by international law in interpreting unconditional surrender to mean a complete transfer of government authority into their hands. The preamble goes on to state that the inhabitants of the Länder concerned were acting for all those Germans who were prevented from taking part. There was still incumbent on the entire German people the task of completing the unity and freedom of Germany in free self-determination. It was at one time argued that these sentences made it necessary for the Basic Law to be amended before any Federal government could reach agreement with another government ruling over Germans in any other part of Germany but in July 1973 the Constitutional Court decided that this was not so, provided that the agreement did nothing to make reunification impossible.

The first chapter of the Law consists of nineteen articles defining fundamental rights. The opening article proclaims the dignity of men to be unassailable and says that in consequence the German people recognise certain inviolable and inalienable human rights as the foundations of every human community, as well as of peace and justice in the world. This wording neatly evades the question whether these rights exist prior to the state or, as the classic German view maintained, are derived from it, so that an individual is precluded from claiming rights against it. There follows however an article which says that personal freedom may only be encroached on pursuant to a law, while Article 19 provides that laws restricting basic rights must apply generally, must name the right encroached on and the article of the Basic Law protecting it and must refrain from infringing the 'essential content' of the right. These limitations bar the police and courts from interfering with rights by virtue of a supposed power given them by nature or customary law to maintain public order or security. This police power was used even under the Weimar Republic to justify considerable interference with private freedom, especially where 'public morals' were supposed to be involved.

The third article provides for equality between the sexes, a radical departure for many Germans. The Parliamentary Council gave a chilly reception to the idea when it was proposed by the Social Democrats but yielded reluctantly to a storm of letters from fervent women. Discrimination on account of sex, descent, race, language, nationality, origin, belief or political views is also forbidden. Other articles provide for freedom of expression (though such freedom is not to justify disloyalty to the free democratic order), of assembly, organisation, communication and movement. Articles protecting marriage and the right of parents to decide on the religious education of their children were put in to meet the wishes of the Christian Democrats, although education is strictly a Land rather than a Federal responsibility.

The Social Democrats wished to include a right to strike but dropped the proposal when its opponents pointed out serious difficulties of interpretation; the Free Democrats did not press a proposal to forbid the 'closed shop'. But Article 12 says that all Germans have the right to a free choice of profession, place of work and place of education and a requirement that somebody must join a union before being able to work in a place where he has obtained a job would probably be held to infringe this. An attempt has also been made to use it to prevent universities from excluding on the ground of lack of room applicants who were otherwise qualified, but the Constitutional Court decided not to uphold this. Property is guaranteed but land, natural resources and means of production can be taken into public ownership by law, provided that compensation is paid.

The next chapter of eighteen articles deals with the relationship between the Federation and the Länder. At all lower levels of government there are to be representative bodies based on general, direct, free, equal and secret voting. Black, red and gold are again the republican colours. An important article provides not merely that the internal organisation of political parties must conform to democratic principles but condemns as unconstitutional parties which by their aims or the behaviour of their members set out to influence (*beeinträchtigen*) or set aside the free democratic order. (The idea that party organisation is something which needs a special law to regulate it is typical of the way in which the German approach to public affairs differs from the British.) Another article authorises the Federal Government to part with sovereign rights in so far as this may be involved by membership of a system which seeks to preserve peace by mutual collective security or to secure peaceful and permanent order in Europe. Actions were declared unconstitutional which threatened to disturb the peace of nations or lead to aggressive war. Unless otherwise provided, the Länder are responsible for the exercise of national powers and the fulfilment of national tasks, though Federal Law takes precedence over Land Law. Foreign relations are declared a Federal matter. If a Land fails to carry out duties imposed on it by the Basic Law or other Federal Laws, the Federal Government can with the approval of the Federal Council (i.e. of the other Länder Governments) step in. Provision is made for boundary changes between the Länder; the only use so far made of this has been the amalgamation of the three original Länder of Baden, Baden-Württemberg and Württemberg-Hohenzollern (p. 130) into a single Land.

The third chapter (12 articles) deals with the Federal Assembly
(*Bundestag*). Originally only those over 21 were allowed to vote but
this was lowered to 18 in 1971. The Bundestag is chosen for four years
and there are provisions to ensure that it is both called together and
(ultimately) dissolved. Ministers do not need to belong to it (and do not
all do so) but have the right to attend all sessions (including committees,
of which one for foreign affairs and one for defence are statutory) and
must do so if summoned. Deputies enjoy the usual immunities and are
paid £22,500 a year plus an expense allowance of £13,500 (1980).
Officials who wish to stand as candidates are not required to resign
their posts beforehand, but, in accordance with previous German and
much European practice, are entitled to go on leave during elections
and, if successful, during their period of office.

The Federal Council (*Bundesrat*) is disposed of in 4 articles. Consisting, as already mentioned (p. 160), of representatives chosen by
the Länder Governments, it provides the forum in which Federal and
Länder officials can work out (largely in committee) problems affecting
their respective spheres of responsibility. It has in consequence been
described as a Parliament of Under-Secretaries (*Oberregierungsräte*)
though, when it comes to plenary sessions, votes are only valid if cast
by Ministers. The Bundesrat now contains 41 members, five each from
Länder with populations of over six million (North Rhine-Westphalia,
Bavaria, Lower Saxony and Baden-Württemberg), four each from Länder
with populations between six and two million (Rhineland-Palatinate,
Schleswig-Holstein and Hesse) and three each from those with populations of under two million. This allocation of seats represented a compromise between the Social Democrats, who wanted all Länder to be
equal (which would have given them initially 18 seats to a CDU 15),
and the other Parties, who wanted representation to be exactly proportionate to population (which would have given the CDU 25 seats to an
SPD 19). In accordance with previous practice (p. 29), the votes for
each Land have to be cast as a block.

The approval of the Bundesrat is required for a wide range of legislation on the ground that in one way or another it affects the affairs of
the Länder. Where such approval is not required, the Bundesrat is still
entitled to vote against such legislation. If it does so by an ordinary
majority, the vote can be overridden by a similar vote in the Bundestag.
Where the Council's adverse vote is carried by a two-thirds majority, the
Assembly must in turn produce a two-thirds majority to give the law
validity. Government proposals for legislation are normally submitted
to the Bundesrat before they go to the Bundestag. Differences between

the two Chambers are ironed out by a joint Committee consisting of eleven members of the Bundestag, chosen in proportion to Party strength, and eleven members of the Bundesrat, with one member for each Land.

The fifth chapter of 8 articles deals with the Federal President who is elected by a Federal Convention consisting of the members of the Bundestag and an equal number of Land representatives chosen by the Land Assemblies on the basis of proportional representation. This arrangement represents a reaction against the Weimar Constitution where the President was elected by direct popular vote. It is one of several points in the Basic Law where the framers showed their distrust of the masses. This is further displayed in the requirement (taken over from the Constitution of 1871) that, with four exceptions, every act of the President requires the countersignature of the Chancellor or responsible Minister in order to be valid. The President holds office for five years and can only be re-elected once; of the four holders of the office thus far, two have had a second term.

Perhaps the most important chapter (of 8 articles) concerns the Federal Government which consists of the Chancellor and Ministers. The Ministers, for whom no number is prescribed, are appointed by the President on the nomination of the Chancellor. The Chancellor himself is elected by the Bundestag without debate on the proposal of the President (here acting on his own authority). If the person proposed does not obtain a majority of votes, the Bundestag can within a fortnight propose its own candidate who, if he obtains the votes of over half the Deputies, must be appointed by the President. If this does not happen, a fresh vote has to be taken immediately the fortnight is over. If anyone then receives the votes of more than half the Deputies, the President must appoint him; if nobody fulfils this requirement, the President has to choose between appointing the man who gets most votes and dissolving the Bundestag (acting again on his own authority). In practice the President has always waited until soundings among the Deputies have disclosed a man whom a majority are prepared to vote for as Chancellor and only then proceeded to nominate him. But this course might not be practicable, if, as the authors of the Basic Law were anticipating, there were a number of small parties.

To deprive a Chancellor of office, the Bundestag must not merely vote by a majority against him but must, at least forty-eight hours previously, nominate a successor, whom the President is then bound to appoint. This 'constructive vote of no-confidence' was taken over from the constitution of Baden-Württemberg where it was suggested by an

American professor; it is intended to obviate the situation where two extremes unite to eject a Chancellor, without being able to agree on a successor. If a Chancellor asks the Bundestag for a vote of confidence, and fails to win a majority, he can (Article 68) demand within three weeks from the President a dissolution of the Assembly and fresh elections. His right to do this lapses however if the Assembly can, before the dissolution takes place, agree on an alternative Chancellor. When this procedure was put into operation in 1972 (p. 238), it proved remarkably difficult to bring about a dissolution although most people wanted one. If the Chancellor does not want a dissolution, the President can, given the approval of the Bundesrat, declare a law passed as a matter of emergency even against the votes of the Bundestag. This procedure can be repeated for six months but cannot thereafter be resorted to again as long as the Chancellor concerned holds office. Laws which amend or otherwise affect the Basic Law cannot be passed in this way. Inside the Cabinet, the Chancellor is responsible for deciding the general principles of policy to be followed, while each Minister is left to apply those principles within his own department. Clashes between Ministers are decided by the Cabinet. This arrangement represents a compromise between a Presidential Cabinet of the American type and the collective responsibility of Ministers on the British pattern. How it works in practice depends on the personalities of the Chancellor and the remaining Ministers; Adenauer frequently interfered with his subordinates and Schmidt is said to keep them under firm control, whereas Erhard, Kiesinger and Brandt in varying degrees found difficulty in establishing their authority.

For a long time there were no Junior Ministers. This considerably reduced the patronage available to, and thus the influence of the government. Moreover it laid a heavy burden on the single Minister in each department, although, in accordance with German tradition, (p. 29) the State Secretary (or senior civil servant in the Department) undertook many responsibilities such as answering parliamentary questions which in Britain would be considered political. In 1967 however the Coalition Government decided to appoint seven Deputies as 'Parliamentary State Secretaries' with a view to improving contact between the political and administrative worlds. Some commentators made heavy weather over this innovation on the ground that it would restrict undesirably the functions of the existing State Secretaries. However, it would seem to have proved its worth as there are now 19 Parliamentary State Secretaries. But a Minister is still regarded as broad-minded if he leaves in position the official State Secretary whom he finds there on taking up office, and does not insist on installing someone who shares his own political views.

The remaining five chapters and 77 articles of the Law deal in considerable detail with the passing of legislation, with its execution and with administration, justice and finance. There are three broad types of legislation:

(a) Exclusive e.g. where the Länder can only legislate if a Federal law gives them express authority to do so. In this field come nationality, freedom of movement, currency, weights and measures, customs and trade treaties, railways, air travel, posts and telecommunications, rights of Federal officials, commercial law, criminal police. Foreign affairs were added in 1952, Defence in 1954.

(b) Concurrent, where the Länder can legislate in so far as the Federal Government makes no use of the powers given to it in fields where legislation, to be effective and avoid clashes, must extend to more than one Land. The Basic Law lists 23 subjects for such legislation, most of which relate to law and economics though matters like environmental protection and infectious diseases and rules for road and sea transport are also included. Subsidies to educational institutes and hospitals were added in 1969.

(c) Other, where Länder are free to legislate as they choose, subject to the Basic Law.

In 1971 the Federation was authorised to pass laws laying down the outlines (*Rahmenvorschriften*) regarding the legal position of officials at all levels of administration, higher education, the preservation of nature, town planning and water supply.

The position is further complicated by the fact that, in accordance with German tradition, much Federal legislation is in fact administered by the Länder. The Federal Government supervises this process and has power to issue general regulations as to how it shall be done which, provided that they obtain the approval of the Bundesrat, are binding on the Länder. Other matters, however, such as Finance, Railways and Posts are administered by federal authorities scattered throughout the country. The Ministers-President in 1948-9 only allowed for 3,225 established posts in the headquarters offices and although this number has since multiplied, the proportion of civil service posts at the centre remains comparatively small.

In the financial field the Americans horrified the German administrators by proposing that both Federal and Länder Governments should be free to levy the same kinds of taxation. Instead, an elaborate division was made, on lines traditional in Germany, by which the proceeds of certain taxes (mainly indirect) were to go to the Federation and others (including property taxes, driving licences and the beer tax) to the Länder, while revenue from income and corporation tax was to be divided between the two on a stated percentage, the adjustment of which has proved a standing bone of contention. A further elaborate compensation arrangement, requiring the approval of the Bundesrat, evens out the burden between the relatively rich and the relatively poor Länder. The net effect of the whole arrangement is to make German financial affairs complex and inelastic since the Federal Government is often unable to make its decisions effective without securing the agreement of the Länder.

Responsibility for ensuring that the Grundgesetz is observed and more particularly for delimiting the constitutional spheres of the Bund and Länder is laid on the Constitutional Court at Karlsruhe. (This is distinct from the Federal High Court in the same city which is the last instance of appeal in non-constitutional cases.) Appointments to this Court are made alternately by the Bundestag and Bundesrat from a list drawn up by the Federal Ministry of Justice; this includes people with legal training who have made a name for themselves in politics, administration or the universities, since only a quarter of the seats in the Court are filled by professional judges. Besides reviewing legislation, the Court deals with complaints from individuals who consider that rights guaranteed to them by the Basic Law have been infringed. But on the major issue of the Federation's right to legislate in the concurrent field, the Court is not entitled to do more than examine alleged abuses of discretion; it may not challenge the need for a particular piece of legislation.

Amendments to the Basic Law require the approval of two-thirds of the members of the Bundestag and two-thirds of the votes in the Bundesrat. No amendment however is admissible which alters the federal character of the state, the rights of the Länder to co-operate in legislation, the democratic basis of the state or the human rights recognised in the opening paragraphs (though amendments have been made amplifying or clarifying those rights).

The Basic Law represents a determined effort to learn from experience and is a good deal more down-to-earth than the Weimar Constitution. Its framers sought to provide against the paralysis of the legislative by the inability of the Assembly to agree, against the consequent resort on a lasting basis to government by emergency decree, against the growth and agitation of anti-democratic radicalism and against the victory of anti-democratic forces in a single Land. Critics have alleged that, if it had been in force in the 1930s, it would not have prevented Hitler from coming to power. The present document would, however, seem to give more opportunities than did its predecessor to anyone who is prepared to defend the kind of system which it has instituted — and that must always be a principal test of any paper formula.

(For a fuller description of Federal election procedure today, see p. 274. An English translation of the text of the Basic Law (with amendments) is published by the Press and Information Office of the Federal Government in Bonn.)

Germany Gets Governments Again

The Parliamentary Council had found life pleasant in the small and relatively undamaged university town of Bonn and when the time came to choose a capital for the Federal Republic, felt that it had many advantages over Frankfurt which, although bigger and more important, was for that reason badly bombed and full of Americans. The popular story is that Adenauer got Bonn chosen because he happened to live just across the river but a more likely explanation of his advocacy is the fact that Schumacher preferred Frankfurt and, after the advantage which the SPD leader had gained over the question of standing up to the Military Governors, the CDU leader welcomed another issue on which to assert his authority. But the alleged Schumacher statement that 'the selection of Frankfurt would be a defeat for the CDU', which is said to have played some part in getting the CDU to vote for Bonn, is believed to have emanated from two newspaper correspondents who were in love and wanted money to set up house. Another factor which played a part was the argument that Bonn would be easier to abandon if Berlin ever became available again. Indeed the transitory character of the Republic was for long reflected in many of the buildings in which the Federal institutions were accommodated. But as the prospects of re-unification have faded, much has been done to refashion Bonn for a long-term function and it is now well on the way to being a handsome and efficient modern capital (although there are still a surprising number of level-crossings!). The choice, however, underlined the character of the Federal Republic as a West European state under Catholic influence.

The General Election on 14 August 1949 brought the CDU/CSU 139 seats, the SPD 131, the FDP 52, the Bavarian Party and the German Party 17 apiece, the Communists 15 and others 31. In the light of these

figures, the Socialists favoured a 'Great Coalition' with the CDU, as did
the left wing of the CDU. The Ministers-President also favoured a Great
Coalition which they guessed would leave them more power. Adenauer
on the other hand was on bad terms with Schumacher but pleased with
the results which had thus far followed from CDU/FDP co-operation
(p. 157) in the Bizonal Economic Council. Indeed the CDU had largely
fought the election on the economic policies of Erhard (who had only
recently joined the Party) but these aroused little enthusiasm in the
groups favouring a Great Coalition. Adenauer inclined instinctively
towards the more conservative solution of a 'Little Coalition' with the
FDP and the German Party which would not only be anti-Socialist but
would be sufficiently far to the right to deprive any more reactionary
groups of their allure and so reduce the danger of anti-democratic elements exploiting their social and economic positions to turn the bureaucracy and professional classes against the Republic. He must also have
seen that his influence in his own Party would be greatest if he could
act as a balancing factor between two divergent wings, and that he
would be more likely to hold this position in a Little coalition since in
a Great one he would himself belong to the right wing. Moreover in a
Little Coalition the CDU/CSU would be the dominating partner.

His behaviour in these circumstances was characteristic. A week after
the Election, he held a tea-party at his home for a hand-picked group of
25 CDU members including those on whom he thought he could count
and those on whom he felt he would need to count. Arnold, although
CDU Minister-President of the Land in which the gathering was held,
was not invited. Kaiser, on the other hand, was a key figure who at an
early stage was talked into supporting the Adenauer solution. Some of
the opponents of this course made the mistake of going away early and
thus leaving the way open for the impression to be created by adroit
handling of the journalists waiting at the gate that all those present had
come down in favour of a Little Coalition. Soon afterwards Adenauer
secured the support of the FDP by promising his backing for their leader
Theodor Heuss as President of the Republic, and of the CSU by promising in a similar way to back Ehard, the Minister-President of Bavaria,
for the chairmanship of the Bundesrat. By the time the rank-and-file
Deputies of the CDU got to Bonn, they found that the die had been
virtually cast. The delegation from North Rhine-Westphalia, however,
voted not for Ehard but for their own leader Arnold, who was in consequence elected. The CSU were furious and if any acceptable CDU
candidate had been standing for the Presidency would probably have
voted for him, since Heuss was too liberal for their tastes. But the only

alternative was Schumacher who had insisted on standing himself and he lost to Heuss on the second ballot. Heuss nominated Adenauer as Chancellor and on 17 September his appointment was confirmed by a majority of one — when asked if he had voted for himself, he replied 'of course'. He told his followers that they must contrive to hold office for eight years.

Earlier planning had contemplated only eight Ministries — Finance, Economics, Justice, Interior, Food, Agriculture, Labour and Posts. Adenauer added Ministries for Bundesrat Affairs, All-German Affairs, Refugees, Housing and the Marshall Plan, thus enlarging the number of people he could reward. (A disarmed Germany naturally had no Defence Ministry and as long as Foreign Affairs consisted of relations with the Occupation Authorities, they were kept in the hands of the Chancellor.) Adenauer gave five of his thirteen posts to the CDU, three to the CSU, three to the FDP and two to the German Party. The CDU left wing, along with those members of the Party who had been prominent in Land Governments, or in the Bizonal Administration, were passed over. Kaiser was made responsible for All-German Affairs but found it a back seat. Except for him, the Cabinet contained nobody who had offered serious opposition to Adenauer's views. It soon fulfilled its promise of being an obsequious body.

Meanwhile those in charge of the Soviet Zone had been following step-by-step behind the West. In March 1948 a deliberative body of 400, the People's Council, was set up by a People's Congress and in March 1949 (during the blockade) approved the constitution of a German Democratic Republic (DDR). In May 1949 a third People's Congress was elected on a single party list and this in turn elected a second People's Council. In the month following Adenauer's assumption of office this constituted itself a Provisional Government. This, however, did not imply any significant relaxation of the Russian grip on the territory.

9 REARMAMENT AND THE RESTORATION OF SOVEREIGNTY, 1949-1955

Saar and Ruhr

The establishment of a German government logically implied the end of foreign rule and the Western Occupying Powers had therefore agreed, as an integral part of the deal, to change the Control Commission into a High Commission and give written definition in an 'Occupation Statute' to their rights and obligations towards the new German authorities. The High Commissioners at one stage intended to deliver the Occupation Statute to the Federal Government in a solemn ceremony and suggested to Adenauer that he should formally present his Cabinet to them at the same time. He, however, demurred: an 'Occupation Statute', though an improvement on the situation in which the Germans had no defined rights, was still in his eyes a disagreeable document and its presentation no occasion for festivities. The High Commissioners therefore decided to hand over the Statute on 21 September 1949 in a formal but private ceremony on the Petersberg above Bonn (where Chamberlain had stayed during the Bad Godesberg talks with Hitler in September 1938).

They would stand together on a carpet while Adenauer waited in front of them and listened to an address by their French chairman. After the speech was over, Adenauer was to step on to the carpet and be given the documents. When, however, Adenauer entered the room, the Chairman took a step forward to greet him. The German went towards the Frenchman and so brought himself on to the carpet before the address had begun. The incident symbolises the way in which the new West German Chancellor exploited every opening given to him for extending the scope of the powers which the Allies had granted. In yielding to one of his demands during the negotiations soon to be described, the American High Commissioner was to say 'All right then. This is now the 122nd concession we have made to the Germans'. Nobody could complain that the Occupiers were committing the frequent mistake of 'too little and too late'.

Yet at the same time fairness calls for a tribute to the extent to which Adenauer worked with the Allies and tried to meet their wishes. There were no doubt two reasons for him to do so. One was that the basic Allied policy of resisting Russia and integrating Western Europe coincided with his own desires and his ideas of what was good for Germany.

But in addition he believed, as Stresemann had done before him (p. 69), that co-operation was likely to release West Germany from her limitations and penalties more rapidly than resistance would do. This attitude involved him in a considerable amount of criticism, particularly from the Social Democrats; Schumacher once taunted him with being 'the Federal Chancellor of the Allies'. But the High Commissioners in the ceremony on the Petersberg had given an unmistakable hint that early changes in the Occupation Statute would be possible if the Federal Government observed their side of it. The Statute itself talked of revision in twelve to eighteen months. The Chancellor however lost no time in driving home the argument that, if the Allies really intended to develop West Germany as a prosperous member of the European community, further demolitions of factories made no sense. The truth was that Allied policy, as so often where several countries are working together, was evolved not so much as a logical whole but as a succession of compromises between different points of view. The transition from the policy of holding Germany down to that of building her up had therefore to be gradual and while it was in progress, contradictory things were capable of happening at the same time. Yet a policy which is patently inconsistent is not easy to defend and by his pressure on this weak point Adenauer not surprisingly obtained quick concessions.

Another sore point concerned the Ruhr. Talk of 'internationalising' this area was of long standing and, in agreeing to hand the government of West Germany back to its inhabitants, the Western Foreign Ministers had sought to allay the fears which this step aroused abroad by including in the package a 'Ruhr Authority'. This body was to include representatives of the USA, Britain, France and the Benelux countries, along with one German. It was to allocate the coal, coke and steel output of the area between the German home market and exports, so as to prevent the Germans from satisfying their own needs at the expense of their neighbours. It was also authorised to fix prices and transport arrangements. Such an interference with liberty, which was moreover to last until a peace treaty was signed, aroused much resentment in Germany and indeed the Authority would probably have belied its name if the West German Government and public had chosen to thwart it. (What the advocates of internationalism in such circumstances overlook is that the establishment of such a body against the will of the inhabitants is inconsistent with democracy.) Much pressure was put on Adenauer to refuse to nominate a German member. He however took a wider view, expressing the hope that the Ruhr arrangement would gradually grow into an organisation embracing the basic industries of other countries besides West Germany, with an underlying hint that otherwise it could not last. Moreover he realised that in this field the decision rested with the French, since it was their desire for security which lay behind both the Authority and the dismantling policy: they too would be the people with the most to contribute, after the Germans, to any organisation of West Europe's basic industries. To win their confidence was imperative and the best way of doing so would be to take part in the Ruhr Authority instead of boycotting it.

There was, however, another apple of discord between the two countries in the shape of the Saar, the area with the second largest exports of coal in Western Europe. France had tried to get possession of it in 1919 but had only obtained control over the mines; the actual territory had been placed under the League of Nations and had then been returned to Germany after a plebiscite in 1935. Immediately on occupying it in 1945, the French had made it into a separate unit and set about detaching it from the rest of their Zone, since their industry was vitally dependent on its coal. On 21 December 1946 a Customs Union was proclaimed between the Saar and France (p. 130) and the area was given a currency of its own (rather than the franc) when the Deutschemark was introduced in the following June. An election in October 1947 gave an 87 per cent majority to parties favouring independence from Germany and close association with France. In March 1950 the resulting Government was induced to sign a convention giving France a fifty-year lease of the mines. While the Americans and British did not much like these arrangements, they preferred tolerating them to meeting French wishes for an independent Rhineland. The Germans resented French behaviour and argued (as events were to show, with justice) that the election results did not represent the considered wishes of the population. Moreover Adenauer, with the full support of the SPD, enunciated over the Saar a doctrine which had even more significance when applied to the East, namely that the Four-Power declarations of 5 June 1945 (p. 112), had left unaffected the continued existence of Germany as a state within the frontiers of 1937 (i.e. before the annexation of Austria and Czechoslovakia) and that no part of the area could be legally and permanently transferred to another state unless the government of a free and united Germany gave its consent.

German feelings were therefore very mixed when the suggestion was made that the Federal Republic and the Saar should simultaneously be made associate (rather than full) members of the Council of Europe which had been set up in May 1949 and held its first meeting the following September. On the one hand West German ability to attend meetings would be a step forward, yet for the Saar to receive the same treatment might imply an admission that the area was no longer German territory. In the end the whole complex of outstanding problems was brought together in the Petersberg Agreement of 24 November 1949 between the High Commission and the Federal Government. West Germany accepted the offer of association with the Council of Europe and agreed to take her seat on the Ruhr Authority. The Saar also became associated with the Council but there was agreement that a final settlement of the area's status could only occur at a Peace Conference. The West German Government was allowed to open consulates (but not embassies) abroad and send its own officials to the OEEC (instead of being represented by the High Commission). Dismantling for reparations and disarmament, although not altogether wound up for another two years, was reduced to a very small scale.

To obtain so many concessions within two months of the entry into force of the Occupation Statute was a distinct score for Adenauer, though the Opposition preferred to concentrate on what he had given rather than on what he had won. Gradually too his longer-term calculations began to work out.

The more far-sighted French statesmen were coming to realise that the chances of pushing through the policy towards Germany advocated by de Gaulle after the war were, in face of American and British determination to rebuild that country, virtually nil. France needed dollars too badly to withhold her co-operation from the Anglo-Saxons and if West Germany was to be allowed to recover, she must be prevented from swinging into hostility to France. In both countries there was a widespread desire, nourished by the mutual experience of defeat and occupation, to end an antagonism which had done so much to disturb and weaken Europe. With this went a belief that such an ending could only be achieved inside the framework of a closer European association. Moreover France needed both German coal and an outlet for some of the steel, surplus to her requirements, which an ambitious investment programme had just put her in a position to produce.

Such was the background which led on 8 May 1950 to the receipt by Adenauer of a letter containing a proposal for a Franco-German Coal and Steel Community, signed by the French Foreign Minister Robert Schuman, himself a Lorrainer who had been born in Luxembourg. As Schuman was well aware, his Plan fitted so closely to Adenauer's desires as to be certain of a sympathetic reception from the West German Government. It was, and was intended as, a first step towards integrating Europe and reconciling France with Germany; it got rid of the Ruhr

Authority, nullified the main advantages of the Customs Union between France and the Saar and restored to the Federal Republic some measure of international equality. The Allied Governments further promised to remove the limitation on West German steel production as soon as the Community was in being. The idea of having to compete with the Germans without tariffs or quotas and on equal terms frightened the French steel industry, although a German industrialist described the Plan as an effort to overcome the difficulties of that industry. The West German Social Democrats attacked the proposal on the ground that it would continue Allied controls in a new form and make reunification harder, but they were fighting against the tide and did not have the trade unions behind them. Within six weeks of Schuman's dramatic step, negotiations were opened to give the Plan concrete shape. The Benelux countries and Italy accepted the invitation to join in, though Britain held aloof, and on 18 April 1951 Adenauer for the first time left the territory of the Federal Republic to sign in Paris the Treaty establishing the Community. Before he did so, however, he insisted on Schuman exchanging with him letters by which the French Government recognised that German signature did not imply definitive acceptance of the Saar's status.

The Defence of Western Europe

Discussions on the Schuman Plan had hardly begun when the whole world situation was changed by the launching of a communist attack on South Korea. Reinforcements, nominally under the United Nations flag but in practice consisting of 85 per cent of American troops, were rushed to the victim of aggression and quickly succeeded in carrying the war into communist territory. The result in November 1950 was the entry of Chinese troops into the fighting and the prolongation of the war for nearly three years.

Not unnaturally, though not necessarily with justification, the communist initiative made many statesmen consider the possibility of its being repeated in other continents and look anxiously to their defences. In such a survey, the West's weakness in Europe leapt to the eye. Since the first atom bomb exploded, the West Europeans had in effect been relying on American nuclear predominance to keep the Russians from risking a forward move. In the summer of 1950 there were only twelve divisions in the area, mostly incompletely equipped, whereas in East Germany or within easy call, the Russians had 175. Not only was Russia known to possess her own fission bombs, even if in far fewer numbers

than the US, but the Korean experience emphasised how unsatisfactory
it was to rely on so devastating a weapon to meet all types of warlike
situations. There was a widespread agreement that the West must greatly
improve its strength in 'conventional' weapons if its determination to
resist aggression was to be made 'credible' to the East. A production
programme was set in hand, the economic effects of which have already
been described (pp. 148-9). The North Atlantic Defence Treaty (p. 143)
was transformed from an Alliance into an organisation, with an integrated staff and troops permanently under its command; in December
1950 General Eisenhower assumed office as Supreme Commander of
Allied Forces in Europe. The divisions in Germany were brought up to
full readiness and reinforced, but it was clear that they would still be
no match for the Russians.

None of the NATO countries was prepared to dislocate its economy
and cut its living standards so as to divert into the armed forces the
manpower needed to match the Russians in numbers. This was not entirely due to selfishness. Both Britain and France had many of their
forces tied down by commitments outside Europe; America could only
finance the rearmament of others as long as she was prosperous herself.
No country could become poorer without risking political upheavals
which would play into the hands of the communists. Only one alternative solution was in sight and that was to rearm the Federal Republic. At
this stage her productive capacity and technical skills were of secondary
interest, except for the need to keep them out of Russian hands. What
the West wanted was men to fight. Ever since 1947 the War Department
in Washington had been pressing for such a policy; now at last they
succeeded in overcoming the political objections of the State Department. At a NATO meeting in September 1950 Dean Acheson, the US
Secretary of State, made it clear that his Government's willingness to
remain in Europe was contingent on agreement to rearm West Germany
as a matter of urgency.

The proposal met on all sides with considerably less than enthusiasm,
particularly among the other members of NATO. Many Europeans were
deeply disturbed at the idea of giving arms back to a nation which
had in the past put them to such brutal and destructive purposes. A
Germany with access to nuclear weapons was a particularly unpleasant
thought. A wave of pacifist revulsion, partly spontaneous, partly the
outcome of Allied indoctrination, swept through West Germany itself.
There was little eagerness to provide the West with cannon-fodder. The
catch-phrase of the time was *ohne mich* or 'include me out'. Rearmament would imperil the economic revival, increase the risk of the area

becoming the first theatre of any East-West clash and above all reduce the likelihood of reuniting the Federal with the Democratic Republic, especially as the Russians had already increased the paramilitary 'People's Police' in the DDR to 55,000 and equipped them with tanks and artillery. Yet these dangers would not necessarily be avoided by remaining disarmed, and the plain facts remained that the rearming of West Germany was the price demanded by the Americans for continuing the protection which the Western Europeans thought essential, and that the Germans were therefore themselves in a position to demand concessions as the price for their consent.

The influential groups of enthusiasts for European integration saw in this situation an opportunity for carrying their aims a large step closer to realisation. In August the Assembly of the Council of Europe, with the encouragement of Churchill, called for the formation of a European Army, subject to democratic control. On 24 October 1950 Monsieur René Pleven, the French Prime Minister, followed the example of his colleague Schuman and proposed to the European Council the creation of 'a European Army attached to political institutions of a united Europe', with a European Minister of Defence.

Adenauer had repeatedly assured the Allies that he did not want to see Germany rearmed, though he also lost no opportunity of emphasising to them how insecure and exposed he considered the Federal Republic to be. He had pressed for authority to establish a Security Corps to match the People's Police and hinted that, if anything more was to be done, it should be inside a European framework. Shortly before the NATO meeting he indicated that, if an international West European Army were to be formed, he would support the inclusion of a German contingent, but at the same time he made it clear that the price of this contribution would approximate to the complete restoration of German sovereignty; any German troops must be on a footing of equality with those of other countries.

On 19 December the Foreign Ministers of America, Britain and France agreed in principle to the idea of a West German defence contingent, and negotiations began to work out what the Pleven Plan would mean in practice. The Occupation Statute was revised in March 1951, eighteen months after its inauguration, to restore to the Federal Republic control of its foreign policy. West German civilian and military representatives took part on a footing of equality in the discussions about the European Defence Community (EDC). These dragged on for over a year and it was not until May 1952 that the Treaty of Paris embodying their result was ready for signature. It proposed a Community with integrated staffs and forces, though the maximum size of a homogeneous national unit was raised in the course of discussion from 4,000 to 13,000. The idea of a single Defence Minister was dropped in favour of a Board of nine Commissioners, supervised by a Council of Ministers from the participating states, with an Assembly elected (at the outset) by national Parliaments and a Court to decide disputes. The Board would prepare a common budget which would need to be approved by the Council (unanimously) and the Assembly. Once that process was complete, each member state would be legally bound to pay its contribution. The Assembly was required within six months of the entry of the Treaty into force to work out plans for a democratically-elected Assembly as one component in a federal Europe.

Parallel with these discussions others went on between the Federal Republic and the Occupying Powers. They produced as preliminary results a declaration of 9 July 1951 bringing to an end the state of war between the negotiating parties and on 14 September 1951 a resolution favouring the inclusion of a democratic West Germany on an equal basis in a Community covering continental Europe. They were however held up by arguments about the repayment of German debts and the status of the Saar. The French wanted not only British membership of the Defence Community but British and American guarantees of protection in case a rearmed Germany were ever to quit the EDC. Not only the British Labour Government but, to continental surprise and disappointment, Churchill's Conservative Ministry which took its place in October 1951 refused to go more than a limited way to meet these wishes. All the same, a Treaty was laboriously worked out and was ready for signature in Bonn on the day before that of Paris. It restored sovereignty to West Germany, cancelling the Occupation Statute and winding up the High Commission. Arrangements were included for the continued stationing in the Federal Republic of American, British and French troops as a matter of mutual security, and for the reassumption of control by the Occupying Powers in the event of an emergency (until the Germans worked out suitable crisis plans of their own). The same Powers retained their status in Berlin, which was to remain outside the Federal Republic, but promised to consult the Bonn Government about the use of their rights in the city. An important article provided that an essential aim in the common policy of all four states would be a 'peace settlement for the whole of Germany freely negotiated between Germany and her former enemies. The final delimitations of the boundaries of Germany must await such a settlement.' Pending its conclusion, all four states would co-operate to achieve, by peaceful means, their common aim of a unified Germany enjoying a liberal-democratic constitution like that of the Federal Republic and integrated within the European Community.

The two Treaties of Bonn and Paris were complementary and it was provided that the first would only come into force when the second did. Moreover although both had been signed, both required ratification by the Parliaments of the states concerned.

In West Germany ratification was never seriously in doubt, and Adenauer had pressed ahead with little reference to his colleagues and almost none to the Bundestag. His Minister of the Interior, Heinemann, who had shown himself a man of principle during the Third Reich and owed his position largely to his influence in the Evangelical Church, resigned on anti-military grounds. The Social Democrats, led by Schumacher and after his death in August 1952 by Ollenhauer, objected not simply because they disliked rearmament but because they believed that Germany was more likely to be reunited by a policy of co-operating with the East than by one of combating it. Adenauer's reply, which was much influenced after January 1953 by President Eisenhower's Secretary of State John Foster Dulles, was that the only thing which the Russians understood and would yield to was force, so that the best prospect of reuniting Germany lay in building up the strength of the West until it was great enough to 'roll back the Iron Curtain'. As he put it in a speech in March 1952:

> The aim of German policy today as yesterday is that the West should become strong enough to conduct reasonable conversations with the Soviet Union. We are firmly convinced that if we continue in this path the moment will not be too distant when Soviet Russia will declare itself ready for reasonable negotiation.

This policy however proved to be based on a false assumption, for the plans to strengthen NATO were never fully realised. The 85 divisions originally said to be required were scaled down in 1951 to 43, with 30 on the central front. In fact the last figure never rose above 22. Arguments could be reasonably advanced to suggest that such a force might be able to resist a communist attack. But there clearly could be no question of it initiating a successful attack on communist territory. The post-war years had already shown how impossible it was for the United States to use their monopoly of nuclear weapons to compel Russian compliance with their wishes, and in any case that monopoly was in rapid process of being converted into an 'equivalence of terror'. In fact the West had probably reached the peak of its strength at the juncture when Adenauer made the speech just quoted.

From the point of view of West German internal politics, there was much to be said for Adenauer's policy of integrating the young Federal Republic as closely as possible into the West and thereby making it as hard as possible for an aggressive anti-Western nationalism to develop again there. Moreover this policy, which so well met the wishes of the most powerful nation in the world, was far more likely to result in a prosperous West Germany than would have followed from either an attempt to remain neutral or co-ordination with the controlled economies of the East. A break with the United States might also have halted West Germany's progress towards the recovery of sovereignty and equality. But such was the importance of refugees in Adenauer's political calculations and such the emphasis which the West German people had been encouraged to place on reunification, that the Adenauer policy could not be sold to the public on its genuine merits alone. For it to be acceptable, they had to be given misplaced hopes of what it would produce in relation to the East. In the long run, this was bound to become obvious and, when it did, to damage the public standing of the Party which had advocated it. But the death of Stalin in 1953 and the uncertainties of the Khrushchev epoch postponed the date at which this would happen until its main author was leaving the political stage.

Even in the short run, however, the policy was put in question by the Soviet Government which clearly saw their worst fears realised in the action of the capitalist world to rearm West Germany. In March 1952, three months before the Treaties of Bonn and Paris were signed, the Russians sent to the three other Occupying Powers two notes suggesting terms for a Peace Treaty to bring about German reunification on a neutral and democratic basis. These notes, which certainly arrived at a rather late stage of the Western negotiations, cannot be said to have been seriously considered. Instead they were regarded as a sign that the policy of 'negotiating from strength' was beginning to yield results and, if pursued, would result in still more conciliatory offers. The Allies argued that they should not therefore allow themselves to be deflected from their purpose by what seemed to them intended as a 'delaying bid'. The Allied reply insisted that free elections throughout Germany were a necessary preliminary to a Peace Treaty and negotiations bogged down in argument as to which should come first. Was this reaction justified or was a real chance of settlement missed?

The Russian proposals provided for a guarantee of democratic rights to the German people so that all Germany could enjoy the rights of man and the basic freedoms. All democratic parties and associations were to be allowed freedom of activity, including liberty to meet, publish and decide on their own international relations. Organisations inimical to democracy and to the maintenance of peace were not to be permitted. Civil and political rights were to be available to all former members of the armed forces and to all former Nazis other than those serving sentences for war crimes. There were to be no limitations on economic activity and Germany was to be free to join the United Nations. She was to have such national armed forces of her own as she needed for defence, and was to be allowed to produce arms, though the quantities and types of these were to be prescribed in the Treaty setting up the arrangement. But she was to promise not to enter into any kind of coalition or military alliance directed against any state which had fought her between 1939 and 1945. All Allied forces were to be withdrawn within twelve months and all foreign military bases on her territory were to be destroyed.

At first sight nothing could have sounded more reasonable, even though the organisations to be assured freedom were obviously going to include the Communist Party. Perhaps too the presence of big and undefined words like 'peace-loving' and 'democratic' might have roused the suspicions of those who remembered the controversies which had flowed from different interpretations of such words in the Control Council. The Russians could get troops back again from Poland more easily than the Americans from across the Atlantic. The Russian offer may well have been seriously intended. But it involved many opportunities for dissension and delay so that its acceptance might have meant the West finding themselves after five years or so back where they had started in 1947-9. The proposal seemed obviously put forward to prevent the Federal Republic from binding itself to the anti-communist bloc but could only have been accepted by someone willing to take the risk of a reunited Germany coming under the control of the pro-communist bloc. German production and manpower could make too much difference to the balance of power for either side to trust the other at that stage to let the reunited country remain genuinely neutral. Such an act of faith was certainly not to be expected from an elderly man who was not only a convinced European and anti-communist but had staked his political reputation on a policy which involved binding his country to the West. By the time the offer was made, things had gone so far that a much higher bid would have been needed to make a reversing of engines seem justifiable to those responsible for Western policy, and so high a bid would have been too much for the East to contemplate at that stage.

The East Germans answered the Bonn and Paris Treaties by establishing a security strip along the inter-Zonal frontier and ending except at a very limited number of points the relatively free local traffic across it which had existed until then.

Disaster and Recovery

The attitude of West Germany towards the European Defence Community could be decided by the obstinacy of a single individual but unfortunately more was needed to bring the Community into being. The Treaty signed in Paris in May 1952 required six ratifications in order to come into force; it only received five. The inroads which the proposal made on national sovereignty, though designed to allay French fears of Germany, proved more than the French, deeply divided as they were at the time by many other issues, could bring themselves to accept. The prospects of obtaining a majority for the Treaty in the French Parliament were so slight that its presentation kept on being put off, while world conditions changed and its main authors lost office. In August 1954 Mendès-France, the then Prime Minister, finally took the plunge but without showing any enthusiasm for the proposal, since if he had, he would have been brought down by his own Cabinet! A large majority accepted a motion agreeing to postpone consideration indefinitely. The country which had sponsored the idea had ended by turning against it; Adenauer's plans appeared to be in ruins.

Although the Treaty of Bonn was only supposed to come into force when the Treaty of Paris did, the world had too easily taken the ratification of the latter for granted. For over two years the Western Occupying Powers had been increasingly treating West Germany, and West Germany had been increasingly behaving, as a sovereign state, except that it had halted its preparations for raising armed forces. Here was a clock which could not be put back. The French had professed themselves nervous about the EDC for fear of it allowing West Germany to become too strong: they had as a result created a position where there would soon be little but her good faith towards her allies to prevent her from re-arming in total independence of all controls.

The blame for this predicament was however as widely laid on Britain as on France since the British reluctance to join the Community was said to have swung the balance against French participation. Though it is hard to believe that British aloofness was more than a contributing factor, it was Britain which now came to the rescue by proposing in October 1954 an organisation of sovereign states, a Western European

Union, instead of a move to a supra-national plane. A Secretariat replaced the proposed Commission and the Assembly (though empowered to take certain decisions by a two-thirds majority) was only allowed consultative rights. Britain undertook to keep four divisions and an air fighter force on the continent until 2000 AD; this was little more than had been offered under EDC and contained a let-out clause of which advantage was taken within three years. But after some initial hesitation the French accepted it.

In some respects WEU was an extension of the Brussels Alliance of 1948 which had preceded NATO (p. 143), but that Alliance had been directed against the possibility of a resurgent Germany and not only was this animus now removed but West Germany and Italy were admitted to the Union. The Federal Republic was however required to incorporate all its forces in NATO, whereas no other member did so. It also renounced the right to manufacture on its territory (though not to acquire or control) atomic, bacteriological and chemical (ABC) weapons. Moreover it undertook never to have recourse to force to achieve reunification or the modification of frontiers. In return the Americans, British and French recognised the Government of the Federal Republic as the only German Government 'freely and legitimately constituted and therefore entitled to speak for Germany as the representative of the German people in international affairs'. They went on to reaffirm that a peace settlement for the whole of Germany freely negotiated between Germany and her former enemies, which should lay the foundations of a lasting peace, remained an essential aim of their policy. The final delimitation of the frontiers of Germany must await such a settlement (a standpoint which was widely taken in West Germany to mean that, failing such delimitation, the legal frontiers remained those of 1937). The Federal Republic was to contribute 500,000 men to NATO (the size of the army of a united Germany when Hitler reoccupied the Rhineland in 1936) but would not maintain a separate General Staff.

The practical obstacles to effective action against the East had already been illustrated on 17 June 1953 when the workers of the Democratic Republic and particularly of East Berlin had been provoked by their harsh conditions of life into staging something approaching a general strike. The People's Police could not or would not cope with the situation and two Russian armoured divisions had to be called in. Though they behaved with restraint, 21 people were killed. Persons variously described as 'interested spectators' and *'agents provocateurs'* came from West Berlin to discover what was happening but the whole affair was over before the Western Governments had had time to decide how to react. In West Germany the anniversary was later proclaimed a day of remembrance, though with the passage of time it turned into just another public holiday. Steps were also taken to rein in the broadcasts by Radio Free Europe, the nominally unofficial US station in Munich which was thought to have encouraged the idea that, if people living behind the Iron Curtain rose against their rulers, the West would come to their aid.

The Western Allies did however seek to exploit Soviet embarrassment by pressing the question of German reunification. At a Conference of the Four Foreign Ministers held in Berlin in January 1954, Eden proposed a Plan for all-German elections as the preliminary to the establishment of an all-German government which would be free to make what alliances it chose. At first the Russians shied away from proposals which seemed designed to work out to their disadvantage, and the Conference broke up without agreement. But in the autumn of 1954, alarmed by the prospect of WEU, the Russians put forward proposals which seemed to come much closer to the Eden Plan, while in February 1955 an inter-parliamentary congress on the German question at Warsaw proposed the virtual acceptance of the Plan subject only to a guarantee of German neutrality by the principal states concerned (including the US). This, however, would have meant the Federal Republic staying out of WEU and the Western Governments were not prepared to let this happen. Almost immediately afterwards Malenkov was replaced as Chairman of the Soviet Council of Ministers by Bulganin and his fall has sometimes been seen as the defeat of the doves in the Kremlin after the Western failure to respond had made their policy of conciliation hopeless. Although his demotion seems to have been decided on a month or two before the Warsaw meeting, the Russians certainly from this time onwards lost interest in reunification and took to treating it as primarily an internal German affair which must be dealt with in the first instance by direct conversations between the two German Governments. The Bonn Government however refused to recognise the legitimacy of the regime in East Germany, let alone negotiate with it. Meanwhile the communist states replied to the WEU by establishing in the Warsaw Pact a military alliance which was clearly intended as a counterpart to it and which included the Democratic Republic among its members.

Prosperity at Home

Germany will blossom as never before. Her destroyed landscapes will be rebuilt with new and more beautiful towns in which happy people will live. The whole of Europe will participate in this upsurge. Once more we shall be friends with all nations who are of good will. Together with them we shall let the deep wounds heal which disfigure the noble face of our continent. In rich cornfields the daily bread will grow, banishing the hunger of millions who are needy and suffering today. There will be plenty of work and out of it as the deepest spring of human happiness there will come bliss and strength for all.

This remarkable vision of the Federal Republic in the 1950s dates from the dark days of April 1945; it comes from Goebbels's last broadcast on the eve of Hitler's last birthday. Its idyllic word-painting was intended by its author to show the Germans what they might hope to achieve by victory. That the dream should instead have been realised in the wake of defeat is not entirely due to Russian policy, for it would be ungrateful to suppose that the generosity of America was exclusively inspired by the wish to save Europe from communism. The liberal trade policies which resulted in the creation of such bodies as the International Monetary Fund, the World Bank and the General Agreement on Tariffs and Trade date from the days of the Russian-American honeymoon. Yet it was these policies and institutions which made possible the widening markets that distinguished the post-war world. And without these markets it is hard to see how there could have come into existence the 'virtuous spiral' on which West German export-led prosperity rested (p. 149). No comparable openings had existed since the years before 1914 and it was equally long since Germany had made comparable efforts in foreign markets. The West German share of world trade in manufactures rose from 7 per cent in 1950 to nearly 19 per cent in 1959, which had been approximately its level (allowing for partition) in 1913, whereas for 1937 the figure had been only 16.5 per cent. The consequence was that the Federal Republic's export surpluses became embarrassing. So far from needing to conduct an 'export drive' the Government was under pressure to get the favourable balances reduced since their accumulation inside the country could not but have an inflationary effect.

One solution to this problem was found in the removal of import quotas and the lowering of tariffs. The population was thus enabled to live better and more cheaply. Arrangements were made to pay off all outstanding external debts. Another step was a Treaty concluded in 1952 by which West Germany undertook to pay to Israel DM 3,000 million to be used in compensating Jews whom the Nazis had driven out of Europe: a further DM 450 million was made available for the same purpose in other countries. From 1953 onwards increasing sums were made officially available in the form of loans at low rates of interest for the benefit of developing countries until by 1962 annual expenditure on this head was running at about the same rate as Britain. Nearly all of this expenditure came back to West Germany in the form of orders but, while it thus increased the income of manufacturers and workers, it did not necessarily add to the country's material resources as much as its use in other directions might have done.

None of these measures proved adequate and in March 1961 the Deutschemark was revalued upwards by approximately 5 per cent. Devaluations of currency have been distressingly frequent in the world but this deliberate move in the opposite direction was almost unprecedented. The step was strongly opposed by the Bundesbank, which would have preferred to see the rest of the world devalue instead, and by industrialists who feared that selling abroad would become harder and competition at home from imports fiercer. It turned out, however, that West German goods sold on quality, delivery and servicing as much as on price while export markets had become so important that manufacturers made an even greater effort so as to retain them, with the result that this and subsequent revaluations only had a temporary effect on the surplus. The truth is that, to make an international monetary system function smoothly, a country which is a persistent creditor must get rid of its surplus by lending abroad and this the Federal Republic was slow to do; whereas her cumulative surplus over the years 1951-61 amounted to DM 24,000 million, her overseas investments in 1966 only totalled DM 8,500 million. One reason for this was the vast amount of capital needed for reconstruction at home. By 1964, 8 million houses had been built (as against 4.8 million in Britain). By 1967 over half the dwelling-units in West Germany were post-war. Over half of the cost was in effect borne by the public authorities either in the form of loans or tax remissions so that the necessary funds could be raised without having to put up interest rates to a level which made rents prohibitively high. (Building Societies of the British type do not exist in West Germany.) Similar tax remissions encouraged individuals and firms to plough back

large parts of their earnings into development. The Government is estimated to have been responsible for 43.5 per cent of total net investment
between 1948 and 1957.

Thus the background to the West Germany of the 1950s was one of
great and growing prosperity, a situation all the more gratifying because
it was unexpected. For the first time in German history democratic
government came to be associated with success and the world owes to
Adenauer and Erhard a considerable debt of gratitude for having proved
that such a conjunction was possible. A preoccupation with material
well-being absorbed the country, illustrated by the story of the girl who
said that the two books to have had most influence on her life were her
father's cheque book and her mother's cookery book. Nor was it only
the rich who profited, in spite of some appearance to the contrary and
of the frequent assertions of foreign critics. Germany had led the world
in devising social insurance (p. 33) and a generous system of social
security was now built up until the West German people were in this
respect the best cared for in the world. In particular a scheme was introduced in 1957 for 'dynamic pensions' which rose automatically with
the cost of living. Although much of the finance for these services came
from contributions by employers and workers, the amount spent by the
state trebled between 1950 and 1962, while Land and communal governments spent even more. A not surprising result was that the level of
taxation also became as heavy as any in the world though less severe on
the highest income groups than in Britain, the US and Scandinavia. (See
Table 9, p. 281).

Control of firms in the Federal Republic, as in much of Western
Europe, is divided between a Supervising Council (*Aufsichtsrat*) and a
Management Board (*Vorstand*). The former meets four or five times a
year, appoints the Management Board, supervises the firm's balance
sheets, and decides on such matters as mergers, take-overs, major expan-
sions or closures; the latter conducts the day-to-day business. During
the occupation period, (p. 146) workers in the coal and steel industries
secured equal representation with the shareholders on the Supervising
Councils (the two groups then combining to elect a chairman). In the
rest of industry a law of 1951 gave the workers a third of the places on
the Supervising Councils. Moreover, every firm with more than five
workers is required to have a Works Council, elected by the entire labour
force (and not merely the union members) in a secret ballot: this body
has a right to co-decision with the management in such matters as job
evaluation, wage structures, working hours and holidays, training and
welfare schemes. Wages are settled by collective bargaining between an

industry and the union which represents all the workers in it, usually on a regional basis; once concluded, such agreements are legally binding on both sides for the full period which they cover; strikes are only permitted when an agreement has expired and then only if three-quarters of the union members concerned have voted in favour in a secret ballot. An elaborate but cheap system of labour courts exists to decide disputes between individual workers and their employers. The net result has been a high level of peace and orderliness in industry. It is hard to say how far this is due to the existence of a fixed and unchallenged legal framework, how far to workers' awareness that they have spokesmen for their interests at the top.

The victims of the war, including those on whom the Currency Reform had borne harshly, were not forgotten when the benefits of prosperity came to be distributed. After a temporary measure in 1949, a Law for the Equalisation of Burdens was passed in 1952. This combined a capital levy, capital gains tax and a levy on mortgages, intended to amount to 50 per cent. From the fund thus created, a variety of compensation payments were to be made. Obviously, however, it was impossible˙to raise so large a levy at one blow and arrangements were made to spread its collection over 27 years, though loans were raised on the strength of the initial contributions so as to allow hand-outs in anticipation of the income. By the end of 1964 benefits totalling over DM 40,000 million had been distributed to communal enterprises of social importance as well as to individuals. Another law of 1953 made the handling of refugees into a Federal rather than a Land matter, so that all should receive comparable treatment, irrespective of where they had come from or of what part of Germany they had gone to. A law passed two years earlier provided for the payment of compensation to those who had suffered at Nazi hands, as well as for their reinstatement in their old posts or pensioning in accordance with the rank which they would have reached had they not been dismissed.

Considerable comment was, however, aroused both inside and outside Germany by the fact that this last law was accompanied by another passed under heavy pressure from the organisations representing civil servants and ex-members of the armed forces. Article 131 of the Grundgesetz called for legislation to regulate the position of all who had been in public service on 8 May 1945, and had since been removed from office for reasons not laid down in the service code. This was now interpreted to require the reinstatement in office at their former rank of all except those actually serving prison sentences as a result of the denazification procedure; it was argued that to do anything else would be to

punish them twice. Their replacements, often victims of Nazism, had
in many cases to make way for them. Any who had passed the age of
retirement were awarded their normal pensions, as were all who had
belonged to the armed forces before 1935. This single act undid much
of the work achieved by the Occupying Powers (already considered by
many to have been inadequate) of eliminating from positions of responsibility men who had shown by their attitude to Nazism that they could
not be relied on as friends of democracy or humanity. Every second
senior civil servant in West Germany in the early 1960s had worked for
the government under the Third Reich. Between December 1949 and
June 1950 23 ex-Nazis were recruited into the Ministry of Economics.
In March 1952 39 out of 49 senior officials in the Foreign Office proved
to have been Nazis. A grotesque situation was disclosed when, as a
result of publicity from Poland and Russia, it emerged that the Baden-
Württemberg Government had in 1958 appointed to the Directorship
of the Central Office for the Investigation of Nazi Crimes a man whom
they knew to have been a storm-trooper and Party member.

Adenauer showed himself insensitive to the undesirability of employing in high office people whose record in the Third Reich had been
unsatisfactory. His 1953 Cabinet included as Minister of the Interior
Gerhard Schröder who had been a Party member; as Minister for Refugees, Theodor Oberländer who had belonged to the SS; and as Minister
of Transport Hans Christian Seebohm, a prominent protagonist of the
Sudeten Germans who was later to define Germany as including all
areas where Germans had ever settled and make many similar utterances
without being seriously reprimanded. Hans Globke, the State Secretary
at the head of the Chancellor's Office, although not a Nazi, had written
the official commentary on the anti-Jewish laws and the other heads of
Departments included several who were similarly compromised.

The tolerance was undoubtedly deliberate. The Chancellor was sufficiently a German and sufficiently a conservative to have a good deal
of sympathy with the attitudes of old-fashioned nationalism. Moreover
he realised that, if such elements in the nation were cold-shouldered by
the regime, they would turn against it. One of the reasons for the failure
of the Weimar Republic has been seen to be the hostility, amounting to
disloyalty, of many who had formed the pillars of society under the
Hohenzollerns. It was important that this should not happen again.
There is a good deal of evidence indicating that, even at the end of the
war, 10 per cent of the adult population, or 4 million people, were
hard-core Nazis (p. 137). The members of the Nazi Party and affiliated
organisations had numbered 12 million. The 8 million or so refugees

and expellees from the East in the Federal Republic were all potential recruits for radical policies. To give the CDU a character which enabled it to appeal to such people was not merely shrewd political tactics (though undoubtedly this aspect was not lost on its leader), it was also calculated to keep within limits the growth of parties further to the right. There can be no doubt that as a result of Adenauer's policy a number of people who might otherwise have sabotaged the democratic experiment were induced to tolerate it until its very success made them think that it might after all have merits. How do you run a liberal democracy if the supply of competent and convinced democrats is inadequate?

Nevertheless West Germany had to pay a price for the Adenauer era. In too many directions it amounted to a restoration of the kind of society which its leading figures had known in their youth. Thus the civil service unions were able to frustrate most of the half-hearted measures taken by the Occupying Powers to reform the administrative corps by widening the area of recruitment in terms both of class and intellectual background. Preference continued to be given to those whose parents had paid for their education and who had then passed an examination in law. In education the British and Americans had deliberately refrained from trying to enforce changes, only to see their advice and example largely disregarded and little done to overhaul the system either as regards curriculum or as regards equality of opportunity. The Universities still concentrated on training students by specialist research and were slow to recognise the need of modern society for large numbers of people with a general higher education. In its treatment of criminals and in its laws on such matters as divorce and abortion, the Federal Republic remained old-fashioned. As a result it increasingly failed to meet the wishes and needs of the generations who came to maturity in it. Had it only lasted a decade, this might not have mattered, especially as its rightward character meant that any change was almost bound to be towards the left. But the success of the 'Miracle' made its beneficiaries reluctant to move away from it and this resulted in an estrangement between the generations which created an explosive situation.

The initial satisfaction of the West German people with the general policy of their government was convincingly demonstrated in the elections of 1953 when the CDU/CSU won 243 of the Bundestag's 487 seats. Adenauer, however, preferred to keep his former allies of the FDP and German Party in the Cabinet, so as to maintain a united anti-Socialist coalition. He even brought into that coalition, and in due course absorbed into the CDU, the Refugee Party which had been established in Schleswig-Holstein in 1950.

In 1956 developments occurred in North Rhine-Westphalia illustrating several characteristics of West German politics. As has been seen (pp. 156, 170) love had never been lost between Adenauer and Karl Arnold, the CDU Minister-President. The Chancellor particularly objected to Arnold's policy of finding his majority by coalition with the SPD. After the Land elections of 1950 had failed to give any party an absolute majority, Adenauer tried to prevent him from resuming this combination, and even to force him out of office; at one stage the unusual spectacle was seen of the Minister-President boycotting the meetings of his own party, at another of the Federal leader ordering the Land leader, in front of all his followers, to 'resign or be faced with the charge of deception'. But the only concession which Arnold would make was to get his majority by coalescing with the archaic Centre Party (only extant in this Land) instead of the SPD. This grouping lasted until the Land elections of 1954 when Arnold was forced to follow Bonn in taking the FDP as his ally.

By 1956, however, elements in the FDP were growing tired of playing second fiddle to the CDU and a group of 'Young Turks' in North Rhine-Westphalia decided to break away and form a coalition with the SPD. Arnold was forced out of office and soon afterwards died; he was a man who might with advantage have played a larger part on the German political stage but for the fact that too many non-Germans were anxious to see him do so. Many of the 52 Federal Deputies of the FDP decided to follow the North Rhine example, but their four Ministers felt no inclination to resign from the Cabinet, and sixteen other Deputies followed the ministerial example. This group of 20, led by Franz Blücher the Vice-Chancellor, formed the Free People's Party (FVP) which a year later joined forces with the German Party. The remainder under Thomas Dehler went into opposition. Two years later the SPD chose to fight the North Rhine elections on the issue of nuclear weapons (p. 200) and lost heavily, after which the former CDU/FDP coalition was re-established there.

Among minor parties without representation in the Bundestag, some attention was attracted by the Socialist Reich Party — a right-wing group centred in Lower Saxony — and the Communists. The first of these was, however, declared by the Constitutional Court in 1952 to contravene Article 21 of the Grundgesetz forbidding parties which sought to alter the democratic character of the State: the second suffered the same fate, on the initiative of the Federal Government, in 1956. There were those who thought it a mistake, particularly with the Communists, to drive them underground where their weakness could not be demonstrated.

The CDU/CSU contested the 1957 Elections with great vigour and spent over £3 million (five times as much as the British Conservatives in the General Election of 1955) in support of the slogan 'No Experiments'. An analysis before this election suggested that there were in the Republic 8.5 million firm CDU/CSU supporters and 3.25 million lukewarm ones, 9 million firm SPD supporters and 3.25 lukewarm ones, 1 million firm supporters of the minor parties and 2 million lukewarm ones, with 3 million voters undecided. In the event most of the lukewarm and undecided voters (many of them women) would seem to have played for safety with the result that Adenauer received an even greater majority than before in the highest poll yet known in Germany (disregarding 1933), while the Refugee and Centre Parties disappeared from Federal politics.

Adenauer was at the height of his prestige. His success presented a serious problem for the Social Democrats. Their Party was taking an active share in several Land Governments, notably Greater-Hesse, Hamburg and Bremen, as well as West Berlin, and it was at this level that their ablest leaders, such as Brauer, Kaisen and Willy Brandt, were deployed. On the Federal plane, however, the CDU/CSU appeared to be so firmly in the saddle that the SPD looked like being condemned to permanent opposition, which in a democratic state is tantamount to slow extinction. The prospect caused the intellectual leaders of the Party, in particular Herbert Wehner, Fritz Erler and Carlo Schmid, to insist that the programme must be drastically revised to take account of the Welfare State and the communist threat. This meant not merely committing the Party to the support of the free democratic order — which after all had been the Socialist position for many years — but also ending its identification as primarily a working-class and Marxist body, which sought the public ownership of key industries. Prosperity was bringing nearer to completion a social process which had been intermittently under way since 1933 and giving to the workers an outlook hitherto characteristic of the middle classes. Unless the Party could be made not merely compatible with, but positively attractive to such an outlook, it would have small hope of picking up the essential marginal votes needed to give it a majority. Moreover the time had come to realise the growing affinity between the Party and the increasing social awareness shown by many members of the Churches; to this the materialism of Marxist doctrine was an obstacle. Finally the Party saw no alternative but to admit that Schumacher's opposition to Western integration had been a costly mistake. In 1957 the SPD voted for entry into the Common Market (p. 197) and in June 1960 Wehner, speaking in the Bundestag, announced the Party's acceptance of Adenauer's foreign policy in its broad principles. Meanwhile the new look of the Party had in 1958 found expression in the Godesberg Programme. The key slogan in the economic field had already been coined by Professor Schiller, 'Competition as far as possible — planning so far as necessary.'

> In the Godesberg programme, the SPD became a Party like the others and ceased to consider itself as a community of political saints. Parliamentary democracy was no longer a halting-place on the road to true Socialism, economic policy no longer a short-cut to nationalisation, the class struggle with the victory of the proletariat no longer the sole way to save the world. Since Godesberg the SPD has sought its justification not in true faith but in good works.[21]

By 1957 Adenauer was 81 and, though remarkably lively for his years, was growing ever more autocratic and high-handed. His success in managing the West German people led him to believe that any change of leader could only be for the worse. Various possible successors were considered but given no real chance to show their paces and then discarded. Particular difficulty was caused by Adenauer's fixed and, as events proved, justified belief that the most successful of his assistants, Ludwig Erhard, was too genial and unsubtle for the post of Chancellor. He therefore determined to ditch him if he could.

In 1959 an opportunity for change arose. Theodor Heuss had for ten years filled the post of President with a good sense, modesty and impartiality which deservedly won him respect and affection. The Grundgesetz laid down that a President could only be re-elected once; Heuss characteristically refused to allow the Law to be modified in his favour so that a successor had to be found. Adenauer failed in an effort to talk Erhard into taking the job, and was then induced to announce his intention of standing as a candidate himself. But he also made remarks in public and private which suggested an intention to exert more political influence than Heuss had done, and to secure the succession to the Chancellorship for a former industrialist Etzel rather than Erhard. Considerable opposition was at once evident to a step which would undo much of Heuss's achievement by bringing the Presidency back into party politics. The CDU flatly refused to consider Etzel for the succession and Erhard flatly refused to refrain from standing as a candidate for it, while close study of the Grundgesetz seems to have convinced the 'Old Man' that a President did not have the powers which he would want to exert. He therefore withdrew his candidature as abruptly as he had announced it, proposing instead Lübke, the Minister of Agriculture. Lübke was duly elected but the impression was given that the CDU leadership thought a second-rate man, and one with strong party affiliations too, good enough for the Presidency. As it was to prove, Adenauer would have done much better for his own reputation if he had withdrawn while his prestige was still intact; his behaviour was the first step of a series which were to cast a shadow over his closing years.

Intransigence Abroad

A minor casualty of the French failure to ratify the EDC had been the idea of using the Community's existence to settle the question of the Saar. Instead, the 1954 Paris Agreement included a Franco-German deal by which the Saar, until the conclusion of a definitive Peace Treaty, was to be administered as an international territory under a European Commissioner responsible to WEU. The population was asked to confirm this imaginative and conciliatory arrangement but was also given the option of joining the Federal Republic. Times had changed since the bleak days after the war when an overwhelming majority had voted for close association with France. Life in prosperous West Germany had recovered its attractions to such an extent that two-thirds of the electorate thought it preferable to becoming a guinea-pig for a federated Europe. There was nothing for the French Government to do but 'faire bonne mine au mauvais jeu' and at the beginning of 1957 the Saar became the tenth Land of the Federal Republic.

The summer of 1955 was eventful. In July, at Geneva, the leaders of the USA, USSR, Britain and France held the first summit meeting for ten years. The chief problem was German reunification, on which neither side was prepared to depart from its prepared position. Consequently neither that meeting nor a Foreign Ministers' Conference which followed it in the autumn achieved in this field anything more than sterile argument. What the summit did do was to reveal to each side that the other realised what an atomic war would mean and had no intention of starting one if it could avoid doing so. Though few at the time appreciated the implications of this discovery, it was fatal to the policy of reunification through strength.

In the following month Adenauer, against the advice of his experts, decided to try his own hand at negotiating and accepted an invitation to visit Moscow. On arrival, he proposed two subjects for discussion with his hosts — reunification and the return to Germany of German prisoners-of-war still in Russian hands. He made no progress whatever on the first and for a limited verbal undertaking on the second had to agree to the establishment of diplomatic relations between the Federal Republic and the Soviet Union. To prevent such relations from being interpreted as implying West German recognition of the 1945 territorial arrangements, he insisted on the Russians accepting from him a note saying that this was not so, though even then the Russians published the note accompanied by a statement joining issue with it. The prisoners — or some of them — later came back, but two days after Adenauer left, a DDR delegation arrived to conclude a Treaty which gave sovereignty to their Government and authorised it to enter into diplomatic relations with other states.

Adenauer's chief justification for making this somewhat unhappy excursion had been that, as reunification was a matter for the Four Powers rather than for the two Germanies, the Federal Republic must have direct relations with the Russians. But by his action he had created the danger that other states would follow the Russian example and establish diplomatic relations with the DDR as well as with the BRD. To counter this the Bonn Government promulgated in December 1955 the Hallstein Doctrine (called after the State Secretary of the Foreign Office) according to which recognition of the DDR by any state would be regarded by the Federal Republic as an 'unfriendly act', since it would involve recognition of the division of Germany into two states for which there was (in Bonn's eyes) no legal justification. When in 1957 the Yugoslav Government accepted a DDR legation, the Federal Republic broke off diplomatic relations and moreover, until February 1967, it did not establish such relations with any of Russia's allies in view of the fact that they possessed relations with the DDR. The main targets of the 'Doctrine' however were the non-aligned states of Asia and Africa and there can be no doubt that, supported by Bonn's extensive programme of aid (which owed a good deal to such political calculations), nearly a hundred states were for some ten years dissuaded from recognising the DDR. On the other hand the Doctrine gave to any neutral state which wished to extort concessions from Bonn a convenient handle for doing so in the shape of a threat that it would otherwise come to terms with the rival.

West Germany did not rest content with the Hallstein Doctrine but proceeded, with that methodical thoroughness which is such a notable national characteristic, to draw all possible consequences from the theory that their neighbours to the east had no right to exist. For one thing, use of the term 'Deutsche Demokratische Republik' was turned into an action tantamount to treachery; if employed at all, it was always prefaced by the adjective 'so-called' and as a rule the term 'Russian Zone of Occupation' was substituted for it. Indeed in many nationalist quarters the favourite description of that section of the country was 'Middle Germany' with the obvious implication that the areas taken over by Russia and Poland within the 1937 frontiers still constituted 'East Germany'.

A more constructive development also began in the summer of 1955 with the decision taken by the Foreign Ministers of the Coal and Steel Community, meeting at Messina, to set up a Committee under a 'political personality' (who proved to be M. Spaak of Belgium) with the task of working out proposals for closer European integration in the economic field. This initiative led to the scheme for the European Economic Community which achieved concrete realisation in the Treaty of Rome (25 March 1957). The elaborate provisions of the Treaty combined respect for the rights of member states with an inexorable advance to a situation in which decisions on such matters as agricultural prices, tariffs, and commercial policy would have to be taken collectively. Once signed, the Treaty allowed for no going back. It has sometimes been described as a compromise between German industry and French agriculture; this is too sweeping but it was largely a bargain between West Germany and France and represented in many ways the culmination of Adenauer's policy. West Germany was henceforward to be mixed with the rest of Western Europe in a way which would be difficult to unscramble. When critics suggested that the course might prove an obstacle to reunification, the habitual answer was that, on the contrary, only in the context of an integrated Europe would reunification become possible. A little-noticed proviso, however, allowed the Federal Republic to treat the Democratic Republic as an associate of the Community, in that goods passing from one to the other did not have to pay duties. A minor advantage of the Community has been that it enabled the vexed issue of decartellisation to be transferred to a European plane. At such a level the question whether a single West German firm holds too big a share of the market changes its character since such a firm must expect to withstand competition on level terms from similar giants in other EEC countries. The job of seeing that these giants did not in turn concert to fix prices or share the market was made the responsibility of the Community (though West Germany has its own legislation against restrictive practices, introduced by Erhard against the wishes of industry).

Meanwhile the Federal Republic had in 1956 put in hand the recruitment and organisation of the armed forces needed to fulfil its obligation
as a member of NATO. With the example of the Weimar Republic in
mind, great precautions were taken to ensure that the new troops should
be loyal to the democratic state; these largely corresponded with current
thinking about the kind of men needed in a modern technological army.
The soldier was to be the 'citizen in uniform'; in a considerable break
with German tradition, he did not wear uniform off duty. Drill was reduced to a minimum, instruction was given in civics and everyone from
general to private was free to join a trade union (as the Grundgesetz
required). Full authority over the armed forces rests in peace time with
the civilian Minister of Defence, who has on several occasions removed
high officers from their posts for talking out of turn. The Defence Committee of the Bundestag was given permanent status. A civilian Personnel Committee was set up to go into the record of each senior officer
before appointment and the Bundestag was authorised to appoint a
Defence Commissioner with the job of watching over the maintenance
of parliamentary control, investigating alleged infringements of basic
rights and acting as a sort of Ombudsman for any member of the forces
who felt himself aggrieved. The first few choices for this office were not
wholly happy and the safeguards, taken as a whole, are so thorough as
to make it a question whether they may not in due course provoke a
reaction by impeding military efficiency; they have already undergone
some modification. Relations between Government and Bundeswehr
are, however, very different from what they were under the Weimar
Republic.

The original target had been to have 95,000 troops under arms by
the end of 1956 and 270,000 by the end of 1957. Long before those
dates, however, complications had set in. The aim of the NATO allies
had been to raise in West Germany the men whom they were not themselves prepared to spare from their peace economies (p. 177). But as the
Economic Miracle got under way the prospect of some 500,000 men
being removed from the labour market began to fill German industrialists with alarm. While there was some doubt as to whether the weapons
needed to arm the Bundeswehr (which at this stage would have to be
largely imported) could be paid for without either inflation or massive
US help, the real fear was that an artificially-induced labour shortage
would make it impossible to hold wage claims in check. As the Ministry
of Defence under Theodor Blank paid little attention to their representatives, the bosses turned elsewhere and found a more receptive ear in
the Minister of Nuclear Power, Franz Josef Strauss, an exceptionally

intelligent butcher's son and ex-bicycling champion of 40 who was working his passage to the top of the CSU.

As early as November 1955 Strauss was publicly attacking his colleague Blank's arrangements. In July 1956 the Bundestag Defence Committee, whose chairman belonged to the same party as Strauss, cut out of the draft bill for raising conscripts the figure stating the length of time (eighteen months) which they were to serve. In mid-September 1956 the CSU leaders laid down principles of rearmament which hardly squared with those of the Government and at the end of the same month the Budget and Defence Committees of the Bundestag combined to cut out of the Defence Estimates the provision for equipping all units with tanks. Adenauer's majority was not such as to let him dispense with CSU support and in October he replaced Blank by Strauss. The new broom immediately cut down the numbers to be raised to 76,000 at the end of 1956 and 120-135,000 twelve months later. By the end of 1958 only 180,000 were to be in service, of whom only 45,000 had to be conscripts. Conscription was reduced to twelve months and it gradually emerged that the final target was to be 350,000 instead of 500,000 while even this level was not to be reached until 1961.[22]

The apprehensions of the industrialists were thus allayed. The Federal Republic had paid the rest of NATO back in their own coin, refusing in turn to allow the economy to be disrupted and the tide of prosperity checked by the need to compete with the Russians in numbers. Nor was this all. The reduction in numerical strength could only be justified if the fire-power of the remainder could be increased. Just at this stage technological advances in the construction of nuclear weapons enabled them to be made in small sizes and used much as artillery. American and other strategists, convinced by German developments and by the response of the rest of NATO that the original target of 96 divisions could never be realised, argued that the use of such 'tactical' weapons offered the only means short of full-scale atomic war by which the West could hope to offset communist superiority in men and conventional weapons. West German industry saw in this development the chance of manufacturing under licence a wide range of modern weapons and thereby gaining not merely profits and government help with research but also know-how which could be turned to effective civil use. Strauss on occasion argued that, as West Germany was on a footing of complete equality with her NATO allies, the Bundeswehr must get nuclear weapons. The Americans however insisted that, while all troops should be equipped with means of firing such weapons and trained in their use, the actual warheads must remain under US control — and American theatre commanders were required to refer to the President before authorising the small bombs to be used. There was soon, however, every sign that an attempt by the President to withhold his sanction would throw the entire defence arrangements of the West into disarray. The paradox of course was that the case for rearming West Germany had rested on the need to match up to the Russians in conventional weapons; as things worked out, German rearmament was accompanied by a decision to abandon for all practical purposes the idea of defending the West conventionally, while the danger of a deliberate Russian attack on Western Europe was becoming steadily more questionable.

But a NATO decision, taken in December 1957, to authorise the use of tactical nuclear weapons in Central Europe unleashed a flood of controversy. For, though smaller than bombs delivered by aircraft or missiles, they were clearly going to be extremely destructive, and the knowledge that the West was equipped with them would almost certainly (and in practice did) lead to the East following suit. Any incident on the East-West frontier, whether provoked deliberately or by accident, would be capable of escalating rapidly into a situation in which atomic weapons devastated considerable areas, and the areas most likely to be devastated lay in Germany. The result was a West German clamour for the stationing of such weapons on German soil to be forbidden, reinforced on the part of many past victims of Germany by a clamour against putting such lethal weapons into the hands of German soldiers under any circumstances.

Adenauer and Strauss refused to make any concessions to this outcry. According to their arguments the knowledge that tactical nuclear weapons were available would in itself be enough to prevent incidents from occurring. When fifteen distinguished scientists from Göttingen University pressed that the Federal Republic should renounce all use of nuclear weapons, Adenauer disparaged them in public, while he was able to quote in his own favour a strong statement by General Norstad, the American NATO Commander. A vote in favour of nuclear arms was forced through the Bundestag in the spring of 1958, largely by the argument that such a step was vital to West German and European security; when the SPD put their opposition to the test in Land elections in North Rhine-Westphalia in July, they were decisively defeated (p. 192).

Yet though inside West Germany the issue had been decided, the fears of Germany's neighbours remained. Communists were not loath to stoke the fires of disquiet, and the period saw a proliferation of plans for the creation of a nuclear-free or even armament-free zone in Central Europe. Adenauer and Strauss poured scorn on any such suggestion, especially when it was accompanied by proposals for a fresh approach to reunification initiated by direct talks between the two German states. They persuaded the Americans to treat the overtures as mere devices to stop the introduction of nuclear weapons into NATO and were rewarded by accusations that their own ultimate aim was to make the Federal Republic a nuclear power in its own right. East and West showed themselves suspicious that the other would somehow evade its undertakings about disarmament, would use provisions for inspecting the genuineness of disarmament to carry out espionage or subversion, and would manage to exploit a disarmed zone for its own purposes. The question whether disarmament should precede or follow reunification also provided a fruitful source of dissension. The actions of both sides had built up an atmosphere of distrust which virtually precluded agreement and there is no point in trying to chronicle negotiations which were doomed from the start. Mutual obstinacy had led to an impasse.

Unfortunately the East could not afford to let things go on as they were. Conditions in the DDR had undoubtedly improved since 1953. Reparations were stopped in 1954 and occupation costs ceased to be levied after 1959. Food rationing was given up in 1958. The Republic was in the process of becoming the biggest producer and exporter of manufactured goods among all the communist satellites and was at last being paid for its deliveries, even if at low rates. Gross National Product rose above the 1936 level (though long after it had done so in the West and chiefly as the result of increased output of capital goods). In 1958 personal consumption per head at last got above the pre-war level. But by that time it was half as high again in the western part of the country, and the contrast between the two economies, when combined with the communist limitations on personal freedom, provided a strong incentive to migration. Over the nine years from 1952, an average of around 600 people crossed to the West (mainly through Berlin) on every day of every year, the total loss coming to over 2 million; and it was mainly the young, the enterprising and the skilled who left. No state can face such a drain and survive. The policy of combating communism by making the West strong and prosperous was succeeding only too well. Its fallacy lay in supposing that counter-measures could not and would not be devised.

In August 1957 the Soviet Union was reported to have launched a missile with an atomic warhead. In the following October came the first 'Sputnik' (i.e. traveller) which gave evidence of a capacity to carry such a warhead from Warsaw to Washington in twenty minutes and guide it with enough accuracy to destroy a target as limited as the Capitol building. For various reasons the Russians were not as far ahead, nor the Americans as far behind, as was at first thought. But the revelation cast doubt upon the long-term willingness of the Americans to use nuclear weapons in the defence of Western Europe since henceforward such an act was going to invite similar retaliation on America. Khrushchev, who was under some criticism at home for his renunciation of Stalin's policies, seems to have decided to exploit his temporary advantage by pressing for a European settlement. The Russians made no response when Adenauer on three occasions in 1958 secretly suggested the application to the DDR of the neutrality formula which in 1955 had made possible the restoration of Austria's independence. Instead Khrushchev in November 1958 made a threatening speech in which he said that the time had come for the signatories of the Potsdam Agreement to 'renounce the remnants of the occupation regime in Berlin' (which had not in fact been mentioned at Potsdam) and thereby make it possible to create a normal situation in the 'capital of the DDR' (a description incompatible with the agreements which had actually been made as to Berlin). Seventeen days later his underlings followed him up by a more accurate but equally sinister note saying that the Russians regarded the pre-surrender agreements regulating the status of Berlin (p. 108) as obsolete. It then proposed that West Berlin should be made into a demilitarised free city under Four-Power guarantee and threatened that unless the West accepted such a solution within six months, control over communications between the city and West Germany would be handed over to the DDR authorities. Apart from the fact that to get into the city thereafter would involve the West in giving practical recognition to the DDR, the authorities of that Republic could be expected to act more provocatively than the Russians, so that the chances of an armed clash would thus become distinctly greater.

The Western Powers replied in effect that their right to be in Berlin derived from the same pre-surrender agreements which gave the Russians a right to be in Germany at all, and which could not be ended by unilateral repudiation. The Soviet Union was not entitled on its own initiative to transfer its responsibility to any other government, let alone one which its co-signatories did not recognise. No doubt was left about the intention of the West to maintain its position in Berlin, if necessary by force. This show of firmness, which was accompanied by expressions of readiness to discuss Berlin in the wider context of Germany as a whole, had its effect. After pressure had been put on the Russian leader Mikoyan when he visited the US in January 1959 and after arguments had been deployed by the British Prime Minister Macmillan when he visited

Moscow the following month, the Russians began to abandon the time limit and in May the four Foreign Ministers met in Geneva.

Whereas the Bonn Government were delighted with the three Western Powers for standing firm, they were distinctly less enthusiastic over the idea of negotiations, and particularly negotiations in which they could not directly take part. Reunification was becoming so improbable that they attached ever-increasing importance to Western pledges of support for it and deprecated any overtures which might suggest a willingness to compromise. Macmillan's trip to Moscow earned him a black mark in Adenauer's books, while German faith in America was never the same after the retirement and death of John Foster Dulles in 1959. The British and American leaders were, however, under increasing pressure from their publics which, while ready to protect West Berlin and West Germany against communist encroachment, were much less concerned than the Germans about reunification and insistent that West German opposition to negotiations should not result in a slide towards atomic war.

The Foreign Ministers argued for four months and at one stage seemed on the verge of agreeing on at least an interim settlement for Berlin. Their failure to do so was chiefly due to disagreement as to whether, at the end of the interim, Western rights in the city were to continue until reunification or to lapse. In the autumn Khrushchev visited the US and agreed with President Eisenhower that another attempt should be made to settle the problem. But the Summit conference at which this was to be set in train was delayed by de Gaulle and, when it was finally convened in Paris in May 1960, was broken off by Khrushchev, ostensibly because of the shooting-down of an American spy-plane but probably because he saw no prospect of emerging from it with any settlement which his colleagues at home would tolerate. Thereafter he refused to negotiate as long as President Eisenhower was in office and the whole question smouldered till May 1961 when, meeting President Kennedy in Vienna, Khrushchev revived his threats and again talked of time limits.

Kennedy, on taking office, had initiated a radical re-examination of NATO's strategic plans, for he shared widespread fears that the West had been preparing for the wrong kind of emergency. A deliberate attack in strength by the East on the West, the spectre of the early 1950s, was coming to seem less and less likely. What were possible were minor probes or border raids, either deliberate or provoked by misunderstandings. Yet if these were met at the outset by tactical nuclear weapons, there seemed a real danger that the situation would get out of hand through escalation. The Kennedy administration set out to develop the theory of the flexible response, which called for the presence of sufficient ground forces, equipped and trained to fight on conventional lines, to hold an attack until its true scale and object became clearer. The efforts to raise NATO's conventional forces were not very successful but in the late 1950s the Russians reduced their strength in Eastern Europe and it became not unreasonable to suppose that as a result the divisions in Western Europe would be just enough to make a communist attack from immediately available forces a risky business. If, however, one should occur on a full scale, the West's plans still required NATO to be the first side to use nuclear weapons.

The new policy was, however, unwelcome to Adenauer, Strauss and German industry. Not only did it undermine the Ministers' position with their home public, to whom they had multiplied assurances that tactical nuclear weapons were essential, but it also seemed to involve abandonment of defence in forward areas for defence in depth, which was likely to make the whole of the Federal Republic east of the Rhine into a battleground. Adenauer would have agreed with Bismarck's view that 'Russia must be treated like bad weather till things are different.' He considered Kennedy a brash young man who was mistaken in preferring politics of movement to those of stone-walling; he once described him as 'a cross between a junior naval person and a Roman Catholic boy-scout'.

During the weeks succeeding the Vienna meeting, however, Kennedy took the lead in combining firmness with conciliation. American troop strengths in West Germany were increased and the Bonn Government announced its intention of raising the Bundeswehr to its original target of 500,000. But at the same time the West made clear that negotiation would be possible if the Soviet Union would accept the freedom of West Berlin, the principle of free access from West Germany to it and the maintenance of the Western garrisons in it as a guarantee of these freedoms. Significantly, nothing was said about reunification and nothing about free access to West Berlin from the East.

The Soviet leadership would seem to have concluded that the West was not to be cajoled or intimidated and that, as a solution involving attacks on West Berlin and the access routes was likely to be met by force, it must be discarded as too risky. Something, however, had to be done to stop the exodus from the DDR which was swelling to a flood as potential emigrants decided that, if they waited any longer, they might find it too late. Pressure from Ulbricht resulted in a decision to put into practice the least risky solution (for which indeed preparations had been begun some time previously). On 13 August 1961 a barbed wire fence, soon converted into a wall, began to go up hermetically sealing East Berlin from the rest of the city (except at a few controlled crossing-points). On 22 August West Berliners (as distinct from West Germans) were barred from entering the Russian Sector without passes and, as the West Berlin authorities refused to allow those passes to be issued on their side of the city, traffic came to a halt. Henceforward Germans had to learn to live with an extra obtrusive symbol of the country's defeated and divided condition.

The people, and possibly the Government, of West Germany were disillusioned to find that their Western Allies took no steps to interfere with the building of Berlin's Wall, or to secure its demolition once it was built. But any attempt by them to use force on the eastern side of the boundary might have provoked Ulbricht into interrupting their communications with West Berlin and thus might well have developed into all-out war. The free world regarded the Wall as an act of unprecedented and inhuman barbarism. But such a reaction was ingenuous. Not merely did it overlook the probability that the alternatives would have been harsher and more dangerous. It overlooked the alternatives because it assumed that an opponent who was conventionally regarded as ruthless and materialistic would act out of character by remaining inactive when pressure was applied to a key point in his system. What the building of the Wall demonstrated was the determination of the Russians to hold on to the parts of Germany which they had won and the inability of the West to shake their grip. Thereby it also demonstrated that the policy of undermining the foundations of the Democratic Republic was as futile as that of rolling back the curtain. The West and the Federal Republic would sooner or later have to recognise that disliking a situation which one cannot change is not an adequate reason for refusing to come to terms with it. There were in any case those in the West who had no objection to Germany's strength being reduced by partition provided it could be prevented from leading to war; a Frenchman said, 'J'aime tellement l'Allemagne que je suis heureux qu'il y en a deux.'

11 THE ERHARD INTERLUDE, 1961-1966

Adenauer Proves His own Worst Enemy

Just over a month after the building of the Wall, on 17 September 1961, West Germany went to the polls. The growing disillusionment with Adenauer was reflected in the loss by the CDU/CSU of 28 seats, which involved into the bargain the loss of their absolute majority. The German Party, which had been their coalition partner, fared even worse; it only won 2.8 per cent of the poll and as a result disappeared from federal politics. The SPD, fighting under the leadership of the young Lord Mayor of Berlin Willy Brandt, gained 21 seats; the FDP 26. Many people inside and outside Germany had hoped that the venerable Chancellor would take the occasion to retire. There were those in his own Party who wanted to see him replaced by Erhard because, although they thought Erhard would make a bad leader (as he did), they reckoned for that reason on being able to get rid of him more easily than Adenauer and to open the way for one of themselves. But Erhard refused to be a party to such intrigues or put himself up against Adenauer while Adenauer, on whom such calculations were by no means lost, regarded the situation as so serious and his colleagues as so unsatisfactory that on the morning immediately following the Election, he announced his intention of continuing in office. To do so, however, he needed the support of a second party – and by now the Parties in the Bundestag had been reduced to four (counting the CSU as distinct from the CDU). The chief gainer at the Election had been the FDP but it owed this success in large part to a promise by its leader Dr Mende not to join in any coalition as long as Adenauer remained at the helm. The alternative of a 'Great Coalition' with the SPD had adherents in many quarters but its opponents in both Parties on this occasion won the day. A coalition between SPD and FDP was at the time ruled out by the Confederation of German Industry which financed the FDP and was not convinced that the SPD had genuinely renounced socialisation. In the end, after seven weeks of bargaining, in the course of which Brentano was succeeded as Foreign Minister by the more conciliatory Schröder, a CDU/CSU/FDP coalition emerged, Mende atoning for his rash commitment by forswearing office. A promise was, however, extorted from Adenauer that he would retire in 1963 at the latest.

The building of the Wall did not end the Berlin crisis which continued to simmer for another eighteen months. Kennedy made clear that he was still ready to discuss solutions which did not impair the fundamental determination of the West to protect West Berlin; as a result he went a long way towards alienating Bonn without quite conciliating the Kremlin. At one point Grewe, the German ambassador in the US, felt compelled to appeal to the article in the 1954 Paris Treaty by which the West had committed itself to seeking a freely negotiated peace settlement for the whole of Germany; at another, great offence was taken in Bonn when Washington suggested making concessions to the East and in Washington when Bonn sought to torpedo the move by deliberately leaking the US proposals. Grewe himself had later to be removed on account of incompatibility with Kennedy and the State Department. Relations improved slightly as East and West measured up to the confrontation which was precipitated in October 1962 over Cuba. The demonstration that Kennedy was not to be intimidated but was anything but brash earned him widespread respect in West Germany. The crisis had clear implications for Russian policy regarding Berlin and Germany; that Khrushchev had learnt them was suggested when on 16 January 1963 he told the East German Party Congress that the problem of the German Peace Treaty was not what it had been before defensive measures (including the building of the Wall) were taken. Thereafter, for the time being at any rate, the chief Russian aim seemed to be to harass sleeping dogs with nothing more than tintacks.

Since the death of Dulles and more particularly since the election of Kennedy the US administration had given Adenauer little encouragement for pursuing his hitherto unyielding line. His disillusionment with the country which he had made one of the two main foundations of his policy inclined him to pay all the more attention to the other and helps to explain the friendship which was struck up from the autumn of 1958 onwards between himself and de Gaulle. The General's previous record towards Germany should hardly have disposed the Chancellor in his favour. His hostility to the EDC and, as was to become evident, to the supranational conception of the EEC might have been thought to show a radical difference of approach. Moreover de Gaulle had as early as March 1959 committed the sin, usually regarded in Bonn as unforgivable, of saying that present frontiers (including presumably the Oder-Neisse line) must be maintained; he also insisted on keeping in touch with the Russians because of his hope that France could prove she was still a Great Power by mediating between East and West. But both the French and the German statesmen were elderly, both Catholic, both inclined to behave as autocrats; their homes were within two hundred miles of one another. Each of the two combined a respect for tradition with an astute eye for political advantage. De Gaulle could have no hope of realising his ambitions in Europe, involving as they did the reduction of American influence, unless he could secure at least one powerful ally and, in her current mood of disappointment, West Germany must have appeared a more likely recruit than Britain. Another factor which could be counted on to work in the same direction was Adenauer's well-known desire to end Franco-German animosities for good and all. The Germans may well have appreciated that France's reasons for disliking America were by no means the same as their own. But the French policy of building up Europe as a 'third Force' must have appeared to Adenauer to offer a chance of maintaining towards the East the unyielding line which seemed otherwise doomed by the withdrawal of American support.

For the rest of the period covered by this chapter, two alternative schools of thought contended inside Bonn government circles for the control of foreign policy. One, represented by Adenauer and Strauss, denied that there had been any fundamental change in Russia's desire for world domination and therefore sought to maintain with as little alteration as possible the attitudes of the Cold War. But they now sought to achieve this policy in association with France rather than America and by building up a 'Europe *des patries*' which, although composed of states still essentially sovereign, would co-operate sufficiently to overcome the inadequacies of sovereign states in the modern world, notably as regards the possession of nuclear weapons. The other school, of which Erhard and Schröder were the protagonists, argued that for the foreseeable future West Germany must continue to depend for her defence on American nuclear might, and that, to maintain American good-will, some (but not too many) concessions must be made to the American desire for a reduction of East-West tension. If Erhard's tenure of office had been more auspicious as a whole, he and Schröder might have been able to make their views prevail. But as it was, they had to make so many concessions in order to carry their Party with them as to remove any real chances of success. Thus the 'Peace Note' which they circulated to all friendly Powers in March 1966 was far too cautious to melt any Eastern ice. But the German Gaullists for their part were frequently embarrassed by the unwillingness of their patron to consider any German interests which did not suit him as well as by the failure of various proposals to evolve a European deterrent.

The SPD not only agreed with Erhard that there was no future in stone-walling but had positive reasons for favouring a positive approach. Their attitude was well expressed by a speech made in 1963 by Egon

Bahr, the Press Officer and policy adviser of Willy Brandt:

> The American strategy for peace can be expressed by the formula
> that the Communist domination has got to be transformed rather
> than superseded.
>
> The first consequence of applying the Strategy for Peace to Ger-
> many is that the policy of all or nothing has got to stop. Today it
> is obvious that reunification is not to be a once-for-all affair but a
> process with many stages and many pauses. There is no need for us
> to be handicapped by our refusal to recognize the Zone as a lawful
> state. This goes without saying and without serious challenge. Our
> first concern must be with human beings and with the exploration of
> every conceivable and defensible means of improving their situation.
> An improvement in material conditions in the Zone must lead to a
> relaxation in tension.
>
> Such a policy can be summed up in the phrase 'Nearness will bring
> change'.

Bahr's attitude was regarded by the 'hard-liners' of the CDU/CSU as
incapable of arousing any response on the part of the East and therefore as involving a gratuitous display of weakness.

This background helps to explain the commotion caused in West
Germany towards the end of 1962 by the 'Spiegel Affair'. *Der Spiegel*
is a weekly paper which combines the format and style of the US *Time*
with the news sense of the British *Daily Mirror*. It performed during the
Adenauer era the useful function of forcing on public attention issues
and scandals which politicians preferred to keep wrapped up. Besides
being frequently critical of Adenauer himself, it had on several occasions
spotlighted actions by Franz Josef Strauss of distinctly questionable
propriety, although he afterwards explained them to the satisfaction
of the Bundestag majority. They included a report that, on one of the
crucial nights of the (then recent) Cuba crisis, the Minister of Defence
had been the worse for drink. At almost the same time *Der Spiegel* published an article on the position of the Bundeswehr in NATO which not
only contained privately-obtained information as to future plans but
claimed that at the Minister's instigation so much attention had been
given to the use of tactical nuclear weapons as to impair the efficiency
of conventional training.

Over a fortnight later police raided the office of *Der Spiegel* and the
homes of some of its senior staff, on the pretext that there had been
a leakage of vital defence secrets. Eleven arrests were made; that of

Conrad Ahlers, the author of the article, was effected by the Spanish police, at the request of the German Embassy, while he was on holiday. Rudolf Augstein, the paper's publisher, was kept in jail for fourteen weeks.

In the subsequent controversy both Adenauer and Strauss at first attempted to minimise their parts, only to have it demonstrated that they both had told lies to the Bundestag. In particular a telephone call to the Madrid Embassy was shown to have been made by Strauss himself, though he subsequently claimed to have been acting on the Chancellor's behalf. Adenauer, who on the whole despised his Cabinet colleagues, recognised in Strauss something of the flair for political manoeuvre on which he prided himself: he is less likely to have recognised as a further common characteristic a blind spot to the feelings of others. He would probably have liked to keep the offender in his Cabinet but was precluded from doing so by the FDP, one of whose Cabinet representatives, as Minister of Justice, had by Adenauer's orders been left in the dark in a matter directly involving his Ministry. Adenauer's first expedient was to dismiss the two senior officials who had done as they were told but this did not suffice to stop the FDP Ministers from resigning in a body and indicating that they were no longer prepared to serve with Strauss. Before they returned, the Cabinet had to be reconstructed, Strauss had to resign and the Chancellor had to confirm his intention of retiring in 1963. The FDP Minister of Justice was, however, left out of the new Cabinet. Meanwhile in the middle of the row the people of Bavaria had gone to the polls and voted for the return to office with an increased majority of the CSU who had in the previous spring chosen Strauss as their chairman.

Hardly was the Cabinet reconstructed than Adenauer in January 1963 visited Paris to put the coping-stone on to his policy of reconciliation by signing a Franco-German Treaty of Friendship. The auspiciousness of the occasion was somewhat impaired by its occurrence midway between the Press Conference at which de Gaulle questioned the qualifications of Britain for joining the Common Market and the meeting in Brussels at which the British application for membership was finally on French insistence suspended. Had Adenauer made his signature of the Treaty conditional on British entry, as some of his colleagues wished, much might have altered. But the development and maintenance of Europe was always his first priority, while for Britain he had at best respect, never affection. British attitudes towards disarmament, nuclear free zones and a compromise with the East smacked altogether too much of appeasement for his tastes. The Bundestag, however, when ratifying the Treaty, insisted on adding a preamble which reaffirmed the German desire to maintain the Atlantic Alliance and strengthen the European Community by the inclusion of Britain. They thus ruled out the use of the document to support Gaullist policies.

Three Years of Fumbling

Adenauer finally retired in October 1963. In spite of all his efforts, Erhard was nominated by the Party as his successor. But they allowed him to remain Party chairman and he did not resign from the Bundestag. From these positions he kept up a running fire of comment about the policy of the new regime and at an early stage a remark that 'I can no longer endure the miserable talk of relaxation' began to make the rounds. Schröder was retained as Foreign Minister and inaugurated a 'policy of movement', the chief feature of which was the development of trade with, and the establishment of trade missions in, the five Communist satellites whose recognition of the DDR made impossible under the Hallstein Doctrine the establishment of full diplomatic relations. In the documents effecting this development, the terms offered by the Federal Republic were said to apply throughout the currency area of the Deutschemark; this formula neatly evaded the controversial question of the Republic's right to act on behalf of West Berlin.

A similar evasion was resorted to at Christmas after the DDR Government had offered to allow citizens of West Berlin facilities for visiting relatives in the east part of the city. A representative of the West Berlin Senate at the last moment negotiated an arrangement which, rather than use terms with implications unacceptable to one or the other side, opened with an admission that the two negotiators had been unable to agree on how to describe their respective areas, superior authorities or positions! The Bonn Government disliked the development but lacked the courage to veto a step which could bring happiness to many, and almost a million people passed through the Wall. The arrangement was repeated in 1964 and 1965 but grew more and more unpopular with the hawks in Bonn who not merely feared that the very act of negotiating with DDR officials might be exploited as involving recognition but also that any steps which eased the evils of partition might weaken the determination to get it abolished completely. The DDR, observing this, thought that they saw an opportunity of putting the hawks at cross-purposes with the doves and, when the 1966 negotiations started, insisted on spades being called spades. As a result no agreement was reached and no visits exchanged.

The virtual cessation of traffic between the two sides of the city was not merely a human tragedy. It called into question the functions which during the 1950s the Western side had been performing of show-window, listening post, reception centre and propaganda factory. Moreover with the ending of replenishment from the east, West Berlin's labour force began to fall and the proportion of pensioners in the population to grow abnormally high. To maintain employment the Federal Government, on top of other financial aid, provided subsidies which enabled raw materials to be brought from the west, made into finished goods in the city and taken back to the west for sale. Even so there were signs of a drift of work, talent and control to West Germany. The unbroken monopoly of political power which the SPD enjoyed began to have its usual corrupting effects. The beleaguered bastion of liberty was showing signs of degenerating into a dead end.

Erhard and Schröder remained faithful to the Atlantic Alliance and their relations with France failed to live up to the aims professed in the Treaty of Friendship. America's attention and resources became increasingly strained by the Vietnam War and after Kennedy's assassination few initiatives were taken in Europe. America's expenditure on aid combined with extensive overseas investment and the rising outlay on Vietnam to create a serious overall deficit. Britain had for some time been endeavouring to make the Federal Republic choose between contributing more to the cost of maintaining British troops in Germany or seeing their numbers reduced, and now the Americans, in search of economies, adopted the same line. De Gaulle made increasingly clear his determination to wreck NATO which had for so long been the sheet anchor of West German defence policy. In the summer of 1965 his high-handed attempt, in defiance of the Rome Treaty, to reshape the Common Market more to his liking added another ground for dissension, since the West Germans stood firm in solidarity with the Italians, Benelux and the EEC Commission. The policy of seeking reunification through a relaxation of tension seemed productive of problems rather than results.

Nor was foreign policy the only field in which things were going wrong. In the economic field much had changed since the early days of the 'Miracle'. Many of the initial advantages had faded away. People who had rebuilt their fortunes no longer felt the same need for effort; by 1966 the average working week in West Germany was 2.5 hours shorter than in Britain. Workers who had tasted the pleasures of the affluent society grew eager for the money and leisure needed to make more of them; in particular the practice grew of taking expensive holidays abroad. The building of the Wall, by stopping the flow of workers from the east, made labour for the first time scarce; the workers who came instead from Southern Europe, besides being less skilled, sent back much of their earnings to their families at home. The West German trade unions began to demand and obtain higher annual wage increases. In 1963 an export boom set in, producing such prosperity that prices and imports began to rise alarmingly. In 1965 the country had a deficit on current account of DM 6,500 million (£550 million), and whereas Britain was accustomed to cancel out her traditional deficit on visible trade by a surplus on invisibles, the Federal Republic was coming to need a substantial visible surplus to offset the expenditure of her tourists, the remittances of her foreign workers and the considerable sums which she was paying as development aid.

Deficits were not confined to foreign trade. In the prosperity of the 1950s, a readiness had developed to quiet the complaints of pressure groups by handing out public money. Pensions had been made up on a lavish scale; many people received 60 per cent of their final salary. Subsidies were given to encourage building, the unnatural economy of West Berlin was bolstered up, compensation paid to all affected by the war, uneconomic industries like textiles, coal-mining and shipbuilding kept in being. The fact that some of these expenditures were sensible did not prevent them from being costly. Such generosity at the expense of the taxpayer was not confined to the Federal Government which only incurred 20 per cent of total public expenditure; many social services in West Germany are the responsibility of the Land Governments, others that of the cities and communes. Extravagance was just as noteworthy here. Moreover the system of government, and in particular the allocation of tax revenues (p. 168) would have made it impossible for the Federal Government to control expenditure elsewhere, even had the desire to do so existed. As the 1965 Election approached, the largesse became more lavish than ever; a particularly untimely step (not unknown in Britain in similar circumstances) was a cut in income tax. The praise accorded to the 'Social Market Economy', by making 'planning' a dirty word, discouraged people from asking how the Budget was going to be balanced or what levels of expenditure would be involved in future years by the commitments already entered into.

Curiously enough, the election campaign of 1965 did not lead to any real debate on the problems facing West Germany in the fields of economic and foreign policy. The Government were too fundamentally divided to encourage discussion, while the Socialists, fighting again under the leadership of Willy Brandt, seem to have feared that talk of the need to economise or suggestions of a more conciliatory policy towards the East might lose them votes. They hoped to win victory by promising to do the same things as the Government but to do them better. These tactics did not pay. Their gain of twelve seats fell far short of their expectations, whereas the CDU/CSU, who had been afraid of losing ground, returned three seats stronger. The real losers by 18 seats were the FDP; no other parties gained any representation at all. Although there was once again talk of a 'Great Coalition' (principally by people who wanted to get rid of Erhard), the Chancellor insisted on keeping the FDP as his partner in government and they were still content to play that role. With their help he beat off attempts to bring Strauss (now leader of the CSU in the Bundestag) back into the Cabinet and to evict Schröder from the Foreign Ministry.

In the succeeding twelve months, however, things got worse rather than better. Dissatisfaction mounted with the lack of progress over reunification. The 'German Gaullists' remained opposed to gratifying American desires for negotiation with the East, but their resistance to all forms of relaxation grew increasingly difficult to reconcile with their advocacy of close co-operation with France and the development of an independent Europe, since de Gaulle showed himself almost as anxious as the Americans to improve relations with the East. The choice open to West Germany began therefore to be seen, not as one between rigidity and movement but between the Social Democratic solution of trying by negotiations with the rulers of the DDR (short of formal recognition) to secure minor alleviations for their population and the official preference for trying by negotiations with other Communist states to isolate and undermine the rulers of the DDR. It became, however, increasingly clear that Erhard was too genial, too much of a technical expert and too little of a politician to impose his authority on his colleagues. He did not dare to threaten resignation because he knew (especially after the Election of 1965 had been won) that many people would have been glad to see him go. Consequently West German policy remained one of little steps because Ministers could not agree in what direction to make big ones.

Much the same story was repeated in economic affairs. The boom of 1963 was gradually waning. In particular the programme of housebuilding, which hitherto had been a major source of growth, was at last beginning to slacken as supply caught up with demand. But there was still a certain amount of inflationary pressure in the economy. The Bundesbank, which was required by its Charter to give overriding priority to maintaining the value of the Mark, had not yet realised how much time modern economies take to answer the monetary helm and insisted on maintaining a deflationary course for longer than was appropriate. Interest rates were kept high, industry became reluctant to borrow, orders began to fall and business confidence to be shaken. As the Bank had been deliberately so constituted as to be independent of official control, the Government could not enforce a change of policy and failed to achieve one by persuasion. The fall in tax revenues further impaired the balance of a budget already upset by the lavish expenditure. Various proposals for savings had no practical result and even the expedient of forming five Ministers into a *Streichquintett* to strike out proposals for expenditure came to little because the Ministers affected by the cuts persuaded the Cabinet to cancel most of them; party discipline was not strong enough to prevent the representatives of pressure groups from getting other economies rejected when they came before the Bundestag. An attempt to reduce defence expenditure was stamped on by the Americans. The Government was therefore unable to comply with the Basic Law's requirement that the Budget must be balanced. The symptoms of a crisis were thus unmistakable. They even induced Erhard to overcome his objections to attempts at guiding the economy and allow his Economics Minister Schmücker to introduce a Stability Bill giving the Government powers to accelerate or slow down the rate of expenditure at Land and local levels as well as centrally. The project however evoked numerous objections, not least from the Land Governments, and became bogged down in Bundestag debates.

When a Bundestag Deputy dies or retires, his place is filled automatically by the next available name on his Party's list for election by proportional representation (p. 275); thus there are no by-elections. As a result, it is elections for Land Governments which in the Federal Republic perform the role of recording changes in public attitudes towards the government. In July 1966 such elections fell due in North Rhine-Westphalia, and in them the SPD came within two seats of winning an absolute majority. This was an omen which the CDU could not afford to disregard. Dissatisfaction with Erhard ceased to be confined to political opponents and personal enemies; even for those who had hitherto supported him, he began to seem more a liability than an asset. The FDP in particular began to worry whether in their electoral position they could afford to be associated much longer with a discredited regime. But Article 67 of the Grundgesetz (Constructive Vote of No Confidence, (p. 165) makes any Chancellor difficult to dislodge, and all the obvious CDU/CSU aspirants for the succession had determined enemies. It took a double manoeuvre at the end of October 1966 to evict Erhard. In the first place the rank-and-file of the FDP Deputies insisted on their representatives in the Cabinet vetoing proposals for balancing the Budget by higher taxes; they hoped by this means to force the CDU/CSU into facing fundamental policy decisions. The rank-and-file of the CDU/CSU, led by Strauss, saw their chance and, by insisting on their Cabinet representatives standing firm, provoked the FDP Ministers into resigning. Though Erhard tried for a time to weather the storm, it became clear that he could not fill the vacancies, that he would therefore have to resign and that a new Cabinet would have to be formed under a new Chancellor. But who should compose it?

The urgency of the situation was underlined by elections in Hesse on 6 November and in Bavaria on 23 November. Not only did the FDP lose ground in both, being completely deprived of representation in the Bavarian Landtag, but the right-wing 'Neo-Nazis' or National Democratic Party (NPD) — which had obtained no seats in the 1965 Federal Election — made striking gains, polling 7.9 per cent of the votes (with 8 seats) in Hesse and 7.4 per cent (with 15 seats) in Bavaria. Some voters were losing patience with democracy.

The first step towards the resolution of the crisis was taken when the CDU/CSU decided, largely on the initiative of Strauss, to bypass all the more obvious rivals for the succession and call back to Bonn, as its candidate for the Chancellorship, Dr Kurt Georg Kiesinger, a former Bundestag Deputy who, after Adenauer had dashed his hopes of becoming Foreign Minister, retired to his native Land of Baden-Württemberg as its Minister-President. The most obvious objection to his appointment was that he had not only joined the Nazi Party in 1933 but had remained a member, even if a relatively inactive one, throughout the Third Reich, with a post as liaison officer between the Foreign Office and the foreign services of the Reich Broadcasting Company; this at least seemed to justify a charge of conformism and thereby to impair the good impression made by his post-war record.

Both the CDU/CSU and the FDP regarded with distaste the idea of working together again. The character of the new Government was thus made dependent on the preference of the SPD. While they still differed from the CDU/CSU on many issues, the gap between the two Parties had been narrowing ever since the Godesberg Programme (p. 194), while the Social Democrats could not be said to see eye to eye with the leaders of the FDP. The greatest objection to a 'Little Coalition' lay in the fact that it would only have a majority of six and there was considerable doubt (to be justified by experience after 1969) as to the loyalty of some members of the FDP right-wing. In a 'Little Coalition' the main responsibility would have rested with the SPD and they were afraid of being discredited, on at last achieving office, by failure to discharge it effectively. Yet if they refused office altogether, they would face criticism for shunning responsibility. They also feared that, in face of an SPD/FDP government, the CDU/CSU would move to the right and criticise Ministers for lacking patriotism, as after 1918. There also seemed to be a good deal in the argument that only a Great Coalition would be strong enough to overcome the difficulties facing the new government abroad and restore business confidence at home.

For all these reasons, under the strong promptings of Herbert Wehner, but against the inclinations of many ordinary party members, and to the disillusion of the young, the SPD Deputies came down at the end of November 1966 in favour of a Great Coalition. The CDU/CSU were delighted with a solution which spared them the unpleasant necessity of giving up office. Under Kiesinger as Chancellor, Brandt became Foreign Minister, Schiller (a Professor of Economics who had distinguished himself as an SPD Senator in Hamburg) Economics Minister, Strauss Finance Minister, Schröder Defence Minister and Wehner Minister for All-German Affairs. In total, the CDU held eight posts, the CSU three and the SPD nine. The first, and as it proved, decisive step had been taken towards ending the domination of Federal politics by the CDU/CSU.

12 THE GREAT COALITION, 1966-1969

Restoring Confidence at Home

The main domestic task of the new Government was to restore confidence in West Germany's continued economic prosperity. But this could best be achieved by success in two other tasks. The first was to reverse the policy of deflation and get the economy expanding again. This was all the easier because by the time the Great Coalition took office, there was unmistakable evidence that the boom had run its full course. Whereas in October there had been 300,000 more unfilled jobs than unemployed, by December the second exceeded the first. The Bundesbank was thereby helped to overcome its hesitations about reducing the interest rate, a step which it was all the readier to take because the very formation of the Coalition was evidence of an intention to tackle the other main source of inflation, namely the Budget. To believers in the Keynesian principle of working against the cyclical trend, the very fact that this was unbalanced was a recommendation in its favour. But not only did the Grundgesetz require it to be balanced; the inbred fear of rising prices and mounting debts, due to memories of 1923 and 1948, made the crude form of deliberately incurred deficit out of the question.

This was where the Great Coalition did most to justify its formation. The presence of two parties in the Cabinet and the division of responsibility between two Ministers (Strauss and Schiller) allowed the problem to be solved by pursuing two policies at once. Strauss pleased the CDU/CSU by balancing the Budget through the orthodox remedy of taxing more and spending less; Schiller pleased the SPD by pursuing a counter-cyclical policy of 'moderated expansion' (*Aufschwung nach Mass*) with a special programme of capital expenditure on communications, public building and the provision of similar 'infrastructure' which had been neglected in previous years and could quite properly be paid for by running into long-term debt. Each Minister backed the other up, so that the performance was said to have 'words by Schiller, music by Strauss', and Kiesinger backed both: their combined weight was sufficient to get the programme through the Cabinet and Bundestag more or less intact. The unions, anxious to avoid unemployment, agreed to co-operate by moderating their demands for higher wages and making the new rates run for two or three years.

The cure was completed by steps to prevent the disease from recurring. July 1967 saw the passing into law of a revised version of Schmücker's Stability Bill (p. 215). It set as the targets of government policy the 'quadrilateral' whose all-round achievement has often been thought impossible — stable prices, full employment, adequate growth and a reasonable external surplus. It allowed for 10 per cent adjustments up or down to be made in certain taxes without Bundestag approval being necessary. Both the Federal and Land Governments were authorised to freeze revenue in booms and release the money in recessions; they could also remit taxes on companies to encourage investment or suspend allowances to deter it. As no increase in Federal authority over expenditure had a hope of being accepted by the Bundesrat, a 'Business Activity Council' (*Konjunkturrat*) was set up to steer the economy, on which the Federal and Land Governments, the Communes and the Bundesbank were all represented. A Council of (five) Experts had already been set up in 1964 to provide economic forecasts and suggest action; the Government was now required to report annually to the Bundestag its reactions to these suggestions. The joke that the country was becoming a 'Republic of Councils' (*Räterepublik* — what the left wing had wanted to set up in 1919) was encouraged by the creation of yet another one to produce rolling forecasts of overall income and expenditure in the public sector for the next three years (*Mittelfristigesplanung*). A Council of Government, Employers and Unions (*Konzentierte Aktion*) was set up to produce in concert forecasts of growth and, in the light of these, recommendations as to the size of wage increases which could be afforded. Finally the Government was required to publish annually a list of all the subsidies which it was paying.

The other notable achievement of the Great Coalition in the economic field was its reorganisation of the coal industry. The drop in demand for coal, highlighted early in 1967 by the near-bankruptcy of Krupps, meant that, if the industry was to remain profitable, it must be reduced in size. But as long as the pits remained in separate hands, often owned in conjunction with enterprises in other fields, diversity of interest would prevent the framing of any rational plan for contraction. Ideology made straightforward public ownership out of the question and only the obstinacy of Schiller brought about the formation at the end of 1968 of an overall Company for the Ruhr Coal Industry, which took over the mining activities of 47 companies, in return for generous compensation to be paid over a long period. Schiller also saw to it that elaborate plans were included for compensating and retraining redundant miners, thereby avoiding obstruction by the unions. He had less success in his efforts to form a single German oil company large enough to compete with Esso, BP and Shell, which dominate the market. An ambitious scheme by the Minister of Transport to transfer heavy long-distance loads to the railways fell foul of the road transport lobby. The idea of extending workers co-determination was as unpalatable to the CDU as it was dear to the SPD and, as a compromise, a commission was given the job of formulating precise proposals. While many favoured the idea of revising the financial relationships between Bund and Länder, everyone had different ideas as to the form which revision should take, so that the most achieved in the end was minor tinkering. In 1969 amendments were passed to the Basic Law giving the Federal Government power to work with the Länder (mainly by contributing cash) on higher education, scientific research, town planning and hospital construction.

Novel as the idea was that the economy could and should be deliberately steered by the Government, the CDU/CSU members of the Coalition came to accept it. What they and still more their SPD colleagues overestimated was the ease and speed with which it could be done. In 1967 progress was slow, largely because the local authorities found it hard to accustom themselves to the idea that the right way to counter falling revenues was to increase expenditure. By July industrial capacity was only 75 per cent employed and Schiller secured authority for a second investment programme. Most of the increasing production went into exports, which led to a favourable trade balance of nearly DM 17 billion. After the New Year, however, home demand began to pick up and by mid-1968 the economy was once again at full stretch. No trace remained of the anxiety which had been so much more widespread than people outside Germany had realised. The budget was back in balance; the growth rate, instead of the forecast 4 per cent, reached 7 per cent while exports were up by 13 per cent (as in most other countries of Western Europe). Everyone who had a chance of holding Marks took it. Money poured into the country, with inflationary results.

The American and British Governments, which were struggling with deficits, called on the West Germans to help by revaluing the Mark upwards. Strauss and Schiller were ready to consider a small rise as part of a general international adjustment. But when this was blocked by de Gaulle's refusal to devalue the franc, Strauss refused to handicap exporters and farmers by making the Mark more expensive abroad. The Bundesbank, giving priority as usual to preventing inflation, wanted a unilateral revaluation. Schiller's concern for the consumer made him sympathetic, but the most he could get his colleagues to accept was a scheme of taxes and rebates on foreign trade which had much the same effect as a revaluation.

But although this resolved the political deadlock, it did not remove the economic difficulty; the trade surplus continued to grow. By March 1969 Schiller was telling the Chancellor that revaluation was inevitable, but he had not got far towards securing agreement on such a step when at the end of April de Gaulle's resignation seemed to remove the obstacle to an international solution. Strauss tried to precipitate one by saying that the Mark needed to go up by 8 to 10 per cent, an ill-considered remark which caused the amount of foreign money in Germany to double within a week. Action by further countries however was not forthcoming and the Cabinet therefore decided to remain inactive too, a decision which produced a protest from 61 Professors of Economics but was approved by 87 per cent of the electorate! The Cabinet spokesman into the bargain described it as being valid 'for ever' (*auf ewig*), a time limit which most observers interpreted as meaning until after the election due in September, and even in that sense considered foolhardy. Schiller disowned responsibility for what might happen in the interval but did not resign since he would thereby have almost certainly broken up the coalition and left a minority government to caretake for five months. The close collaboration between the two Ministers had been ended by the very success which it had made possible. The views of the two Parties had become diametrically opposed and, although this was partly due to discrepant guesses as to which line would bring most votes, the chances of them ever being able to work together again harmoniously seemed small. Paradoxically it was the SPD who favoured leaving market forces free to act and the CDU/CSU who wanted them to be directed by the government.

Small Steps only Get a Small Distance

In its policy towards Communist East Europe (*Ostpolitik*), the Coalition professed an intention to advance by a series of small steps, which the Democratic Republic unkindly rephrased as 'aggression in carpet slippers'. From the outset there were two distinct ideas about how to pursue this. One school of thought wanted to build on the foundations already laid by Schröder of developing relationships with all the non-German satellite states, hoping in this way to weaken the ties between those states and the 'hard-line' regimes in Russia and East Germany. The other, considering this tactic too obvious and therefore doomed to

failure, favoured approaches to all states at once. Kiesinger, in his initial
declaration of policy, had said that 'we want to relax rather than stiffen,
to bridge differences rather than deepen them'. He offered to establish
diplomatic relations with all states which did not demand unacceptable
conditions in return. But that was precisely what the Russians and East
Germans did, making clear that as an essential to any progress the Federal Republic must recognise the Democratic Republic and the 1945
frontiers.

Only the Rumanians showed themselves more amenable. The Federal
Republic had already become their largest supplier after the Soviet
Union and, true to their Latin origins, they were showing in the Warsaw
Pact much the same independence as the French were doing in NATO.
In January 1967 they agreed to the upgrading into full-scale embassies
of the trade missions in the two countries. They allowed a clause to be
inserted in the agreement which explicitly recorded that its conclusion
did not imply any change in Bonn's views about the illegality of the
DDR. This, and the invention of a theory that Rumania could not be
criticised for recognising that state since she had never been left any
choice by the Russians (*Geburtsfehlertheorie*), enabled Kiesinger to
conciliate the more intransigent members of his right wing.

Ulbricht for his part had hoped to use West Germany's desire for
trade with south-east Europe as a lever for forcing the members of the
Atlantic Alliance to recognise the existence of his own state. His party
paper minced no words about Rumania's sale of the pass; the Rumanian
party paper replied, at four times the length, to the effect that that
country's leaders intended to run their own foreign policy. They further
refused to go to East Berlin for a conference to co-ordinate action,
though they were not able to prevent a later conference in Czechoslovakia from vowing never to follow their example. Feelers which Bonn
had been putting out, particularly towards Hungary, were as a result
rebuffed. This outcome bore out the misgivings of those West Germans
who had questioned the wisdom of approaching the Eastern bloc through
its deviant member — but no other approach had at that juncture any
better prospects.

In April 1967 Kiesinger proposed to the DDR a 16-point programme
for easing mutual relations. No immediate answer was made but in May
a letter arrived at the Chancellor's office containing an offer from Willi
Stoph, the East German Prime Minister, to meet Kiesinger with a view
to creating 'normal relations' — what Willy Brandt at about the same
time described as 'regulated co-existence' (*geregeltes Nebeneinander*). A
pre-condition, however, was that the Federal Republic should give up its

claim to represent all Germans. As all previous letters of the kind had been returned unopened, the very reading of this one was an advance. But the problem of what to say in reply and even of how to address the writer (who could hardly be called Prime Minister if his state did not officially exist) meant that a month went by before an answer was despatched to the 'Dear Chairman' (of an unspecified body) suggesting that, at any rate to begin with, conversations would be best left to subordinates, and adding that if Herr Stoph insisted on prior recognition, Dr Kiesinger would be obliged in return to demand a secret plebiscite of all Germans about their future. Stoph returned to the charge in September but with an 'all-or-nothing' demand which showed that Bonn had to choose between changing its attitudes altogether and making no progress. Meanwhile Moscow and East Berlin dilated on the electoral successes of the National Democratic Party (p. 224), while the more that the CDU leaders tried to calm their hawks by saying that the new policies meant only a change of methods and not of aims, the easier it was for Communist publicists to argue that the capitalists were as dangerous as ever.

There remained Yugoslavia, which sent so many workers to the Federal Republic and entertained so many tourists from it as to make the absence of formal diplomatic contact between the two countries (p. 196) exceptionally nonsensical. But although there was wide agreement that enforcing the Hallstein Doctrine in this case had been a mistake, the reversal of that step would imply abandoning it as a principle, and this the right wing of the Coalition was reluctant to do. Late in 1967 however the Yugoslavs lost patience and induced Brandt to follow suit. In January 1968 he insisted on concluding an agreement with Belgrade which, in spite of a face-saving clause, effectively admitted that West Germany no longer objected to other states recognising two Germanies at once.

For the next nine months attention was dominated by events in Czechoslovakia, which themselves indicated the successes and limits of the new Ostpolitik. There could be no doubt about the desire of the Dubček regime to take up the West's offers of closer relations. But it was precisely for that reason that the Russians (egged on throughout by Ulbricht) set limits on the relaxation which they would permit. Early in the summer a couple of West German politicians went to Prague and there seems to have been talk of a West German loan. But Brandt left unheeded Czech hints that a visit from him would be welcome, while in July he persuaded Kiesinger to shift away from the Czech-Bavarian frontier manoeuvres which were planned to take place there in September, so as to give the Russians no ground for using a supposed threat from the West as an excuse for intervening in Czech affairs. When nevertheless they did intervene, the revulsion throughout the free world was such that efforts at relaxing tension became for a period futile.

During the same summer, much play was made by the communists about West Berlin being no more than a temporary Allied enclave on East German territory and not, as Bonn maintained, an integral part of the Federal Republic. Several limitations were imposed on the passage of West German (though not of Allied) nationals over the surface access routes to West Berlin, culminating in a refusal to allow members of the Federal Convention to go there for the Presidential Election in March 1969 (p. 228). But as the Allies regarded the choice of the city for that Election as possibly illegal and certainly tactless, and as it was always possible to get there unimpeded by air, no show-down resulted.

Soon afterwards Cambodia, Iraq and the Sudan recognised the DDR; the CDU/CSU pressed for diplomatic relations with them to be broken off and aid to be stopped but the SPD were not to be lured into exasperation. Brandt for his part paid more attention to overtures from Poland than Strauss thought appropriate. Both Parties were by this time angling for votes, with opinion polls suggesting that over half the population saw no point in continued intransigence, so that the SPD's attitude was more likely to win them than the CDU's. Everything moreover went to show that no real improvement with the East was possible until the Federal Republic accepted that the 1945 settlement was lasting, if not permanent. The Great Coalition could not do this for, had the CDU and CSU Ministers agreed, they would have split their Parties.

The Opposition Goes Outside Parliament

The overwhelming majority which the Great Coalition possessed in the Bundestag deprived opposition inside Parliament of much of its point but stimulated opposition outside Parliament on both extremes, a development which may have been inevitable in any circumstances. Fortunately neither radical left nor radical right produced a leader of any real ability. The NPD won 5.8 per cent of the vote in the Schleswig-Holstein Land elections in April 1967, 6.9 per cent in the Rhineland-Palatinate ones in the same month and an ominous 9.8 per cent in Baden-Württemberg a year later. The imminent prospect was that they would win more than 5 per cent in the Federal Election due in September 1969 and consequently enter the Bundestag. There was as a result much talk about the desirability of changing over to a British-type electoral system with single-member constituencies, since this was expected to prevent the NPD – and the FDP – from winning any seats at all. But the SPD were afraid that such a change would provide the CDU/CSU with a permanent majority and in 1968 decided to postpone a decision on the matter until 1970. Attention then switched to the desirability of banning the NPD as unconstitutional.

In the summer of 1967 the Government stirred up a hornet's nest of controversy by trying to solve the problem of an Emergency Law. In the 1952 settlement (p. 179) the Western Occupying Powers had reserved the right to reassume authority if any emergency threatened to undermine the security of West Germany before the Federal Government had passed legislation enabling it to deal with such a contingency. Although there had ever since been a natural desire to expunge this last vestige of a subordinate status, the Parties had been unable to agree on the kind of legislation which would be appropriate and the circumstances in which it could be applied. A nuclear war or Russian attack might obviously make it impracticable to observe all the due processes of law but memories of how such legislation had been applied in 1930-2 (p. 73) made many people reluctant to renew it. In the end the Government proposed that the Bundestag should elect an emergency committee of 22 members, to whom the Bundesrat would add one representative from each Land. This body would have the right to decide by a two-thirds majority that the Bundestag was incapable of acting, after which it could proclaim an emergency and bring into operation some forty previously prepared (and debated) decrees. The task of enabling a government to act effectively in a crisis without thereby enabling it to act arbitrarily is always delicate and was in this case complicated by the national predilection for precise definitions. The difficulty found in reaching a compromise illustrates the healthy suspicion by which many Germans have come to view their rulers.

The agitation and demonstrations against the Emergency Law were only one aspect of a disenchantment with the established affluence which was boiling up among the young. This was not of course confined to West Germany but special reasons fostered it there. The generation which was coming of age had been born in the chaotic years 1943-9 and had often been neglected in their 'teens by parents whose long hours of work had been so important in achieving the 'Miracle'. As has been said (p. 190), the Federal Republic was basically fortunate in starting its existence under a government of a decidedly right-wing complexion but Adenauer's over-long tenure of power had meant that many reforms needed to modernise society had gone unmade. Now, instead of a Socialist Government turning out the old order and embarking on a thorough programme of reform, the SPD appeared to have come to the rescue of their opponents, to be gratuitously prolonging the CDU/CSU hold on power and as a result to be themselves debarred from making changes. Many of the young, accepting the world's condemnation of the Third Reich, found the record of their parents during it and the toleration of ex-Nazis in high places hard to stomach. They were not prepared to take for granted the revulsion felt by their elders towards communism or to regard recognition of the *status quo* in Eastern Europe as unthinkable. The Western Alliance was seen as linking them with a country which in Vietnam was behaving much as the Nazis had done. The less lovely aspects of the Affluent Society were felt to cancel out its advantages.

The focus of discontent was to be found in the institutions of higher education. A higher proportion of each age group than ever before was seeking such education and tradition required that everyone who had a grammar-school leaving certificate (*Abitur*) was entitled to enter whatever university he or she chose. The expansion of the universities was, however, one of the things which had been neglected. To help the professors teach the extra numbers, many junior posts had been created. But decisions about appointments to such posts and about the research to be done in each faculty had been left in the hands of the professors. Junior staff were consequently dissatisfied about their lack of say in their conditions of work, while students complained about overcrowding, lack of guidance from and contact with their teachers and the irrelevance of many courses to contemporary life. Demonstrations and sit-ins were regular events. The chief degree conferred by universities remained the doctorate, though this was mitigated by the large variety of diplomas which were issued, often by official bodies. Reasonable changes had been too long resisted, with the result that the politicians intervened. Laws reforming the system began to be passed in one Land after another, led by those where the SPD was in power. New universities were founded with more liberal constitutions. The most radical novelty was a tripartite scheme by which the teaching staff (including juniors along with professors), the non-teaching staff and the students were given an equal say. This was not unnaturally unpopular with professors (who often migrated to universities where it was not in force) and damaged standards of thoroughness and objectivity.

When the Shah of Persia visited Berlin in June 1967, a demonstration against him was organised, in the course of which a student called Bruno Ohnesorg was shot. This was one of many occasions when charges of high-handed action were made, as it would seem with some justification, against the police. There was a further crisis in the city at Easter 1968 when a young man who could not abide communists (but fortunately had no other traceable political connection) tried to assassinate the student leader Rudi Dutschke. Prominent among the targets of the ensuing riots were the papers and premises owned by Herr Axel Springer who was resented not merely as an outspoken anti-communist but even more as the owner of 80 per cent of the daily papers with nation-wide circulation (three-quarters of which was provided by the tabloid illustrated *Bild*).

In the end the Emergency Law was got through the Bundestag after a number of safeguards had been added but without drastic modification. Kiesinger lived up to his reputation as an adroit conciliator; he was not unfairly described as a 'Super-Erhard'. There were those in his own Party who criticised him for not pressing their preferred policies more strongly, oblivious of the fact that, had he done so, he would have broken up the Coalition. To begin with, however, relief at not finding themselves ousted from office reconciled the CDU/CSU to the unpleasant necessity of making concessions to the SPD, while later their ability to keep those concessions limited had much the same effect. Whereas hitherto the CDU had almost exalted its lack of a formal programme into an actual programme, it now realised the need to establish a profile distinct from those of the other Parties and in 1967-8 formulated the Aktion (or Berlin) Programme which, on matters of social and economic policy, and even on relations with the East, showed a distinct liberalisation of outlook. The Party's aim was said to be the promotion of freedom, justice and peace. The pride of place which had once been assigned to Christianity now went to efficiency.

The Socialist rank-and-file at first found it highly uncongenial to be running in harness with their habitual opponents. At a Party Congress in March 1968 they refused to bless in retrospect the decision to enter the Great Coalition and only approved by 147 votes to 143 the way their leaders had conducted themselves inside it. Particular resentment was aroused by the tendency of the CDU/CSU to annex credit for an economic recovery which owed more to Schiller than to anyone else. Few appreciated how much their Party had gained by taking office (and thereby acquiring experience) for the first time in circumstances which inhibited the backwoodsmen of the right from accusing it of betraying national interests for fear of involving their own leaders in that charge. As time went on, however, confidence in Social Democratic ability to govern grew hand in hand with credit for Social Democratic achievements in governing. The SPD began to think that they would like to go on governing without having to bother about CDU/CSU susceptibilities.

As 1968 passed into 1969, the two major Parties came increasingly to resemble a cat and dog tied together by their tails. The closer that the election came, the greater was the repugnance on both sides against renewing the Coalition. The chances of avoiding such a fate would however be reduced if, as seemed well on the cards, the NPD surmounted the 5 per cent hurdle and as a result had 25 or more Deputies in the Bundestag. For their presence would reduce the strength of the other parties and make it less likely that any could obtain an outright majority. As the idea of a government dependent on NPD votes was by general consent ruled out, the only alternative to a Great Coalition would be one with the FDP. But the FDP was itself being gradually transformed. It had long been a marriage between liberal (and anti-clerical) idealism and middle-class (and often reactionary) property owners; as has been mentioned (p. 206), it had depended for part of its funds on contributions from industry. But the younger generations of well-to-do bourgeois were gravitating to the CDU as their natural home. The FDP's role in opposition made it want to find some way of looking different from both the governing Parties. To try to overtake the Great Coalition on the right would have lost it its left-wing members. Consequently the obvious tactic was to overtake on the left, with a programme of individualist radicalism. The move in that direction was personified towards the end of 1967 when Erich Mende was replaced as leader by Walter Scheel, since Scheel, though no revolutionary, was open to new ideas and quick to spot tactical opportunities. His main problem was whether he had enough authority over his rank-and-file to deliver their votes in whatever direction he might promise them.

This question seemed to receive a clear answer in March 1969. About a year earlier, stories began to be put about from East Germany that President Lübke had during the war been involved in building death camps. Though largely malicious lies, they had a small substratum of truth. Lübke mistakenly began by blanket denials only to be forced later into partial admissions. Calls were made for his resignation and in the end he agreed to go before his (second) constitutional term was up; this had the extra advantage of avoiding a close conjunction between a Bundestag election and a Presidential one. The CDU put up Schröder as their candidate, the SPD Gustav Heinemann (p. 180) who, as the Great Coalition's Minister of Justice, had carried through a number of liberal alterations to the penal laws; his general attitude can be gathered from his statements that 'Christ died for us — not against Marx' and 'I love my wife — not the state.' The FDP were persuaded to back him, whereas the 22 NPD votes in the Electoral College went to Schröder. On the third ballot, where a plain rather than a two-thirds majority was called for, Heinemann was elected. His comment that a clear shift of power had been brought about by democratic methods did nothing to reconcile the CDU/CSU to their defeat. But the SPD saw in the episode ground for reassessing the doubts about the FDP's reliability which had kept them from forming a coalition with the Party in 1966. They showed good-will and gratitude by dropping finally the idea of eliminating proportional representation (p. 225).

The Great Coalition performed a useful function which had much influence on the subsequent course of politics, but its final months were inglorious. *Geregeltes Nebeneinander* applied just as much, and had as many imperfections, at home as abroad. The Parties constituting it could agree on practically nothing except to extend for a further ten years the period during which Nazi crimes could be punished. The proposal to ban the NPD was dropped, while an international treaty renouncing the acquisition of nuclear weapons had to be left unsigned. As the elections came closer, pressure on the Mark increased while the refusal to revalue meant that imports cost more. Thanks to the moderation shown by the unions in 1967, the workers had fallen behind in the race for purchasing power and their resentment over the rising cost of living led to a sudden wave of spontaneous strikes. Everything suggested that Schiller had been right in urging revaluation as compared with Strauss who had opposed it. This impression became even stronger immediately before polling day when foreign demand for Marks became so strong that the exchanges had to be shut until the voting was over.

The Transfer of Power

In the Election held on 28 September 1969, the SPD won 224 seats, the CDU 193, the CSU 49 and the FDP 30. To the general relief, the NPD only obtained 4.5 per cent of the votes overall, so that they remained unrepresented in the Bundestag; the support which they received in the southern Länder failed to outweigh their weakness in the north and above all in North Rhine-Westphalia.

Although the FDP had only won its presence in the Bundestag by the narrow margin of 0.8 per cent, it was the Party in a position to decide the character of the new government. The indications which Scheel had already given as to what this decision would be, enabled Brandt to tell President Heinemann forthwith that he was prepared to accept office. The CDU/CSU (who are in the happy position of being able to represent themselves as one party or two according to the convenience of the moment) made a show of protesting that the President's first approach should be to them, as the strongest Party. But, in spite of the strenuous efforts which they made in all sorts of ways to lure over the FDP's right wing, their prospects of securing a majority were never firm enough to justify a formal claim to power. After more than three weeks of negotiation (a lapse of time more usual on the Continent than in Britain) Brandt obtained 251 out of 496 votes, with 3 FDP Deputies abstaining. Scheel became Foreign Minister and Genscher Minister of the Interior while the post of Minister of Agriculture went, with lasting results for the EEC's Common Agricultural Policy, to the right-wing leader of the Bavarian FDP, Josef Ertl; Schiller, who had done as much as anyone to win the victory, remained Minister of Economics. Helmut Schmidt became Minister of Defence while his previous post as leader of the SPD Parliamentary Party (*Fraktion*) was taken over by Herbert Wehner, whose strategy for obtaining power through a Great Coalition had been triumphantly vindicated (though only because the FDP had changed sides). The extent to which the German civil service takes part in politics was illustrated by the fact that 13 out of 26 permanent State Secretaries were changed, though only 11 out of 110 officials at the next level down (*Ministerialdirektor*).

The election thus marked the close of a chapter in German politics. The Federal Republic obtained — for the first and presumably the only time in its history — a President and a Chancellor simultaneously who had both been actively associated with the *Widerstand* to the Nazis (p. 82); Brandt is said to have remarked as the results came in that 'tonight, finally and for ever, Hitler lost the war'. Such a remark may sound unfair to the Adenauer and Erhard regimes, but both had been more prepared to be reconciled with ex-Nazis than with the full consequences of defeat. The vital question for the future had hitherto been whether a majority could be found for a left-of-centre regime or whether (as in Italy) the right was to be a permanent element in government. For the next three years Brandt's position was to be precarious but in fact he had on his side the factor which came to be known as 'Comrade Trend'. In each of the elections of 1965, 1969 and 1972 the SPD share of the vote grew by 3.1 per cent.

To counter the impression that external affairs would get prior attention, Brandt described himself as 'a Chancellor of inner reforms', but in practice he was able to achieve disappointingly few of them. Some were blocked by the FDP, the most notable being the extension of parity in workers' co-determination from coal.and steel (p. 188) to the whole of industry, though the Plant Constitution Law (*Betriebsverfassungsgesetz*) of 1972 considerably extended the range of matters over which management were required to consult Works Councils. Other reforms, particularly in the field of taxation, required the co-operation of Land Governments whose inherent suspicion of the centre was reinforced in half of them by CDU/CSU participation in their Ministries. A number of schemes to benefit the weak and poor had to be shelved for lack of cash. A final group of social reforms (eg. divorce and abortion) might be cheap but were disproportionately controversial and needed Bundesrat approval which was often not forthcoming.

Two days after the election, the Kiesinger Government, as still legally in charge, announced that the Mark would be left to float. After it had done so for 26 days the Brandt Government fixed its value again 8.5 per cent higher. This was a logical consequence of fidelity to a free market system by a country distinguished from its neighbours through an exceptionally low rate of inflation and an abnormal bias towards exports, particularly of capital goods. The home public's readiness to co-operate in keeping prices down increased the competitiveness of West German goods abroad and swelled the export surplus. Unless the Mark's value was continually adjusted upwards in compensation, foreign demand for Marks increased the money supply and thereby threatened to cancel out the achievements of domestic restraint. West Germany had become so dependent on exports that she could not afford to isolate

herself from the outside world, even if her rulers had not been dominated by a belief that this was a wrong thing to do. But as long as that
world was living beyond its means, the Federal Republic's attempts to
do otherwise meant a continual struggle against the stream.

Schiller had hoped to balance the revaluation by relaxing credit so as
to increase home demand at the same time as the rise in their prices was
discouraging sales of West German goods abroad. This strategy assumed
that goods made for export could be equally well disposed of domestic-
ally; in reality any extra home demand would more probably have been
in other directions (e.g. consumer goods and services), so that, for the
policy to succeed, a long-term shift in resources would have been needed.
Moreover the revaluation came too late (or alternatively was not big
enough) to shield the home economy from the inflation going on outside. Between the autumn of 1969 and the spring of 1971 prices rose at
an annual rate of 4.5 per cent. This imported inflation was reinforced
by a 'home-made' variety when the unions, feeling that their moderation
had been exploited, insisted for the first time on wage rises which outstripped gains in productivity. The Bundesbank and the public, to whom
any inflation rate over 3 per cent was high, demanded controls halting
expansion at home while the continued ability of exporters to make
profits abroad removed the incentive to shift their sales efforts. Yet if
in the struggle against inflation interest rates were pushed too high,
employment might suffer and unwelcome foreign money be drawn in.
The federal policy-makers had to pick a precarious path between risking
inflation and risking unemployment.

The Ostpolitik Scrapes Through

Even if there had been more room for manoeuvre at home, the lion's
share of attention during these years would have gone to the main un-
solved problem in the Federal Republic's affairs, namely relations with
the Communist world. Not that relations with the West were neglected.
Brandt repeatedly emphasised that conciliation with the East was only
possible for a Republic securely integrated with the West. At a Prime
Ministers' meeting at the Hague in December 1969 he played a leading
part in opening the way for Britain to join the Common Market. In his
initial declaration of policy, he expressed the wish to prevent a further
'growing apart' between the two German Republics so that 'regulated
neighbourliness' could operate. He made no mention of reunification or
sole representation or the Hallstein Doctrine, and described the DDR as

a state, though adding that, if there were two German states, their relationship must be of a special kind, as was the case between members of the British Commonwealth. Before 1969 ended Moscow had accepted his offer to negotiate an undertaking that neither the Federal Republic nor the Soviet Union would attack one another, while Warsaw had agreed to talks on Polish-West German relations. Both sets of negotiations started early in 1970. They proved detailed and laborious but not wholly unpromising.

The man in the brake-van, however, was Ulbricht who clearly found the whole business unpalatable. This last-surviving Stalinist had long been holding together the inhabitants of his Republic by presenting them with a picture of an unregenerate, revengeful and dangerous next-door neighbour — what the Germans call a 'Boo-man'. Brandt seemed set on depriving this presentation of its credibility. Shortly before Christmas, an East German draft for a Treaty was sent to Bonn. It began by insisting on the DDR being recognised as a foreign state in international law — the one thing which Brandt had declared to be impossible. It went on to demand that West Germany should repeal all laws contrary to the proposed Treaty — a stipulation which could be read as requiring the Federal Republic to leave NATO and the EEC. The terms were such as to be politically impossible for Brandt to accept and seemed deliberately intended to provoke a refusal. Realising that such a reaction would be exploited to put the blame on him, Brandt carefully refrained from making it but instead reiterated his desire to negotiate.

At this point the advantage of dealing with the Soviet Union, Poland and East Germany simultaneously was demonstrated. The talks in Moscow and Warsaw went forward too well for Ulbricht to be able to rely on them breaking down, but if they were going to succeed, he could not afford to be the only man left out. Accordingly Brandt was invited to visit East Germany and on 19 March met Stoph, the DDR Prime Minister, at Erfurt. The most remarkable feature of the visit was a silent but unmistakable demonstration of welcome by the population. Whereas the Eastern Willi repeated the demand for full recognition, the Western Willy emphasised the need to mitigate the human hardships caused by partition. But the only thing on which they could agree was to meet again at Kassel on 21 May and, when they did, to the accompaniment of noisy demonstrations from both neo-Nazis and Communists, they found the going even tougher than ever. Both sides decided that a pause for thought was advisable.

In the Kremlin, however, desire for better relations with the West, presumably fed by worry over China, was gaining the upper hand. The

Politburo realised that no subsequent Bonn government was likely to be more conciliatory than the existing one while a rebuff to it would increase the chances of a successor being more hostile. The idea was floated of the general Security Conference which in due course was to meet in Helsinki. But the Western Governments stood firmly together in saying that a German settlement must come first. With great dexterity a formula was evolved to which both Bonn and Moscow could agree without eating too many of their previous words and in August 1970 a Treaty of Non-Aggression was signed.

Both sides promised to 'promote the normalisation of the situation in Europe, taking as their starting point the actual situation existing in the area'. They agreed 'to acknowledge that peace can only be maintained if nobody infringes the present borders' and to 'respect without reservation the territorial integrity of all states in Europe' in their borders of today. In addition to declaring that they had no territorial claims against anyone and would not raise any in future, they described the borders of all states in Europe, including the Oder-Neisse line and the BRD-DDR frontier, as 'inviolable'. In addition, however, the Russians agreed to accept a letter saying that, in the West German Government's opinion, the Treaty did not conflict with the political goal of a state of peace in Europe in which the German people regained its unity in free self-determination. In other words, the Treaty did not close the door to reunification by agreement (however distant such a prospect might be) but only to the possibility of one side imposing it on the other (something which the experience of the previous twenty years had shown to be impracticable). The Federal Republic was also authorised to tell the United States, Britain and France that in the opinion of both signatories the Treaty did not affect the rights and responsibilities in Germany (and particularly in Berlin) of the four Occupying Powers. Finally the Russians were given unmistakably to understand that the Treaty's ratification would depend on a Four-Power Agreement being reached about Berlin. An unmentioned attraction of the Treaty for the Russians was undoubtedly the prospect of easier access to German credits, industrial skills and equipment; the preparatory negotiations had been given a 'sweetener' in the shape of a contract for oil pipes on favourable terms.

Next came Poland. Here agreement was complicated by the West German insistence that Polish citizens of German extraction must be allowed to leave for the West if they wished to go. The Poles did not reject the demand but held back from making any promises until the actual Treaty had been concluded. The vital clause in this contained Bonn's admission that the Oder-Neisse line constituted Poland's western frontier and was 'inviolable'. The text, however, was so drafted as to avoid use of the word 'recognition'. The Anglo-Americans were left free to maintain their Potsdam provision that a final settlement of the frontier must await a peace conference, but the sting of this had been drawn by clear indications from them that they did not intend at such a conference to press for any revision. The Poles then issued a statement that 'people of indisputably German nationality' who wished to emigrate to either German Republic could do so if they respected Polish rules and regulations. In December 1970 Brandt went to Warsaw for the signing of the Treaty and, during a visit to the site of the Jewish ghetto (p. 106), dropped on his knees in front of a memorial to the victims. This courageous gesture received more widespread acclaim outside the Federal Republic than inside.

As regards Berlin, the Bonn Government insisted that prime responsibility rested not with itself but with the Four Powers. Their ambassadors had indeed met to discuss the problem on various occasions since March 1970 but without making much progress. Even when the signature of the Moscow and Warsaw Treaties put a premium on agreement, it failed to emerge. The whereabouts of the impediment became clear when at the end of April 1971 Ulbricht, then aged 77, was 'promoted' from being First Secretary of the Party to a post which looked purely honorific, and still clearer when in June a speech which he was to have made at the Party Congress was read in his absence. It was not only in West Germany that there had to be a change of leadership before an agreement could be reached. Ulbricht's successor Erich Honecker was to prove almost as obdurate but at the outset was too insecure to frustrate Moscow's wishes.

Two months later the ambassadors announced what was in effect a compromise. The three Western ones had stood out for what became known as the three Zs: *Zugang*, i.e. unimpeded movement between West Berlin and West Germany for West Berliners and West Germans as well as for Americans, British and French; *Zutritt*, i.e. the extension to West Berliners of the facilities allowing West Germans to visit East Germany; and *Zuordnung*, i.e. recognition by the East of the fact that West Berlin was tied to West Germany (as against the East German thesis that it was merely a special enclave in the territory of the DDR). All three demands were recognised in the agreement. The three Western Governments declared, however, that 'the ties between the western Sectors of Berlin and the Federal Republic of Germany would be maintained and developed, taking into account that these Sectors continue not to be a constituent part of the Federal Republic and are not to be governed by it'. The last 24 words corresponded with the position which the Allies had steadily maintained over West Berlin but contradicted the West German position as stated in the Preamble to and Article 23 of the Basic Law and the West Berlin Constitution. The Federal Assembly to elect the President was not henceforward to meet in West Berlin, while the Bundestag and Bundesrat and their committees could only do so to discuss matters directly affecting West Berlin. On the other hand representatives of West Berlin might continue to sit (but not vote) in both bodies and West German laws could still apply in the city, provided they had been adopted (at least tacitly) by the Senate of West Berlin. The Federal Republic was authorised to act for West Berlin in dealings with foreign countries. Federal institutions such as the Cartel Office already established in the city might stay there (at considerable inconvenience). Finally the Russians were allowed to open a consulate in West Berlin to deal with the commanders of the Western forces, which implied that they no longer had any responsibility themselves for governing the area, whereas their retention of such a responsibility in East Berlin was their justification in international law for being in the city at all. The Four-Power agreement was supplemented four months later by three separate inter-German ones. Between them the documents amounted to little more than a confirmation of the *status quo* but gave to that status a precision which it had hitherto lacked (but which was to prove, perhaps inevitably, rather short of absolute).

To work out such a package deal was a considerable achievement. Though Brandt had left the detailed work to others, notably Egon Bahr, it was his determination to reach a settlement which led to compromise formulas being found. But the package could still be frustrated if the Bundestag were to refuse ratification. The CDU/CSU were of course hostile. They complained that the vital cards which West Germany held for bargaining, consisting essentially of refusal to recognise the 1945 settlement, had been played without anything being obtained in return other than imprecise assurances of good intent. The SPD answer was that after 25 years the settlement was so well established as to deprive the refusal to recognise it of almost all political value, while the only way to improve relations and get concessions was to behave reasonably and hope thereby to encourage reasonable reactions. A great deal thus hung upon the FDP. Although their leader Scheel had played a large part in negotiating the agreements, the Party had showed up badly in Land elections early in 1970, which its right wing attributed to its association with Socialist policies. In October Mende and two other Deputies went over openly to the CDU (which promised to put them on its list at the next Election). With the Government's majority thus reduced to six, the doubts expressed by three more FDP Deputies became a crucial matter. A further complication was that in the Bundesrat the CDU/CSU had a majority of 21 to 20 (largely because the number of votes possessed by a Land did not correspond exactly to its population (p. 164) and had all to be cast in the same direction). To overcome an adverse vote in the Bundesrat, the Government required an absolute majority of all members of the Bundestag (and not simply a majority of those voting).

Parliamentary discussion of the agreements began late in 1971 and the crucial vote was due in the following April. Kiesinger's skill in achieving compromises had become less of an asset when the CDU shifted into opposition and he had been succeeded as leader by Rainer Barzel, a nimble tactician and articulate critic rather than a forceful commander. In April Barzel seems to have thought that the FDP Deputies could be prevailed on to defect and therefore tabled for the first time in the history of the Republic a 'constructive vote of no confidence' (p. 165). While demonstrations in favour of the agreements filled the streets, most of the SPD Deputies, in obedience to orders, abstained from voting. On 27 April the motion obtained 247 votes against 10, two short of the absolute majority which it needed. Three Deputies abstained and two FDP ones voted for the motion, so that at least one CDU or CSU Deputy must have voted against it. Just over a year later, a newspaper named as the culprit a none-too-reputable CSU Deputy. Further 'investigative journalism' strongly suggested that he had received some £25,000 as an inducement from an SPD Whip, Karl Wienand. The latter denied the story and was shielded by Wehner, so that a Bundestag inquiry failed to reach any conclusion. But in another more or less contemporary scandal Wienand was shown not to be a witness of truth and a few years later had to quit the Bundestag under a cloud. The episode left an unpleasant taste but there were equally strong stories, to which Willy Brandt gave support in the autumn of 1972, that bribery had been used by the Opposition to induce some of the FDP desertions.

Barzel's fiasco did not improve the Opposition's prospect of defeating the Treaties. Moreover he and some of the more realistic CDU members were belatedly beginning to examine their strategy. The Russians were making clear that no regime responsible for frustrating the settlement could expect any co-operation from them thereafter. West Germany's NATO allies left no doubt of their desire for ratification. Opinion polls suggested that a majority of West German voters were ready to accept it. The alternative to ratification would not be a return to the 1970 position but to something more strained in which the chances of getting alleviations for the inhabitants of the DDR would be minimal. Barzel accordingly negotiated with Brandt and Scheel a declaration 'interpreting' the Treaties in a way which left a door open for the German nation as a whole to be free at some date in the future to determine freely its form of government and for the existing frontiers to be capable of adjustment at a Peace Conference. The Russians raised no objection to the declaration, though pointing out that what counted in international law was the text of Treaties and not that of unilateral statements!

Barzel had originally intended that his followers should, on the strength of the declaration, vote for the Treaties. But some of them, and still more of the CSU, objected so strongly that he had to be content with their abstention and on 17 May the Treaty with the USSR was accepted on this basis by 248 votes to 10 and that with Poland by 248 votes to 17. The Bundesrat decided to abandon opposition and the Brandt Ostpolitik could thus take effect. Barzel had hardly cut an impressive figure but the real blame for defeat must rest with the backwoodsmen of his Party and still more with Strauss and the CSU. They had refused to face up to the consequences of a lost war and had shut their minds to the way politics were developing outside the Federal Republic. Too much emotion had been attached to the so-called 'Right to the Homeland' and to the idea that members of an individual nation have an exclusive right to settle its frontiers, with the result that the practicability of exercising such rights was disregarded. But some blame attaches to the Americans and British who, in their anxiety to secure West German support in the Cold War, had encouraged such intransigence and given a false impression of the extent to which they would support it.

Though the Treaties had been passed, the Bundestag remained in deadlock. A vote on one part of the Budget resulted in a tie, suggesting that the Government could no longer get its proposals passed into law. The natural way out was a dissolution followed by an election. But Article 68 of the Grundgesetz provided that a Chancellor could only ask for a dissolution if defeated on a vote of confidence and then only provided that the Bundestag did not with a majority of its members vote confidence in an alternative Chancellor. But if the Opposition were strong enough to defeat a motion of confidence, what would there be to stop them from using their strength to vote Barzel into power? The position was further complicated by the establishment a few years previously — after a Deputy's widow was found to be practically penniless — of a generous pension scheme which rose sharply with each year of service. This made the members of the Bundestag, irrespective of party, reluctant to bring about an election before the maximum term of four years had run out. Barzel at first refused to make any promises as to what he would do if Brandt, in order to secure a dissolution, engineered his own Party's defeat. But the Opposition would then have come into office, if at all, with as tenuous a majority as was already making the task of government difficult and the disadvantages of taking power in such circumstances were so clear as to induce Brandt to take the risk. By the time the Bundestag went on its summer holidays, an election in the autumn was taken for granted.

Before it occurred, however, a distraction was created by Karl Schiller. The Economics Minister had as time went by become increasingly high-handed and made himself unloved by many, including most of his colleagues and the French Government. In the summer of 1971 the Finance Minister, frustrated by his inability to secure desirable but drastic reforms in the taxation system, was provoked by a dispute with Schiller into resigning. Brandt, to ensure a unified economic policy, invited Schiller to take over the Finance Ministry while keeping his own, thus making him to all appearances the second most powerful man in the Cabinet. In 1972 a fresh wave of prosperity renewed the need to choose between risking more inflation and risking more unemployment. Schiller staked his position on the former and the general view was that the Government would not be able to afford his resignation. But the Governor of the Bundesbank, whom Schiller himself had appointed, persuaded the other Ministers to restrict instead the freedom of foreigners to increase inflation by buying German securities. Brandt put up no fight for his 'Super-Minister' and Schiller resigned, being replaced in his double function by Helmut Schmidt, whose record at the Ministry of Defence had greatly enhanced his reputation. The expected crisis of economic confidence did not occur.

In the meantime negotiations had been proceeding in Berlin between the two German Republics and on 8 November a Basic Treaty between them was initialled. It was described as taking for its point of departure 'historical facts' without prejudice to the differing views of the signatories on fundamental questions including the national one. The two Governments declared that they would develop good relationships with one another on the basis of equal rights, that they would solve their disagreements only by peaceful means, that present frontiers were 'inviolable both now and in the future' and that neither would interfere in the affairs of the other. They affirmed their intention to abide by the principles of the UN Charter, in particular the sovereign equality of all states, respect for independence, autonomy and territorial integrity, the right of self-determination, the protection of human rights and non-discrimination. They would proceed on the assumption that neither of the two states could represent the other internationally or act in its name. They undertook to conclude further detailed agreements on such matters as science, traffic, postal communications, health, sports and environmental protection. The exchange of 'permanent representatives' (rather than ambassadors) was also provided for in one of 17 appendices. Both sides agreed to apply for membership of the United Nations (hitherto blocked by the vetoes of one or other of the Great Powers).

The basis on which settlements had been reached with Russia and Poland was thus extended to inter-German relations. The Federal Republic, except that it did not explicitly 'recognise' the other state, abandoned almost completely the positions which it had been maintaining since its creation. The Democratic Republic on the other hand gave up its insistence on being explicitly recognised as a foreign state in international law (though continuing to maintain that it was one). West German voters were thus enabled to go to the polls with their eyes open to the full range of concessions which they were being asked to approve.

For at the end of September Brandt tabled a motion of confidence and, when the time came to vote on it, refrained in common with the other Ministers from supporting his own Government. The Opposition mustered their full strength with the result that the motion was rejected by 248 votes to 233. This extraordinary manoeuvre, rendered necessary by the fact that the Basic Law had been designed for a Republic with many rather than with few parties, opened the way for the President to dissolve the Bundestag. In a 91 per cent poll on 19 November 1972, the CDU, even taken in combination with the CSU, found itself replaced as strongest party by the SPD, winning only 225 seats as against 229. The FDP rose from 30 seats to 42; the NPD only obtained 0.6 per cent of the poll. Brandt may have been described by his critics as the 'Chancellor of renunciation' but his policy of facing unpalatable realities had been endorsed by the West German people. The man who had been overshadowed by Adenauer in 1961 and by Erhard in 1965 had so improved his stature by his performance in office that he put Barzel into the background.

No Longer the Man for the Season

As so often, however, triumph soon turned sour and the next eighteen months were a time of anti-climax in which little went right for Brandt.

His Party's unity was threatened, reform at home remained elusive and the results of the Ostpolitik fell short of expectations.

After the unrest of 1968, the more moderate of the young intellectuals decided that they were unlikely to succeed in transforming society by revolution and must therefore set out on 'the long march through the institutions' so as to win a position where they could effect reforms peacefully. The old-established members of the Party were lethargic by comparison and baffled by the sociological jargon in which they now found political arguments being clothed. The young socialists (*Jusos*) thus gained a prominence disproportionate to their numbers and dominated the organisation to which every SPD member under 35 automatically belonged. Their support for the Ostpolitik had been welcome; their increasing concentration on internal problems proved less so. They were not content with modifying the existing order of society but wanted to sweep it – and private enterprise – away. Yet, although they admitted to being Socialists rather than Social Democrats, bureaucracy and centralisation figured high among their bugbears. Their ideal was a society which in all its manifestations, political, economic, and social, was controlled by the rank-and-file. Whether, if choice were inevitable, liberty or equality should come first was not a question to which they much addressed themselves.

The SPD, however, would never have achieved their victories of 1969 and 1972 if they had not jettisoned their tradition as a Marxist party devoted to the interests of the working classes and, by becoming instead a popular party (*Volkspartei*) of pragmatic reform, won over a substantial proportion of the 'middle ground' (which was of course coming to include more and more affluent workers – the 'new bourgeoisie'). The Jusos, along with various groups among the over-35s, were challenging this transformation and thereby creating an obvious danger of alienating the essential middle vote. There was the further danger of estranging the FDP, who believed with much justification that the extra votes won by them in 1972 had come from people who wanted a government which was neither reactionary nor radical and looked to them to hold the SPD left wing in check. As one of them put it, 'the economic system may not be a sacred cow but neither is it a lamb waiting for slaughter'. In the past German parties, and particularly those in the middle, had resolved their internal quarrels by splitting in two. The damage which this had done to good government, however, had brought the 5 per cent rule into existence to discourage it. But if parties are not to split, then they must act as umbrellas sheltering a variety of views within their ranks. But this is a situation unpalatable to enthusiasts who are reluctant to make the compromises needed to sustain it.

To the Jusos the SPD was the dominant partner in the Coalition and as such entitled to decide its policies. They discounted the danger of the FDP changing partners again on the ground that another turnabout would do the Party such discredit as to bring it below the 5 per cent line. They argued further that for a progressive party to stop introducing changes meant stagnation, which would soon lead to votes being lost to parties more on the left. Brandt saw the force of this argument. He had done his best to reduce the gulf of distrust between the generations which had appeared so alarmingly during the Great Coalition and he did not wish such success as he had achieved to be dissipated. He described the Jusos as 'the salt in our soup' and, though adding 'we must see that they don't make it too salty', exerted himself, as did Wehner, to keep the enthusiasm of the left wing harnessed to the Party's cause. As a result he was accused by the right wing, and still more by the Opposition, of weakness in the face of crypto-communism.

The atmosphere in the CDU/CSU camp was hardly more harmonious. There too a familiar struggle was in progress between those who argued that the Election had been lost by too much moderation and those who argued that the mistake had lain in not being moderate enough. Strauss had reacted to the defeat by calling for 'the helmet to be bound on more firmly'. He believed that the way to attract votes was to be more aggressive, pointing out that in Bavaria and Hesse where this had been done, the Party had fared best. He denied that the Government had settled the German problem — and events soon began to suggest that he was right. He argued that a lasting solution could only be found within a European context, by bringing about a Federation embracing the whole of Europe — an echo of de Gaulle's 'from the Atlantic to the Urals' which seemed to imply that the Curtain could be rolled back. How far he was in earnest is hard to say. He has been described as one of those tragic figures who cannot find the place in history to which their abilities entitle them. He has seemed unable to reconcile himself to the fact that the causes in which he has invested his emotions are not those which a majority of his fellow-countrymen are prepared to back. With such a handicap, his energy and eloquence make him a disturbing influence in any organisation to which he belongs. The position was complicated by the unusual relationship between the CDU and CSU. Although the latter claimed to be a separate party with views of its own, its activities were confined to Bavaria, so that it could not hope to obtain more than about a third of the number of seats obtained by the CDU; in consequence the common assumption for long was that it could not provide the right-wing candidate for the Chancellorship. (Both Bavarians in general and Strauss in particular were in addition viewed with suspicion in other parts of Germany, somewhat as Welshmen are in Britain.) Although Strauss accepted this bar, it did not prevent him from constantly belittling the man who was chosen instead and from trying to dictate to the CDU on matters of policy.

In May 1972 Strauss had embarrassed Barzel by rejecting the compromise over the Treaties which he had helped to work out and insisting that the joint Parties abstain in the vote. When in the spring of 1973 the Basic Treaty came before the Bundestag, Barzel found his advice as to its treatment rejected by his own Party who preferred to follow Strauss up what proved to be a blind alley. Coming on top of the lost election, the rebuff discouraged him; he resigned and was succeeded as head of the Parliamentary Party by Karl Carstens, a former official State Secretary in the Foreign Office who had only been elected to the Bundestag in the previous November. The post of Party Chairman went to Helmut Kohl, a man of 43 who had made a considerable name for himself as Minister-President of Rhineland-Palatinate. Kohl was one of the most progressive spirits in the CDU and a good administrator but he lacked personality and spoke badly; Strauss was thus provided with both an incentive and a basis for making mischief.

A fresh bout of inflation developed in 1973 but unlike earlier ones this was largely home produced. For in the spring the Mark had been set free to float, in common with other Common Market currencies and following the breaking of the link between the dollar and gold in 1972. The Bundesbank reacted by pushing up interest rates and thereby checking the incentive to invest at home. But this effect was counterbalanced by a flow of funds into the country and by union demands for wage increases exceeding the natural rate of growth. The Union of Public Servants secured by the threat of a strike a rise which for the first time in West German history went into double figures. There was much talk about Germany catching the English disease and the widespread belief that the Government had given way too easily strengthened the impression that Brandt was too kind.

The principal internal reforms which the Government succeeded in carrying through in its first year of existence were those establishing the breakdown of a marriage as the sole ground for divorce and exempting pornography from prosecution unless it caused social offence. Although both changes scandalised the old-fashioned, they had been virtually agreed by all the Parties before the Election. In January 1974 the FDP finally gave way to SPD insistence that workers' co-determination

(*Mitbestimmung*) must be extended to all firms employing more than 2000 persons (pp. 188, 231). After 1976 Supervising Councils in such firms were to consist of shareholders and workers' representatives in equal numbers, but the SPD and trade unions agreed reluctantly to a requirement that one of the seats on the workers' side should go to a representative of the senior executives. Controversy continued, however, as to how the workers' representatives should be chosen and how deadlocks between the two sides were to be resolved. The employers (led by their chairman Hans-Martin Schleyer) challenged the legality of the law. In due course the Constitutional Court pronounced against them but in the meantime the unions, out of resentment against the refusal to accept a parliamentary decision, withdrew from the *Konzentierte Aktion* (p. 219). The FDP also accepted a scheme by which firms were to pay part of their profits into a central fund which would then pay out to some 24 million workers 200 Marks annually in the shape of certificates to serve as capital. Agreement could not be reached, however, on a proposal to tax increases in land values and subject property owners to closer social control.

To the left-wing SPD and Jusos, these reforms were temporary palliatives rather than final solutions. To give workers a say and share in their firms was not considered enough. What it was held that they should have was sole control and exclusive ownership. Indeed the limited reforms were regarded as questionable in case they damped down the demand for further-reaching ones. To get a majority for such sweeping changes was of course out of the question but the awareness of this only made the radicals more impatient with the FDP — and indeed with the Government as a whole. A further cause of strife was the 'Radical Decision' (*Radikalen Beschluss*). The complex story of this matter merits explanation, not least because of the light which it throws on the Federal Republic generally.

Article 21 of the Grundgesetz branded as unconstitutional any party which by its aims or actions set out to influence or set aside the free democratic order. In a consequential spirit, the law regulating the public service (in Länder and communes as well as at Federal level) confined appointments to persons who showed that they could be 'relied on to support at all times the free democratic system established by the Basic Law'. This concept was inherited from a law passed in the Weimar Republic after the murders of Erzberger and Rathenau (p. 65). The requirement came into prominence during the spring of 1972 when, as part of the dispute over the Eastern Treaties, the Opposition were making much of the left-wing sympathies of the SPD and the danger of communists in the public service. (The Communist Party, having been prohibited under the Basic Law in 1952 (p. 192) had been allowed to re-establish itself in a slightly different form in 1968.) The Constitutional Court had laid down that nobody should be disqualified simply for belonging to a party which had not itself been proscribed; activity rather than membership had to be the criterion. At a meeting between Brandt and the Ministers-President of the Land Governments, it was decided that, in order to establish uniformity of practice throughout the country, every applicant for appointment as an established official (*Beamte*) must be examined as an individual case, that membership of an organisation hostile to the Constitution raised doubts as to the loyalty of the individual concerned and that such doubts should as a rule justify rejection. By making 'hostility to the Constitution' rather than 'incompatibility with the Constitution' into the test, this decision outflanked the more liberal ruling of the Court. It also raised the awkward question of who were to decide, and on what grounds, which organisations were to be classed as 'hostile'. Those Land Governments in which the CDU or CSU were participating tended to be more strict than those where the SPD predominated. But all were able to answer the charge of allowing communists to infiltrate the government machine without having to take the step, judged politically inopportune, of once again proscribing the Communist Party and driving it underground.

To appreciate the repercussions of this decision, however, one has to remember that in Germany not only are the senior staff of government departments graded as Beamte but also teachers, judges, engine-drivers, dustmen and grave-diggers. Many legal and medical posts require a period of training with the government. To exclude persons on the ground of political opinion was often therefore equivalent to forbidding them to follow the profession of their choice, although Article 12 of the Grundgesetz ostensibly guarantees freedom to choose. Between January 1973 and June 1975 over 455,000 applications were examined; in 5,700, grounds for doubt were established and 235 refusals occurred. Already in 1973 one or two prominent cases attracted a great deal of attention and Brandt was beginning to reconsider the wisdom of the course to which he had committed himself, but any relaxation of it was bound to be criticised by right-wing Social Democrats and Free Democrats, not to mention the Opposition. The solution might seem to lie in reducing drastically the number of posts for which evidence of loyalty is required. But not only may the West Germans be wise in doubting the desirability of allowing communists to be teachers or to operate official computers. For officials to turn into politicians (and back again) has always been made easy in Germany (pp. 30, 164) and many as a result do so. Any reform which in any way reduced the status of a Beamte would be unlikely to find favour in a Bundestag where 34 per cent of the Deputies possess that status!

In May 1973 the Consitutional Court gave a fresh turn to the controversy about university government. A case was brought before it on behalf of 400 Professors in Lower Saxony arguing that the establishment of threefold parity on university senates (p. 226) was incompatible with the freedom of learning guaranteed by Article 5 of the Grundgesetz. The Court's judgment was long and, as often, couched in theoretical terms from which practical conclusions had to be deduced. It began by saying that the participation of all teaching staff (and not exclusively professors) in matters of self-government did not infringe the freedom of learning. It laid down that the state, in deciding how universities were to govern themselves, must respect the special position of 'those who are qualified and appointed to represent their field of knowledge in research and teaching'. It left open the question of whether students and non-teaching staff had a right to a voice, though conceding that such a voice was not ruled out by the Grundgesetz, but it ended by requiring that the teaching staff should have 'an authoritative voice'. This was interpreted to mean that, provided the professors were agreed among themselves (which, owing to radical influence on appointments during the immediately preceding years, they often were not) they could not be outvoted. In matters of research and appointments (two particularly tender spots), their voice was to be decisive. Junior teaching staff were thus assured of a say in university affairs but threefold parity was declared unconstitutional. The judgment chimed in with a widespread feeling that the democratisation of universities had been carried to lengths at which the quality of their work was being damaged; it went a long way to restore authority and order. But it was naturally unpopular with those who equated authority with tyranny and order with refusal to change. To set it aside however would involve amending the Basic Law, for which the necessary two-thirds majorities in both houses of Parliament were most unlikely to be forthcoming.

In May 1973 Brezhnev paid the first visit that a Russian head of government had made to a non-Communist German state for sixty years. It was said, with an excess of optimism, to mark the end of both the Second World War and the Cold War. In talking to industrial leaders, the First Secretary held out rosy prospects of long-term Russo-German co-operation in exploiting Soviet raw material resources. He pictured the two countries as advancing from coexistence to interdependence, a process which would necessarily bring with it both external and internal relaxation. The underlying motive was not hard to guess. The Soviet Union needed the technical help of the West if it was to retain its military position as a Great Power and at the same time meet the desires of its peoples for better living. Nor was West German industry blind to the possibility of what had always been for it a useful market, and one which would gain in importance if a recession set in elsewhere. But at the moment Russian desires were something of an embarrassment to a country whose industry was at full stretch and whose economic problems were bound up with an excessive propensity to export. East-West trade showed a clear surplus in favour of the Federal Republic to which the Soviet Union and the Eastern bloc generally were heavily in debt. On the other hand the best prospect of getting paid lay in developing the Eastern output of raw materials and energy, which could only be achieved by further credits. The outlook was neither hopeless nor straightforward but the moment of sobriety reduced the Kremlin's willingness to twist the arms of the satellites when difficulties arose in their relations with West Germany.

With Poland these difficulties, though including similar stickiness over credits, concentrated on the question of refugees. Following the promises which the Polish Government had made at the time of, though not as an integral part of, the 1970 Treaty (p. 234), 25,000 people of German origin had been allowed to leave the country in 1971 but in 1972 the number dropped to 13,500 and showed signs of drying up completely. Though the Bonn estimate of 250,000 anxious to leave must have included a number of people with mixed nationality (as to whom no specific promise had been given), it was hard to believe that there were no more qualified and willing to come. The Poles were not only nervous of the effect on their economy if too many skilled workers left too quickly but were loath to admit that their efforts to turn Germans and half-Germans into Poles had had little success. They raised as a distraction the question of compensation for those of their citizens who had suffered in concentration camps. The West German answer was to point to the vast areas of German territory which had passed into Polish hands and to the financial burden caused by having to support their compatriots who had fled virtually destitute from that territory. The Poles were told that they could not sell the same horse twice but this did not stop them from continuing to try and for a time negotiations languished.

With the DDR still more, a happy life ever after was proving something of a fairy tale. Certainly the number of people crossing the frontier in both directions increased, though East Germans were only allowed to do so if they were over working age, while the East's action in doubling without consultation its charge for entry permits was regarded as a piece of sharp practice. In spite of the promise to allow traffic to pass freely on the roads to West Berlin, periodical police checks were staged and difficulties made over the staff of Federal offices and over parties of schoolchildren being taken to demonstrate against the Wall. Remonstrations received the reply that searches had to be made for criminals and undoubtedly a certain number of people were exploiting the access roads in order to escape. The Bonn decision to locate the new Federal Office on Environmental Questions in West Berlin evoked a protest on the ground that, although the Four-Power Treaty had recognised existing ties with the West, it had said nothing about the creation of new ones. The decision was certainly ill-considered – it is said to have slipped through the Cabinet without its full implications being realised (the sort of thing which was rather too liable to happen under Brandt's easy-going management). Negotiations about it were complicated by the fact that the German translation of the Treaty (of which the authentic texts were in English and Russian) was not identical in the two Republics and the Eastern addition of three letters at one point (*Verbindungen* rather than *Bindungen*) reduced appreciably the scope of the clause. There were further arguments as to whether the 'permanent representatives' which the two Governments were to exchange should deal with the Foreign Office as though they were ambassadors or with the Chancelleries on the ground that they represented not foreign countries but two parts of the same nation. The squabble was settled by letting each side have its own way in its own area, but it illustrated how tenaciously each stuck to its own point of view and how little the conclusion of the Treaty had fostered the good-will and reasonableness for which Brandt had hoped. The Democratic Republic did not want relaxation but only the advantages flowing from it in such matters as international recognition.

During a visit to Moscow in October 1973 however Wehner said that he considered the Federal Republic to have overdrawn its credit under the Treaties. However, the basic difficulty was that the two German regimes had contradictory aims which the agreements had not reconciled. For the West, reunification remained the ideal which it had merely agreed not to seek by force; had Brandt refused to leave open the possibility of it being achieved by agreement at some date in the indefinite future, he would never have got the Treaties ratified. The political form which a reunited nation would take was left vague, but the conversion of the Federal Republic into a communist state hardly seemed likely.

But without such a conversion, reunification must mean for the East Germans the partial if not complete dismantling of their system, which was to them unthinkable. The West hoped that relaxation would gradually lead to the disappearance of communism, the East to its consolidation. The two sides were, as the Chinese say, 'dreaming discrepant dreams in the same bed'. Honecker's Government set out on a campaign of 'distinction-drawing' (*Abgrenzung*), doing all in its power to make its country look different from the one next door. One of these steps was to cut down the use of the word 'German', another, paradoxically, was to re-emphasise links with the Prussian tradition in such matters as army insignia. Indeed the DDR had much in common with the state of Frederick the Great.

Although the two Governments had promised that they would not interfere in one another's affairs, neither did much to reduce the efforts it had long been making to infiltrate the other's ranks, in order to discover secrets and influence policy. The situation made the checking of espionage unusually difficult. Not only did the identity of language make it easier for spies to operate undetected but absconders were positively welcomed and the Federal Republic would have been distinctly less well served if it had employed no refugees from the East. In spite of elaborate precautions and extensive organisations for counter-intelligence, a long series of agents had been uncovered in high places. The most spectacular of these came at the end of April 1974 when it was announced that Günther Guillaume, one of Brandt's personal staff whom he had taken with him on a holiday in Norway the previous summer, had admitted to being a communist spy. Guillaume had come from East Germany in the early 1950s, ostensibly as a faithful Socialist whose prospects had been ruined by the communists. He built up a position for himself in the SPD Party machine whence in due course he got a transfer to the Chancellor's office. If several slips had not been made during his security screening, the fact that he had been suspected of espionage in 1955 should have come to light. (It is not altogether impossible that rabid anti-communists in the security service deliberately overlooked this so as to discredit Brandt whose policies were anathema to them.) Responsibility for the omissions rested with the FDP Minister of the Interior, Genscher, (who had himself come from East Germany in 1952 as a faithful Liberal whose prospects had been ruined by communists) or with Ehmke, the Minister at the head of Brandt's office. But on 7 May Brandt announced that he was taking the blame personally and had resigned as Chancellor. His successor was to be Helmut Schmidt.

Brandt's step did him credit but was not strictly necessary. He could well have left the consequences to be shouldered by others such as Genscher, though the position was complicated by Scheel having just announced his intention of standing for the Presidency when Heinemann retired later in the year; Genscher was booked to succeed him both as Foreign Minister and leader of the FDP. Rumours were rife that Guillaume had discovered some discreditable secret in Brandt's personal life, which he threatened to reveal if the Chancellor stayed in office. Brandt was well-known to have his weaknesses but if there had been anything serious to hide, it might have been expected to leak out in the years which have elapsed since then, while his colleagues would hardly have exerted themselves as they did to make him go back on his decision. Moreover it is hard to see why Guillaume should have wanted to force him from office. A paradoxical element in the whole affair is that all Guillaume's masters succeeded in doing by their sensational infiltration was to cause the downfall of the most sympathetic Chancellor they were ever likely to have.

A more probable explanation is that Brandt was losing heart and interest in the job, in face of all the difficulties which have been described, the continual sniping at him for treating the left wing at home and communists abroad too gently and the losses in Land and communal elections which the SPD had recently suffered. He had achieved his main object of realigning West German policy towards the East in such a way that it could never be wholly reversed. He had made the SPD into the strongest party and, in coalition, one with a clear majority in the Bundestag. He could hardly hope, by staying on, to improve his record: the previous eighteen months suggested that he would only blot it. If he judged that it was better to go at a moment of his own choice rather than wait like Adenauer till retirement was forced on him, there would be plenty to be said for the decision. A friendly critic remarked that he had put too much trust in good faith and too little in power; he had set out to rouse conviction and sympathy rather than to mobilise supporters.[23]

THE SCHMIDT GOVERNMENT, 1974-1980

Schmidt Saves the Situation

The new Chancellor, 54 years old, was a man of many accomplishments, including the ability to speak English fluently and play the organ. His orderly mind enabled him to see to the roots of a problem and his fluency of speech to say clearly what he saw. Senses of responsibility and proportion added to his equipment as a leader. His chief weakness was impatience with people who saw less well, dithered more or took longer to express themselves; he had little time for proponents of plans which he believed to be impracticable in current circumstances. These circumstances included the need to find a happy medium between inflation and unemployment, to halt the clear right-wing trend in Land elections and to keep the support of the FDP. Although the Government mishandled tax changes in January 1975 (as it was to mishandle pension increases two years later), its management of affairs improved but its ambitions became more limited. The left wing and particularly the Jusos grew restive but had to face clear evidence that, where they got the upper hand in party affairs (as they did in Munich and Frankfurt), the result was loss of votes and office.

Freedom of manoeuvre was further limited early in 1976 when a revolt of the Hanover SPD (against a central attempt to dictate who should lead them) led to the Land Government being taken over by the CDU. The new Cabinet under Ernst Albrecht could only survive because it was tolerated by the FDP (who later in the year actually accepted office in it). As the Saar already had a 'Black-White' CDU/FDP Coalition Government, this brought the number of 'Zebra-Länder' to two and gave them eight votes in the Bundesrat where the SPD-ruled states had 15 and the CDU ones 18. The FDP thus acquired the casting vote, and mostly used it to put back into legislation those provisions which they had been unable to get the SPD to accept in the Bundestag; the chance of getting radical legislation through the Upper House virtually vanished. The Mediation Committee of eleven members of each House (p. 165) was increasingly called on to devise compromises; where they failed, the Government had small choice but to abandon its proposals. The FDP, however, welcomed the chance of showing that it was no mere lackey of the SPD.

Internal affairs once more took pride of place. The chief exception, other than chronic bickering about the interpretation of the Eastern Treaties, arose from a decision of the Federal Government early in 1976 to yield to the Polish demands for compensation so as to restart the flow of emigrants (p. 247). Both CDU and CSU condemned the bargain, which for a time seemed bound to be thrown out by the Bundesrat. But Kohl, who had inherited Barzel's doubts about the wisdom of intransigence, brought off a deal by which the Poles accepted some last-minute modifications in the text (something Schmidt had declared out of the question) while in return first Albrecht and then even the Bavarians were induced to vote 'Yes' and the Treaty was passed unanimously. The FDP had done much to help the compromise and Kohl undoubtedly hoped that his tactics would win him favour with them and even start them thinking about changing sides again after the Election due in October 1976.

That, however, was reckoning without Strauss who particularly resented a defeat in which his Bavarian colleagues had had a hand. He was largely responsible for the decision to make the election issue into a choice between Freedom and Socialism. Such a formula would only have been justified if the SPD left wing had had a major say in framing policy, which was just what Schmidt was denying them; it polarised the voters instead of attracting floating ones. All the same, the CDU started favourites in a campaign fought primarily on internal issues. Kohl made superhuman efforts and 140 speeches; the SPD only pulled out the stops at the end, perhaps as deliberate tactics, perhaps because they were slow to recognise danger. They ended by losing 17 seats and the FDP two, but they won back over a million of the voters who had deserted them in the Land elections. The CDU/CSU recovered their position as the strongest Party and polled more votes than in any election since 1957 but, as the overall total of votes had been increasing, their gains were not quite enough to turn the scale. The Schmidt Government was more relieved than exhilarated at the prospect of continuing in power with a majority of at best eight (in the first vote of confidence it dropped to one!). The Chancellor's personal prestige had done much to decide the issue; if Brandt had still been in charge, the other side might have got its nose in front.

Terrorism and Nuclear Energy Excite Passions

Terrorism dominated the next twelve months. There had been sporadic acts since 1968, with a first peak in 1972; starting from Berlin, they spread round the country and outside it. A number of bomb attacks were made on public buildings, embassies and military installations; banks were robbed to obtain funds. In the course of these actions and consequential arrests, several policemen and still more terrorists were killed and some of the ensuing actions were declared to be revenges. After a terrorist, Holger Meins, had died on hunger strike in November 1974, a senior judge was murdered in Berlin where, four months later, the local CDU leader was kidnapped just before the city elections; in spite of misgivings, five terrorists were set free to secure his release. Between April and September 1977 a prosecuting counsel was assassinated in Karlsruhe, a banker Jürgen Ponto shot by his god-daughter in his house near Frankfurt and the employers' leader Hans-Martin Schleyer (p. 244) kidnapped in Cologne. The police did not show up too well in the pursuit of the criminals, partly because of rivalries between the Federal Criminal Office and the Land forces. But it was a different story when on 17 October a German airliner returning from Majorca was hijacked and taken to Mogadishu. A specially-trained squad of Federal Frontier Police was sent out and, with the consent of the Somali Government, the plane was recovered, the passengers freed and three terrorists killed. Three other notable terrorists, Baader, Rasper and Gudrun Ensslin, who were already serving life sentences, committed suicide on hearing the news in prison near Stuttgart. Next day Schleyer's body was found in the back of a car in Alsace.

The outcome owed much to the Chancellor's determination and contributed correspondingly to his prestige; there were no serious acts of terrorism in the next 35 months. Over the whole period 1970-80, 41 people were killed, including 11 policemen, but 21 terrorists also lost their lives, while about 400 more received sentences.

The wave of terrorism was not of course peculiar to West Germany — indeed the German terrorists had close links with gangs, and particularly Arabs, elsewhere. But most of the others had clear political objectives, whereas the Germans merely claimed to be using violence in the interests of 'humanity' without any definite ideas as to what they would do if they overthrew the established system. The terrorist epidemic is best seen as an extension of the student unrest of 1968 and a further price which West Germany had to pay for the social immobility of the Republic's first twenty years. The people involved were alienated from society and frustrated at its slowness to change. Nearly all of them were young middle-class intellectuals with psychological problems aggravated by some sort of personal failure. They were the flotsam of the generation which grew up while their parents were absorbed in the war or in achieving the 'Economic Miracle', so that they had not known stable family life. Women were as numerous as men. They were estranged from the older generation by revulsion at the acquiescence of that generation in Nazi crimes; they considered themselves justified in using violence against a society which had condoned it in the Third Reich and Vietnam War and employed it against Ohnesorge, Dutschke and Martin Luther King. (Schleyer had held high rank in the SS.) Their hostility to the established order with its affluence made them sympathetic to Marxism and other revolutionary dogmas which provided rational justification for courses of action attractive to them on emotional grounds. They were more the children of 'Marx and Coca-Cola' than of Hitler.

They could have done serious damage to the Federal Republic if they had succeeded in driving it into blind repression. But when they were most active, liberal men were fortunately in power who saw the danger and refused to panic; instead they merely increased the number and co-ordination of the police, improved intelligence and limited the traditional right of defence lawyers to free access to their clients when this had been palpably abused. As soon as the situation seemed to be under control, the FDP Minister of the Interior Baum began making minor relaxations, only to be bitterly criticised by the Opposition in the election campaign of 1980. The number of active terrorists probably never reached three figures, nor did that of those giving them aid and comfort reach four. They were able to exploit the vulnerability of pluralist society to ill-willed individuals but they did not find in the population as a whole the sympathy which alone could have made them a serious political threat. As soon as the committed ring-leaders had been rounded up, without achieving any positive results, potential successors seem to have given up attempts at imitation as being both difficult and unrewarding.

Energy however was to prove a more intractable problem. Like most industrialised Western countries, the Federal Republic depends for all its oil on imports, principally from the Middle East. Accordingly the sudden and drastic increase in prices imposed by that area's producers at the end of 1973 added significantly to the import bill. Some countries, such as Britain and the US, refused to alter their pattern of expenditure to accommodate the extra amounts which they needed to spend on oil, preferring to increase their money supply and let prices rise generally, thus reducing the real cost to them of the extra oil and depriving its producers of part of the gain which they hoped to draw from the higher prices. But West Germany managed to increase its exports, particularly to the Middle East, and its extra earnings, taken with some Middle

Eastern investment in its own economy, enabled it to pay for the oil without putting its overall balance into deficit or seriously raising the rate of inflation. The record 1974 surplus of DM 26,000 million sank to DM 9,900 million in 1975 but by 1978, it was back at DM 18,400 million. However, this success increased the problems for the rest of the world, since the large surplus won by the oil producers had to be matched by a deficit somewhere else. Accordingly the Schmidt Government came under considerable pressure not to indulge in repressive measures in order to contain inflation but to keep its market open for other countries. The stimulus which it gave to its economy in due course resulted in it doing what it had previously managed to avoid and 1979 saw a payments deficit of DM 9,000 million ($5,000 million) – the first for fourteen years. The further rise following on the cutting of Iranian supplies drove the 1980 deficit to DM 29,000 million. The size of West German reserves prevented such a result from causing an immediate crisis but would not go on doing so indefinitely.

An obvious way of easing the situation would be to consume less oil. Yet, on any scientific projection of growth, West Germany's need for oil will rise rather than fall. In 1977 energy consumption totalled 369 million tons of coal equivalent; by 1985 it is expected to be in the neighbourhood of 450 million tons. Two hundred million of these can be met from coal but to use any more would create serious pollution problems and require expensive imports. Fifty million might come from natural gas and other miscellaneous sources. Gasification of coal or lignite may provide a long-term solution but the processes are not economically viable at today's costs and no plant for the purpose is yet under construction. The only short-term substitute for the 200 million or so tons of oil is nuclear energy. The 30 reactors in existence or at various stages of construction were intended to produce 20,000 mw by 1985, though the programme has slipped. Double that amount would be needed to fill the gap but this would involve putting in hand at least four stations every year.

Nobody denies that such a programme involves dangers. These have been seen not only in the risk that accidents in power-stations would release radioactive material into the environment but also in the need to store increasing quantities of lethal spent-fuel over centuries. The Federal Republic has only a short coastline and is densely populated; isolated sites for reactors and for storage pits are hard to find. The electrical industry favours the American light-water type of reactor rather than the British gas-cooled type which is arguably safer though more expensive. Figures like those just quoted make it hard to deny the need to do something. Opponents of nuclear power have therefore been driven to challenge the estimated pace at which demand will grow and have come close to saying that no harm will be done to the quality of life if lack of energy forces a halt in growth. The advocates of the programme dismissed its dangers with an assurance which events inside and outside Germany showed to be excessive. Part of the difficulty lies in the length of time which seems bound to elapse between the decision to build a reactor and its coming into use; to foresee what decision it would be right to make is as hard as to remedy the consequences of making a wrong one. The Government, well aware that it would be blamed for an economic breakdown, was unwilling to take the risk of doing nothing; in this, it was supported not only by industry, afraid that lack of contracts at home might lead to a loss of contracts abroad, but also by the unions, concerned for the jobs which would be provided if reactors were built as well as for those which would be lost if power shortages forced close downs. Refuge was had to the formula 'As much coal as possible; as much nuclear power as necessary.'

Opposition to nuclear expansion provided a focus for all those dissatisfied with things as they were; the student upheavals of 1968-70 were replaced by mass demonstrations and obstruction at reactor-sites, some of which ended as pitched battles with the police. Every legal opening provided by the Grundgesetz and other laws was exploited. A number of verdicts were obtained delaying the building of reactors, so that the paradoxical situation arose of decisions on policy being taken by judges rather than by ministers. Feeling was strong among the SPD rank-and-file; in Hanover and Baden-Württemberg the local leadership (perhaps because it was not in office) refused to toe the line set by Bonn. But opposition was not confined to existing parties. A number of groups who felt keenly about environmental problems began banding together into a new party 'the Greens', with the intention of putting up candidates at forthcoming Land elections and at the Federal Election of 1980. They were an ill-assorted collection of high-minded worriers and cranks, infiltrated by political extremists and, as events were to show, agreed only in their dislikes. Their chances of winning power were minimal; those of surmounting the 5 per cent hurdle problematical. But in the autumn of 1979, after a success at Bremen, they seemed capable of winning 4 per cent of the voters, chiefly at the expense of the SPD and FDP. As votes given to them in this quantity would not count in the allocation of Bundestag seats, a result would mean that the CDU/CSU could get an absolute majority with only 48 per cent of the total vote — and an opinion poll had already given them 47 per cent.

The Undoing of Franz Josef Strauss

Their prospects had, however, been complicated by Kohl's announcement in May that he would not accept nomination as candidate for the Chancellorship in 1980. He pressed instead the choice of Albrecht, the young Minister-President of Lower Saxony. This was more than the CSU could stomach, since Albrecht, though full of promise, was short on experience (especially in Federal politics) and could not compare in force of character with Franz Josef Strauss, who was induced to stand against him. In a combined vote of the two Parties, the Bavarian leader received 57 per cent. As nearly all the CSU must have voted for him, this figure showed that less than half the CDU could have done so, and the motives of many who did were questionable. For some were frightened of losing their seats if Strauss, in revenge for being rejected, got the CSU to put up candidates for the Bundestag outside Bavaria (as he had often threatened to do). Others, sick of the way Strauss had denigrated Barzel and Kohl, and foreseeing similar treatment of Albrecht, thought that the best way of drawing his political sting was to put him up in an election which he was unlikely to win. For his record reinforced the habitual North German distrust of Bavarians. He was unlikely to attract floating voters and there was no chance of the FDP turning back to coalition with the CDU/CSU as long as that combination was under his leadership. These considerations however did not prevent some Social Democrats from fearing that, during the months before the Election, trouble over energy, or a revival of terrorism, or rising prices or unemployment, or a Russian violation of the Eastern Treaties, could turn the crucial margin of opinion against them.

Instead, the Iranian students stormed the US Embassy in Tehran, the Russians invaded Afghanistan and the Carter Administration reverted to the attitudes of the Cold War. Schmidt had already sized Carter up as a lightweight and the tension between the two men was enhanced by the President's tendency to change policies suddenly without consulting his allies. The Chancellor knew that, in the last resort, the Federal Republic must stand by the United States and indeed did not wish to do otherwise. But he was not prepared to jeopardise the achievements of the Ostpolitik without compelling reason and, though he went further than Britain in acting as the Americans wished, he doubted whether the course they favoured would have its intended effects in Moscow. Had he done otherwise, he would have intensified his existing difficulties with his Party. As it was, he found himself supported not only by a majority of West Germans, whose dominating concern was to avoid having a war fought over their territory, but by moderate opinion throughout Western Europe. He was helped too by the obvious anxiety of the Russians and East Germans to maintain contact with him. The political shrewdness of his course was illustrated by the restraint which Strauss at first showed in attacking it and by the striking gains which the SPD made in Land elections in the Saar and in North Rhine-Westphalia in May. In neither Land did the Greens get 5 per cent (though they did win 5.3 per cent in Baden-Württemberg in March) and, as their disarray was becoming steadily more evident, the danger from them seemed to have passed. Strauss, disillusioned by the results of trying to play the statesman, relapsed into the more congenial role of demagogue and attacked the Government for betraying the North Atlantic Alliance, but there were no indications that the change brought him votes.

In July the Chancellor went to Moscow and persuaded the Russians to resume talks with the Americans; he justifiably represented this as a service to humanity which few other people could perform. Probably he would have liked to base his whole campaign on such a profile. But he had to cancel visits to Poland and to the Democratic Republic in September because the 'Solidarity' strikes started in the former country; it would not have done for the leader of a free state to be the guest of people who were using violence to suppress freedom and there was no assurance that this would not happen (though in fact it did not). As a result home affairs got more attention in the election campaign and here the Government was more vulnerable, in spite of the fact that the Federal Republic, with unemployment at 3.7 per cent, inflation at 5.5 per cent and growth at 2.5 per cent, compared favourably with any other country in the world.

Fifty million dollars are said to have been spent on campaign publicity, much of it being paid for out of public funds. Strauss, having clearly decided that his best chance of victory lay in exciting the voters by emotionalising issues, accused the SDP of extravagance and weakness towards communism and terrorism. He launched a series of allegations, in each of which the truth was more or less twisted, but by the time his opponents had got around to putting the record straight, he had diverted the public's attention to the next charge. Personal abuse abounded, with even the Chancellor stooping to it. The left wing, its dissident factions for once united under the banner 'Stop Strauss', itself stopped at little, but its victim would have gained more sympathy if he had shown more restraint himself. The Catholic bishops, in a pastoral letter, advised the faithful to vote for a list of aims remarkably similar to those professed by the CDU/CSU; this reversion to old habits was duly deplored by those likely to lose by it. The terrorist act which everyone had been expecting duly occurred when a bomb at the Munich Beer Festival killed 13 people, but its value as ammunition was impaired by the discovery that it had been planted by a hanger-on of a right-wing organisation which the Interior Minister had been criticised by the Opposition for prosecuting.

The electorate would seem to have tired of the scurrilities and noticed the lack of solid argument. In a poll a little lower than that of 1976, the SPD failed to realise either their maximal hope of a clear majority or their more modest one of becoming the strongest party again, and had to be content with a marginal rise in their proportion to 42.9 per cent. The CDU/CSU lost nearly 4 per cent, falling to 44.5 per cent, their lowest figure for 20 years; Strauss must bear at least some of the blame for this. The beneficiaries were the FDP who had fought a more moderate campaign — perhaps because the Opposition's fire was concentrated on the SPD; having fallen below the 5 per cent line in North Rhine-Westphalia in May, they were more than a little gratified to emerge at 10.6 per cent albeit without winning a single constituency. The hollowness of the Green menace was shown by their mere 1.5 per cent.

15 A LOOK FORWARD

Previous chapters have charted the unique course by which West Germany has developed into a pluralist, liberal and industrialised society. But while the route has left her with many cultural idiosyncrasies, the result causes her to share many features in common with the other countries of Western Europe and North America. Like most of them, she is closely integrated politically, economically and strategically with the entire area. Consequently her future depends more than ever before on what happens to her neighbours, allies and enemies. There are three extreme possibilities: (a) a nuclear war; (b) the disintegration of Western society as a result of economic difficulties and divergent views about how to solve them; (c) the disintegration of communist society, thanks to disputes about the succession or to the refusal of its people to tolerate any longer the limitations placed on their freedom and welfare. But any attempt to forecast how the Federal Republic would be affected by any of these eventualities involves so many incalculables as to be worth little. It may be unrealistic to assume that national conditions and international relations are going to remain much as they are today indefinitely, but a hypothesis which may be improbable is better than a guess which is bound to be wild.

Population

The population of the Federal Republic reached a peak of 58 million in 1973; there were in addition some four million foreigners. Since then, deaths have exceeded births so that the total has been falling. This process is likely to continue; if existing rates were maintained, the figure would be 52 million by 2000 AD, 39.4 million by 2030. Such a development has been seen in some quarters as a national disaster. It is of course one common to most industrialised states (including the European parts of the Soviet Union) and one which has been developing for some time.

The first reason given for apprehension is the difficulty of maintaining growth when the labour force is falling. But this disregards the microchip. Other futurologists are worried by the problem of finding employment for all who want it in a highly-automated economy, and while this fear in turn may be exaggerated, a fall in the labour force would afford relief. It is also a development to be welcomed by those concerned with the environment, for the housing stock will only need to be renewed and not extended. Pressure on social services (hospitals, water and sewage supplies) and on the transport system will drop. After a few years during which congestion in schools is going to be heavy, it too will wane, offering an opportunity to reduce the student:teacher ratio (23.2:1 in 1977) and will provide places in nursery schools for all likely to want them. In the 1930s there were 39 million people living in the area now occupied by the Federal Republic and they were said to be short of space (*'Volk ohne Raum'*). Why should the same number a hundred years later be regarded as underpopulation?

A further fear concerns the high percentage of pensioners to be expected in the population and the burden placed as a result on the workforce, each member of which will have to produce both for him(her)self and a pensioner, whereas today three are maintaining two pensioners. But, apart from the higher output resulting from higher productivity, the number of children in the population will be falling so that the overall ratio of active to inactive may improve.

Finally comes the problem of defence. How can a country with a falling population hope to maintain its relative power in relation to lands in the underdeveloped world which are increasing so fast as to provoke despair over feeding the extra mouths? Difficulty is already envisaged in keeping the Bundeswehr up to strength and the suggestion has been made that girls will have to be conscripted to do auxiliary work. What is more, this is a problem to which a quick remedy is excluded; the number of people available for calling up in 2000 has already been virtually settled by the current birth-rate. But defence forces are themselves feeling the impact of technology. Their equipment gets steadily more costly. To keep the defence budget within bounds, it might make sense to reduce the size of the force so as to save on pay and have more to spare for spending on arms.

During the years 1960-75 the number of employed Germans sank by two million but that of foreign workers rose by 1.9 million. The Government began restricting the issue of entry permits for foreigners in 1973 and by July 1976 the total number of foreigners had fallen to 3.76 million, among whom Turks, Yugoslavs and Italians were the most prominent. In theory all these aliens are only temporarily in the country and could be sent home if unemployment among Germans became acute. In practice, many of them have been living there with their families for a considerable time and must be regarded as a permanent element in the population (besides being needed to do necessary chores which Germans despise). One of the problems for the future which has hitherto received less attention than in Britain is that of integrating them with the native inhabitants.

Economic Affairs

West Germany's economy is dominated by two facts:

(a) its dependence, in common with most other European countries (except Britain, Russia and Rumania) on imports of oil – not to mention iron ore, aluminium, copper and tin. Any increase in the prices of these commodities has a serious effect on the trade balance; if that is to be kept out of heavy deficit, exports have to be increased. Unless this can be done by raising their prices, or by higher production, there will be a reduction in the proportion of resources available for use at home. But an increase in total production means an increase in the quantities of imports. Moreover oil is priced in dollars, so that a rise in the dollar–Deutschemark exchange rate (such as results from a strengthening dollar) means a bigger bill. Any lasting interruption in the supply of oil from the Middle East would disrupt the whole economy drastically.

(b) its reliance on export markets to absorb a large proportion of its industrial output. As has just been said, exports need to rise to pay the higher bill for imports. If they were to fall, not only would the payments situation become serious but the home market could not absorb the goods set free, so that unemployment would rise. Assuming that in such deteriorating international conditions, home consumers could afford to increase their purchases at all, they would, as Schiller found in 1970 (p. 232), want different things and the process of shifting resources to make those different things would be slow and painful.

In 1979 four-fifths of West German exports went to other countries in Western Europe or to North America. (See Table 14, p. 285.) This underlines the already mentioned dependence of the Federal Republic's prosperity on that of its neighbours. All the indications are, however, that for some time to come, the struggle against inflation in these countries will lead to restrictive policies which discourage investment and growth. In addition, West Germany has shown itself little less immune than other developed countries to competition from Japanese and newly-industrialising producers in Asia and South America. In 1980 three out of four men's shirts and seven out of ten pairs of shoes sold in the BRD came from abroad.

An obvious alternative would be to offset stagnant or falling sales to other Western countries by increased sales to the communist and developing worlds. This idea has played its part in encouraging the Ostpolitik. But if the West were depressed, these alternative markets would be unlikely to be able to raise their sales of raw materials, foodstuffs and simpler manufactures and thereby earn the foreign currency needed to expand purchases from West Germany. Increased sales to them would therefore have to be financed by loans, but many of them are already heavily burdened by debt, making it doubtful wisdom to give them further credits. Ideally such credits would be financed, in conformity with the Brandt Report, by triangular deals between West Germany, the oil-producing countries and the developing ones but this is a solution which the oil-producers seem slow to adopt. In so far as such credits are provided by West Germany, that country's balance of payments would be burdened and the stock of funds available for investment at home correspondingly reduced. Without such home investment, the vulnerability of domestic industry to import competition will grow. Hitherto one of the great strengths of the economy has been the high rate of investment, the will to go on keeping industry competitive by constant re-equipping and the consequent growth of productivity. But as Table 8 on p. 281 shows, the proportion of the West German Gross Domestic Product devoted to capital formation has recently tended to fall from the very high figures of 1953-73.

As has been said, the country in 1979 ran a deficit on current account for the first time in fourteen years, but it was much exceeded by that of 1980 while that in 1981 threatens to be higher still. But the willingness of the Government to run a constant deficit and thus in effect to act as a reserve currency has been important for the stability of other West European countries since otherwise they themselves would have to provide more of the counterpart to the consistent surplus run by the oil-producers. Experience with the pound and the dollar discourages hope that any economy is strong enough to run such a deficit indefinitely.

Internally, growing government expenditure, largely on social services, has produced a rising budget deficit over the last eight years. Borrowing to cover this has caused overall public indebtedness to increase from DM 167,800 million in 1973 (18.2 per cent of GNP) to DM 464,100 million in 1980 (31.3 per cent of GNP). Insistence by the Finance Ministry and Bundesbank on halting this led in July 1981 to cuts of

DM 18,000 million in the budget for 1981-2 being agreed on. Whether the agreement can be translated into reality remains to be seen.

The question is often asked whether West Germany is not catching 'the English sickness'. The essential symptom of that sickness is not strikes or inadequate hours of work or even wage increases measured by the rate of inflation rather than by that of growth in productivity per head. It is a rate of productivity which is both relatively low and growing too slowly. The root cause of this is inadequate investment, due to excessive application of economic resources to consumption and welfare benefits which do not directly improve rates of production. The slow growth intensifies the struggle between the various sections of the population to maintain standards of life unimpaired and make others take the cuts involved by the persistent inflation. The organised strength of labour enables it to secure disproportionate wage increases i.e. to reduce the effect on consumption by its members. The struggle against inflation leads to high interest rates as well as to restrictions and other devices to restrain profits. As a result management loses both the spare resources with which to invest and the incentive to do so, since in such circumstances investment will seldom pay.

There are some signs of the same thing happening in West Germany. Capital for investment is clearly going to be harder to find there in the future than in the past. But it may be that the growth achieved between 1953 and 1973 was something which no economy can sustain indefinitely. Hitherto there has been general recognition of the importance of investment and the unions have been notable for their restraint in demanding higher wages. There are signs that this restraint is being eroded. Resentment has been roused among the workers by management's opposition to any extension of co-determination, as shown by the appeal to the Constitutional Court (p. 244) and opposition in the summer of 1980 to re-organisation of the Mannesman metal company which would have had the incidental effect of reducing the number of workers' representatives on the Supervising Council. If such resentment led to intransigence over wages, the result could be serious.

One of today's paradoxes is that it is the two defeated nations, West Germany and Japan, which (except for their Achilles' heel of oil supplies) possess the strongest economies. The West German economy has repeatedly given the lie to predictions that its success was ending. It may do so again; if it does decline, it is likely to do so more slowly than the prophets foretell. But the improvement in living standards does seem likely to slow down or even cease. (See Table 7 on p. 280.) If the public struggle to resist this trend, and politicians abet them, the foundations of the 'Miracle' could be shaken.

Home Politics

The 1980 Election proved, as far as anything can be proved in politics, that even in an atmosphere of East-West tension, a majority will not be forthcoming in the Federal Republic for a policy which is militantly anti-communist abroad and anti-socialist at home. There are many in the CDU who will wish to draw from this evidence the conclusion that the Party should revert to the policy of conserving things as they are instead of seeking to put them back to what they once were. If however the result is that the CDU stop trying to blur the distinction between Social Democracy and Socialism, the Coalition Government may find itself deprived of its main cohesive force. 'Stop Strauss' was a cry rallying to a united effort all the forces of the country which could be regarded as in any way progressive, from the right wing of the FDP to the left wing of the Jusos. But if the Opposition abandons a policy of radical reaction, the Socialist demand for one of radical progress will grow all the louder. The Election brought with it, as always, the replacing of a number of older men by younger ones who naturally tend to be more sympathetic to change. The left have not failed to notice that Schmidt's policy has strengthened his Government by strengthening his Liberal allies rather than his own Party. As the economic situation becomes more difficult, tension will grow between those who say that change cannot be afforded (or even that existing benefits must be cut) and those who say that a party tending to be progressive must push ahead with proposals for social change at all costs.

It is easy to draw the conclusion that the future will see a split between the SPD and FDP, as a result of which the latter Party, holding as it does the key position, will transfer its favours away from the left and back to a rejuvenated CDU under the leadership of someone like Stoltenberg of Schleswig-Holstein or Albrecht of Lower Saxony. As a recent opinion poll has shown, strength is ebbing from the argument that the FDP, by going back on its 1969 change of course, would make itself look irresponsible in the eyes of the voters and risk falling below the 5 per cent line as a result. For a number of people are known to have voted for the FDP because, although they did not want a reactionary government, they did not want a Socialist one either and relied on the FDP to block radical innovations; the Party could therefore claim with justice that it has a duty to fulfil that expectation. If it were to remain permanently an ally of the SPD, it would risk losing its identity and being absorbed by the larger partner. Moreover there would be a very respectable argument in favour of a switch. Liberal democracy requires for its efficient functioning not merely that several political parties should coexist but that responsibility for government should periodically change hands. By 1984 the CDU/CSU will have been out of office at the Federal level for 15 years, longer than is healthy for any party's morale, least of all for one which during most of the time has been the strongest party in Parliament.

Not all currents, however, run in this direction. The FDP contains a variety of elements; some of the more progressive (such as the Minister of the Interior, Gerhart Baum) share some of the Jusos standpoints and might prefer to split the Party rather than join in with any kind of CDU. Even if the CDU were ready to make the concessions which seem essential for its return to power, the same does not necessarily apply to the CSU (though even in that quarter there is talk of the Strauss era 'nearing its end'), and without the CSU, a Coalition of the CDU and FDP would, on the 1980 figures, be in a minority of 43. The fact that Schmidt has a majority of 45 instead of eight makes him better able to withstand pressure from his left. Hamburg and West Berlin have in 1981 provided further evidence that, where the SPD left gets too much influence, trouble ensues. The restive members of the SPD realise more clearly than it would sometimes appear that if they behave in such a way as to provoke the FDP into secession, they will get a government which is less rather than more to their taste. The Coalition at least survived the financial crisis of July 1981. The poor showing of the CDU in Schleswig-Holstein and Lower Saxony in 1980 damaged the prospects of Stoltenberg and Albrecht; Kohl has been re-elected as CDU leader for the next three years and, though he clearly aims at winning over the FDP, his close association with Strauss in the election campaign will take some living down. Finally the Federal Republic has not often seen a party with seats in one Cabinet immediately join in a new Cabinet with the Party hitherto in opposition; the transition is not unthinkable but in normal circumstances would look awkward.

For all these reasons a good deal will depend on the personalities and constitutions of the men leading the two government Parties. The prestige and authority of Helmut Schmidt is such that, although he did not bring his Party the overwhelming success for which he and it had once hoped, he can probably remain its leader for as long as he wishes to stay, but by 1984 he will be 64 and will have had ten years in office

(Adenauer had fourteen but the precedent is hardly auspicious). His health is not assured and might force him to retire. The same is even more true of Genscher. The latter's obvious successor is Count Lambsdorff, the Economics Minister, but he is bidding fair to become a second Erhard with a similar allegiance to the market economy and would therefore be unlikely to go along with interventionist or socialist remedies. The probability therefore is that between now and 1986 Schmidt will retire and the FDP again change partners. Which of these two events will occur first is anybody's guess; either might precipitate the other.

Education

One controversy likely to be materially affected by the victory of the Schmidt Coalition (though one which received little attention in the election campaign) is that over comprehensive schools. There are at present about 300 such schools (*Gesamtschulen*) in West Germany out of about 26,000. They are regarded as experiments and are all situated in thickly-populated areas where schools of the familiar triple pattern (*Gymnasien, Realschulen, Hauptschulen*) are not far away, so that parents can up to a point choose whichever type they prefer. But Gesamtschulen are said to be popular and to have more applicants than they can take. They also appear to get better results with less gifted children (though there is argument as to the validity of the investigations into this).

As has been said, education is primarily a responsibility of the individual Länder and there is widespread agreement that the last word about the introduction of Gesamtschulen should rest with the Landtäge. Hamburg recently decided to make them the norm; Hesse and West Berlin made moves in the same direction. So, in spite of a set back in a referendum, is North Rhine-Westphalia. Bavaria, not surprisingly, has very few and the CSU threatened at one point to block their extension not merely in that Land but throughout the Federation. Strictly speaking, it has no legal power to do this and, if it were to try holding up the introduction of Gesamtschulen in an area where most parents could be shown to want one, the Constitutional Court might invoke Article 6(2) of the Grundgesetz (which makes the care and education of children the natural right of the parents) to override the politicians. But children often move from one Land to another in the course of their education and the sort of question which can arise is whether a pupil who has attended a comprehensive school in a Land where they are the norm, and obtained the appropriate leaving certificate, is entitled to enter an institution of higher education in a Land where such entry depends on having a different form of certificate based on attendance at a different form of school.

In 1978 the Federal Government, in a report on the structural problems of the educational system, called attention to five matters which in its view required to be settled in a uniform way throughout the country: (1) whether the proposed (and agreed) extension of compulsory full-time education from 9 to 10 years should be achieved by lowering the age of entry from 6 to 5 or raising the leaving age from 15 to 16; (2) whether the two years which children are to be allowed between 10+ and 12+ before deciding finally on their intermediate school (*Orientierungsstufe*) should be spent at the top of the primary school or at the bottom of the intermediate school and whether, if the latter is chosen, the relevant forms should be comprehensive or streamed; (3) what types of examinations should be taken at the end of the first stage of secondary education (at 15+) and the rights which success in them should confer; (4) what types of examination should be taken at the end of the second stage, a question complicated by the fact that some of the pupils taking these examinations will already be working part-time in industry; (5) the courses to be followed in professional and technical education, so as to ensure adequate uniformity between those given in schools and those given in administration and industry. (All children are compelled to undergo part-time education up to 18 but some of them receive it at their place of work while others go to special schools.)

The Federal Government was of the opinion that the Grundgesetz needed revising to give authority for these matters to be regulated centrally. Otherwise the equality of opportunity and freedom of movement throughout the country which is guaranteed to the individual by Articles 3 and 11 of the Grundgesetz would be lacking. The Land Ministers (and particularly those of Länder where the CDU or CSU were in power) objected to any step likely to diminish their powers further, particularly in matters of culture which they saw as the core of their existence as distinct states. Accordingly they argued that the questions could be settled satisfactorily by negotiation between themselves in the Standing Conference of Land Ministers of Culture.

The Federal Government in reply expressed doubt, based on previous experience, as to whether agreement in adequate detail could be reached with adequate speed. Moreover they pointed to a difficulty which goes to the heart of the federal system. The only way of reaching agreement would be by negotiation between the Governments concerned (which, since the amendment to the Grundgesetz in 1971 (p. 167) include the Federal Government). If such negotiations were to succeed, widespread concessions would have to be made all round. But such compromises were undermining the right of the voters, as represented in the Landtäge, to decide on vital social institutions. In many cases, the agreements already reached by the Governments had been put into force by administrative order, without being laid before the Landtäge at all. German legal thinking was turning against such a procedure as undemocratic. But even if the agreements were to be treated as laws and submitted for parliamentary approval, it would be virtually impossible to amend them, since an amendment proposed by one Land would only be valid if agreed to by all the others, which would involve reopening the whole process of negotiation.

The Federal Government maintains that the true democratic solution is to amend the Grundgesetz in such a way as to confer on itself power to legislate on all matters which require uniformity throughout the country and leave to the Länder only such things as are amenable to variety. Federal Ministers would then be responsible to the electorate through the Bundestag and Bundesrat (and, through the latter, to the Land Governments) while the Ministers of each Land would be responsible to their particular Landtag for matters within their competence. The need for negotiations between Federation and Länder should thus be removed. The proposal seems to place great faith in the ability of those drafting the laws to produce texts which are free from any kind of ambiguity.

The next few years are likely to see an extension both of comprehensive schools and of the co-ordinating activities of the central Government in education. Article 6(2) of the Grundgesetz, however, is likely to set limits to the former and give parents more say than has sometimes been the case in Britain, while the anxiety of the Länder to maintain their powers is likely to set limits to the latter.

A great deal has been done in the last fifteen years to develop the educational system. This applies not only to academic but equally to vocational and technical education, in which the arrangements are, as usual, in advance of those in Britain. There are a bewildering variety of Advanced Technical Schools, Advanced Vocational Schools, Technical Colleges, Specialised Colleges, Specialised High Schools, Intermediate Technical Schools, Part-time Vocational Schools and Teacher Training Colleges. Virtually no child leaves the educational system without having received training for a definite kind of employment (though it does not necessarily follow that he or she gets a job for which the training is intended).

One Nation or Two in the Twenty-first Century?

West Germany's external relations are for obvious reasons dominated by the existence of East Germany and are likely to go on being so dominated for the foreseeable future. The official doctrine of the Federal Republic sees Germany as a single nation divided into two states. The question whether the inhabitants of Austria belong to the same nation goes unasked but there seems to be general agreement that those of the German-speaking Cantons of Switzerland do not. Presumably it is the length of time over which those two states have led a separate existence which would decide whether their populations are to be regarded as separate nations. The question therefore presents itself as to how long the Democratic Republic must maintain a separate existence in order to become entitled to the same treatment. There is also of course the consideration that the Swiss and (for the present at any rate) the Austrian Germans desire to be separate whereas it is claimed that the East Germans do not. How far is this claim justified and what are the prospects of it continuing to be justified?

No government can maintain itself for long, even with the help of foreign bayonets, unless it can enlist the loyalty, or at least the acquiescence, of a considerable section of its inhabitants. How big that section must be depends on whether the remainder are actively hostile or merely indifferent and what degree of support the foreign bayonets provide. But the longer that a government maintains itself in existence (which indicates a certain degree of success), the more it creates a number of institutions, practices and cultural idiosyncrasies which distinguish it from its neighbours. The German language as used in the Democratic Republic, for instance, is already noticeably different from that in the Federal Republic. The effort which participating citizens make to bring these distinctive characteristics into existence and thereafter to maintain and develop them creates a shared awareness of endeavour and, in so far as they are successful, of achievement. The state creates the nation even more than the nation creates the state, though the gradual nature of the process makes it impossible to say at any particular moment 'the inhabitants of this state have become a distinct nation'. This power of the state to create a nation explains the efforts which the Government of the Democratic Republic has been making to draw distinctions between its society and that of the Federal Republic (*Abgrenzung*), as well as its efforts to appropriate to itself some part of the German tradition (which undeniably contains autocratic as well as liberal elements).

It is, however, an article of liberal faith that this process of integration will fail in any society where the inhabitants are denied free speech and where participation depends on acceptance of the system. Such states will undoubtedly have trouble with dissidents. But it is a big assumption that this will reach the scale where the governing class will be permanently unable to get itself accepted by the majority of its citizens. The Soviet Union has practically never known a non-autocratic regime. The inhabitants of East Germany have by now been denied the free expression of opinion for almost fifty years, and a great deal can be achieved by conditioning individuals from childhood onwards. On the other hand, the Democratic Republic has to compete with the existence of another German state next door which has three particular ways of making its differences known.

One is the West German television programmes which can be received almost anywhere in its territories and seem to be found more interesting or entertaining by many of its inhabitants (though others are repelled by the luxury and violence which feature in them). The second is the number of visitors from West Germany who, since 1972, have been coming into the Democratic Republic (in spite of recent efforts to discourage them by raising the charges for entry): it must be presumed that they have been making their divergent points of view known. The third is the higher value placed on West than on East German currency by its inclusion, along with other capitalist monies, in those whose possession enables the holder to buy coveted rarities in special shops. As long as these three features continue, the process of Abgrenzung probably cannot be carried to the point at which the inhabitants of East Germany could be allowed freedom of movement into, and freedom of contact with, the West, for fear that too many of them would take the opportunity to stay outside, and a state which cannot hold its citizens can hardly be called a nation. Of course the special shops could be shut, the visitors completely forbidden and television screens supplied by cable from central receiving points under official control. If these things do not happen, it must be presumed to be because the damage done by the holes in the Iron Curtain is outweighed by the compensating gains which they allow.

Even though the existence of West Germany is likely to go on preventing the Communists from achieving in East Germany the degree of consolidation which they desire, the last thirty years have shown that the risks which would be involved by active interference to upset their rule are perilously high. Few events would be more calculated to precipitate a world war than a rising in the DDR which was not immediately suppressed. The Soviet Union will deploy all its resources rather than see its satellites pass out of its control. All sensible people in the West are therefore as apprehensive of unrest in the East as they are from another point of view anxious for it. The result is a stalemate which is regarded as likely to continue as long as the European political scene remains substantially unaltered. Whereas in 1966 only 28 per cent of West Germans thought reunification unlikely in the near future, by 1980 the figure had risen to 52 per cent.

But that does not mean a general abandonment of reunification as a long-term goal. Helmut Schmidt can hardly be regarded as an extreme nationalist but in October 1979 he said in an interview with *The Economist*:

> I do not foresee under what auspices and conditions the Germans will get together again, but they will. Maybe only in the twenty-first century. I don't know. It would obviously be wrong for any European nation to believe that the nation-state is normal for any nation but not for the Germans ... One Germany is not something which anybody thinks of as being round the next corner, or even the corner after next. It's a real desire in the soul of the German nation, whether in the west or the east.

But, however strong the desire for reunification may be, it is weaker than the desire to avoid becoming the theatre of a major war. Those West Germans who want to see the country's defence forces kept strong enough to deter aggression are almost certainly in a majority (despite the noise sometimes made by the minority). But it is unlikely that a majority could be found for a policy which sought to achieve reunification by intimidation.

The main objections to such a policy, which would in any case be inconsistent with the Eastern Treaties, are three. One is that the experience of the years 1949-69, as recorded in this book, does not justify much hope of it succeeding. The second is that (as a glance at Table 16 on p. 286 suggests) its execution would involve switching resources from welfare to defence on a scale unlikely to be accepted in any state where (as in the Federal Republic) such a switch has to be approved by popular vote and there is a vocal body of opinion which considers the switch misguided. The Chancellor has already had to tell the Reagan Administration that the need to cut the Federal Republic's welfare expenditure (partly as a result of the high US interest rates) makes it impossible to fulfil promises to increase defence expenditure. The communist system has a built-in advantage here. The third objection is the fear that threats of violence will only too easily lead to acts of violence, from which West Germany stands to suffer more than most. In this respect, lessons have been learnt from 1914-18 and 1933-45.

The results of seeking reunification by negotiation may have been smaller than was once hoped but even so they compare favourably with those achieved by alternative policies. All the indications are that the West German people will want to keep the possibility of negotiation open and that any attempt to frustrate such a policy by insisting on rearmament first will be counter-productive.

ANNEXE

The Current West German Voting System for Federal Elections

Each voter has two votes. To exercise them, he/she must have resided in a constituency district for at least three months prior to an election. He can then vote without further formality in that district. If he is unable to do so, he can apply for a voting card which enables him to vote (a) in any other district of that constituency or (b) by post.

West Germany is divided into 248 constituencies roughly equal in population; their boundaries have to be reappraised in the year following each election by a commission of seven appointed by the President; the Commission reports to the Government which is bound to submit the report to the Bundestag. There are in addition 11 seats for West Berlin but the holders of these, though they sit in the Bundestag, may not vote.

The individual's first vote has to be exercised for an individual candidate in the relevant constituency. Whichever candidate gets a simple majority on the first ballot is elected.

The second vote, which can be cast independently of the first, is for a party. Each party draws up a list of candidates for each Land. No candidate can stand on more than one Land list or in more than one constituency. This provision is intended to ensure that candidates are chosen by the Land organisation, not centrally. He may, however, stand both for one Land list and for one constituency. If he is elected for the constituency, his name is automatically removed from the Land list.

The number of votes cast for each party in each Land are added up. Parties can, however, and usually do, combine their lists for all the Länder (though the CSU is not able to combine its list for Bavaria with those of the CDU in other Länder). The total votes cast for each party in the Federation are then tabulated and divided by 1, by 2, by 3 and so on. The resulting quotients are then arranged in order of size, irrespective of party, the procedure being continued until 496 quotients have been established. These are then divided among the parties according to the number of quotients which each has obtained.

If the Land lists of a party have been combined, the same procedure is then used to divide the seats obtained by the party between the various Länder.

The number of seats won by each party in constituency contests in

274

each Land is then subtracted from the total number of seats to which it is entitled in that Land. The remaining seats are then allocated to the appropriate number of candidates on its Land list. If, as happened in Schleswig-Holstein in 1980, a party has won more constituency seats than its proportional vote justifies, it retains them, the total number of seats being raised accordingly. This explains why there are 497 seats in the current Bundestag.

No party can have its Land list taken into consideration unless it wins three constituencies or obtains 5 per cent of the votes cast in the Federation as a whole. Votes cast for candidates of such parties are not reckoned in working out the share of seats. Accordingly the shares of second votes shown in Table 3 (see p. 278 below) do not add up to 100.

If a Deputy dies or retires, he is automatically succeeded by the first candidate left on the Land list for his party at the previous election who did not get a seat.

Illustration

Taking the votes cast in the 1980 election and assuming only four parties and twelve seats to distribute, the results for the Federation were that the SPD obtained 16.26 million votes, the CDU 12.93 million, the FDP 4.03 million and the CSU 3.97 million.

	Dividing factor					
	1	2	3	4	5	6
SPD	16.26 (1)	8.13 (3)	5.42 (5)	4.06 (7)	3.25 (10)	2.71 (12)
CDU	12.93 (2)	6.46 (4)	4.31 (6)	3.23 (11)	2.58	2.15
FDP	4.03 (8)	2.01	1.34 etc.			
CSU	3.97 (9)	1.98	1.32 etc.			

The SPD would thus have obtained six seats, the CDU four and the other Parties one each. These would then have to be distributed by a similar process inside each Party between the various Länder. (At this point the illustration becomes inadequate. If it were carried far enough, there would of course be more seats than Länder.)

Supposing that the SPD were thus allocated 70 seats in North Rhine-Westphalia, where SPD candidates won 44 constituencies. Then the total number of 70 would be made up by taking the 26 top names off the SPD Land list after the names of those winning constituencies had been removed from it.

STATISTICAL APPENDIX

List of Tables

276

Table 1: The Federal Cabinet — Autumn 1981

Chancellor: Helmut Schmidt SPD
Minister for Foreign Affairs and Deputy Chancellor: Hans-Dietrich Genscher FDP

Ministers
Defence: Hans Apel SPD
Economic Co-operation: Rainer Offergeld SPD
Economics: Otto Count Lambsdorff FDP
Education and Science: Björn Engholm SPD
Finance: Hans Matthöfer SPD
Food, Agriculture and Forestry: Josef Ertl FDP
Interior: Gerhart Baum FDP
Intra-German Relations: Egon Franke SPD
Justice: Jürgen Schmude SPD
Labour and Social Affairs: Herbert Ehrenberg SPD
Posts and Communications: Kurt Gscheidle SPD
Regional Planning, Building and Urban Development: Dieter Haack SPD
Research and Technology: Andreas von Bülow SPD
Transport: Volker Hauff SPD
Youth, Family Affairs and Health: Antje Hüber SPD

Minister of State in Chancellor's Office: Günther Huonker SPD

Table 2: Party Strengths in Bundestag, 1949-80[a]

Year of Election	1949	1953	1957	1961	1965	1969	1972	1976	1980
Party
CDU	115	187	215	192	195	192	176	190	174
CSU	24	57	55	50	50	50	49	53	52
SPD	131	150	169	190	202	224	229	214	218
FDP	52	48	41	67	49	30	42	39	53
KPD	15	–	–	–	–	–	–	–	–
Refugees	–	27	–	–	–	–	–	–	–
German	17	15	17	–	–	–	–	–	–
Centre	10	3	–	–	–	–	–	–	–
Others	38	–	–	–	–	–	–	–	–
TOTAL	402	487	497	499	496	496	496	496	497[b]

Notes: a. Figures exclude Deputies for West Berlin. b. For the explanation of why there is one more seat in the 1980 *Bundestag* than in its four predecessors, see p. 275.

Table 3: Party Strengths in Länder (Bundestag Election, October 1980)

Name of Land	First Vote Seats obtained by		Second Vote Percentage obtained by		
	SPD	CDU	SPD	CDU	FDP
Baden-Württemberg	6	31	37.2	48.5	12.0
Bavaria	5	40 (CSU)	32.7	57.6 (CSU)	7.8
Bremen	3	0	52.5	28.8	15.1
Greater Hesse	19	3	46.4	40.8	10.6
Hamburg	7	0	51.7	31.2	14.1
Lower Saxony	23	8	46.9	39.8	11.3
North Rhine-Westphalia	44	27	46.8	40.6	10.9
Rhineland-Palatinate	6	10	42.8	45.6	9.8
Saar	4	1	48.3	42.3	7.8
Schleswig-Holstein	11	0	46.7	38.9	12.7
TOTAL	128	120 OVERALL	42.9	44.5	10.6

Table 4: The Länder

Name	Area in sq km	Population ('000) in 1978	% of total Population	Population per sq km	Capital	Minister-President (autumn '81)	Composition of Government	Date of next election
Baden-Württemberg	35,751	9,138	14.7	255	Stuttgart	L. Späth	CDU	1984
Bavaria	70,547	10,831	17.5	153	Munich	F.J. Strauss	CSU	1982
Bremen	404	698	1.2	1,736	Bremen	H. Koschnick	SPD	1983
Greater Hesse	21,113	5,554	8.9	263	Wiesbaden	H. Börner	SPD/FDP	1982
Hamburg	753	1,664	2.6	2,237	Hamburg	K. von Dohmanyi	SPD	1982
Lower Saxony	47,430	7,225	11.5	152	Hanover	E. Albrecht	CDU/FDP	1982
North Rhine-Westphalia	34,057	17,006	29.0	499	Düsseldorf	J. Rau	SPD	1982
Rhineland-Palatinate	19,838	3,631	5.8	183	Mainz	B. Vogel	CDU	1983
Schleswig-Holstein	15,696	2,591	4.1	165	Kiel	G. Stoltenberg	CDU	1983
Saar	2,568	1,073	1.7	419	Saarbrücken	W. Zeyer	CDU/FDP	1983
West Berlin	480	1,910	3.0	3,994	West Berlin	R. von Weizsäcker	CDU	1985

Note: Total area: 248,637 sq km (UK: 240,779; Oregon: 251,000). In 1978 the Republic contained 26.72 million Protestants and 26.79 million Roman Catholics.

Table 5: Growth of Population in Eight Countries, 1871-1980 (in millions)

Year	1871	1891	1913	1936	1946	1956	1966	1980
Country								
Germany	41	49.4	66.8	68.8[a]	65.2[b]	69.2	76.1	78.2
W. Germany	–	–	–	39	46.7[c]	51.6[d]	59.3	61.4
France[e]	36.1	38.2	39.7	41.9	40.5	43.4	49.1	53.4
Italy	n.a.	30.2	34.7	42.4	45.6	49.2	53.0	56.0
Sweden	4.2	4.8	5.6	6.2	6.8	7.2	7.8	8.3
UK	27.4	34.2	45.6	47.1[f]	46.8	51.2	54.7	55.1
USA[g]	38.5	63.0	97.0	128.0	143.7	168.0	197.6	218.5
Russia/USSR	76.5	118.0	175.0	193.0	n.a.	202.0	227.3	262.4
Japan	35.0	40.0	53.0	69.0	80.0	89.0	99.7	116.1

Notes: a. Within 1936 frontiers b. Excluding areas under Russian and Polish administration c. Including W. Berlin d. Including the Saar e. Metropolitan France f. Excluding Eire g. Continental USA

Table 6: Gross Domestic Product[a] in Six Countries, 1899-1978

Year	1899	1913	1929	1937	1950	1957	1960	1970	1978
Country			1935 prices				1975 prices		
Germany	525	560	625	687	–	–	–	–	–
West Germany	–	–	–	775	665	1070	4323	6256	7840
France	360	400	605	540	775	1015	3547	5486	7120
Italy	185	225	275	260	360	520	1949	3176	3751
Sweden	360	475	720	705	1020	1225	5384	7824	8484
UK	830	920	915	1055	1245	1280	2988	3729	4446
USA	790	1000	1380	1330	1940	2185	5160	6644	8101

Note: a. At factor cost per head. Constant prices in US dollars.
Sources: 1899-1957 A. Maizels: *Industrial Growth and World Trade*; 1960-1978: OECD National Accounts 1950-78.

Table 7: Growth Rates in Gross Domestic Products, 1955-81 (annual percentage increase)

	Average 1955-60	Average 1960-5	Average 1965-70	Average 1970-5	Average 1976-7	Average 1979-81
Canada	3.3	5.3	4.8	5.2	2.9	2.6
France	4.6	5.9	5.8	4.3	3.1	0.8
W. Germany	6.3	4.8	4.5	2.4	2.8	0.3
Italy	5.5	5.1	6.0	3.1	1.7	3.2
Japan	9.7	10.0	11.8	5.6	6.0	7.7
UK	2.3	3.2	2.5	2.2	1.2	–3.3
USA	2.2	4.9	3.2	2.6	4.8	2.3

Source: OECD National Accounts.

Table 8: National Expenditures on Consumption and Investment

Proportion of Gross Domestic Product devoted to:

Private Consumption

	1938	1948	1957-9 average	1971	1978
France	n.a.	72	66	59	62
West Germany	60	65	59	54	60
Italy	62	70	64	64	63
Japan	n.a.	n.a.	55	52	57
Sweden	71	69	61	54	53
UK	77	72	66	62	60
USA	75	72	66	63	64

Public Consumption

	1938	1948	1957-9 average	1971	1978
France	n.a.	12	14	12	15
West Germany	20	18	13	17	14
Italy	20	12	14	14	16
Japan	n.a.	n.a.	18	9	10
Sweden	11	13	18	23	29
UK	14	15	16	19	20
USA	12	11	18	21	18

Domestic Capital Formation (Home Investment)

	1938	1948	1957-9 average	1971	1978
France	n.a.	19	21	26	21
West Germany	19	20	24	27	21
Italy	19	21	21	20	19
Japan	n.a.	n.a.	22	35	32
Sweden	19	19	21	21	19
UK	10	13	16	18	18
USA	11	18	18	17	18

Source: EEC Basic Statistics of the Community 1980.

Table 9: Comparative Burdens of Taxation

Tax paid by single individual 1980

Country	Percentage rate of tax min-max.	Limit up to which income is free of tax. DM per annum
France	5 – 60	7992
West Germany	22 – 56	4200
Italy	23.5 – 76.2	780
Sweden	30 – 80	3011
UK	30 – 60	5624
USA	15.7 – 74.2	1850

Source: *Die Zeit*, 13 June 1980.

Table 10: Civil Employment

Country	Civilian workers as % of total population, 1978	Unemployed as % of total population, October 1980	Average weekly hours of work, 1978	% of labour force employed in 1978 in Agriculture	Industry	Services
France	41.2	6.9	41.0	9.8	37.8	52.0
West Germany	41.6	3.8	41.6	7.1	45.6	47.3
Italy	37.5	7.6	40.4	16.5	38.6	45.0
Japan	48.0	2.0	n.a.	12.0	36.0	52.0
Sweden	51.0	2.1	n.a.	6.0	35.0	58.0
UK	46.0	8.5	39.9	2.7	40.0	57.3
USA	44.0	7.1	40.4	4.0	29.0	67.0
USSR	50.0	n.a.	40.4	22.0	38.0	40.0

Table 11: Time Lost in Strikes[a]

	1953	1964	1970	1978
France	730	179.4	43.7	49.2
West Germany	88.7	0.9	1.8	80.0
Italy	n.a.	942.9	518	227
UK	134.8	130.1	211	171.4
USA	679	424.6	371	169.7

Note: a. Minutes per year of economically active population.

Table 12: Consumer Price Index, 1948-79[a]

Country	1948	1953	1963	1970	1979
France	57	82	105	145.9	319.7
West Germany	92	92	111	133.75	209.6
Italy	78	88	117	142.9	447.6
Sweden	65	84	115	156.2	328.5
UK	64	84	112	151.5	454.6
USA	83	93	106	134.4	249.6

Note: a. 1958 = 100.

Table 13: Balance of Payments of Federal Republic, 1950-80 (DM million)

Year	Current Account	Capital Account
1950	−407	207
51	2341	87
52	2528	116
53	3793	82
54	3609	−186
55	2205	−450
56	4379	148
57	5761	−2305
58	5798	−2049
59	3961	−6108
1960	4493	1782
61	2843	4259
62	−1950	−267
63	68	2260
64	−16	−1765
65	−6723	2362
66	68	881
67	9463	−9998
68	10906	−7235
69	6226	−19008
1970	2679	11005
71	2888	10614
72	2561	12017
73	12289	13226
74	26578	−25335
75	9932	−13228
76	9915	−1033
77	9498	−287
78	18419	5436
79	−9644	9869
1980	−29052	5476

Source: *Bundesbank* Reports.

Table 14: Exports of Federal Republic, 1979

By commodities, percentage of total

	1952	1959	1966	1979
Food and agriculture	2.2	2.5	2.5	5.4
Raw materials	7.4	4.8	3.6	2.3
Semi-finished products	15.0	10.5	9.0	8.2
Components	21.0	19.4	18.3	18.7
Finished articles	54.4	62.8	66.6	65.4
of which				
Machines	22.0	18.7	21.4	24.1
Vehicles	5.7	13.5	13.9	14.8
Chemicals	8.9	12.8	13.9	13.1
Electrical goods	5.9	9.0	8.8	5.1
Textiles and clothing	5.6	5.0	4.5	1.5

By destinations, percentage of total

EEC	28.0	28.0	36.5	49.7
Rest of Europe	39.5	32.4	31.5	22.3
E. bloc	3.1	4.5	4.4	5.7
US and Canada	6.7	10.5	10.0	7.6
Rest of America	10.3	7.6	4.8	3.2
Africa	4.6	5.0	3.8	3.7
Asia	7.0	10.7	8.0	7.0
Pacific	1.1	1.3	1.0	0.8

Source: *Statistisches Jahrbuch.*

Table 15: Percentage Shares of World Trade in Manufactures, 1899-1979

	France	Germany/West Germany	Japan	UK	USA	Others
1899	14.4	22.4	1.5	33.2	11.7	13.4
1913	12.1	26.6	2.3	30.2	13.0	13.4
1929	10.9	20.5	3.9	22.4	20.4	18.6
1937	5.8	16.5	6.9	20.9	19.2	23.5
1950	9.9	7.3	3.4	25.5	27.3	26.6
1958	8.6	18.5	6.0	18.1	23.3	25.5
1970	8.7	19.8	11.7	10.8	18.5	23.3
1979	10.8	20.7	13.6	9.7	15.9	21.2

Sources: 1899-1958 Maizels: *Industrial Growth and World Trade*; 1970, 1979: National Institute of Economic and Social Research.

Table 16: The Burden of Defence, 1980

	$ per head 1980	% of GNP 1979	Numbers in active service 1980	% of population
France	374	3.9	494,000	0.93
West Germany	410	3.3	495,000	0.8
Italy	124	2.4	366,000	0.66
UK	437	4.9	329,000	0.6
USA	644	5.2	2,050,000	0.9
USSR	?	11-13	3,568,000	1.9
East Germany	285	6.3	162,000	0.96

Source: International Institute of Strategic Studies: *The Strategic Balance* 1980.

Table 17: Provision of School Places as Percentage of Age-groups[a] in Eight Countries, 1977

	3 – 6	6 – 10	10 – 19	19 – 26
France	105	115	85	16
Germany: East	117	100	93	11
West	79	107	92	18
Italy	70	105	72	18
Japan	39	93	107	18
Sweden	33	88	72	17
UK	22	104	85	9
USA	49	72	86	26

Note: a. The dividing-lines between age-groups and the exact period under reference vary slightly from country to country.
Source: *Bundesministerium für Bildung und Wissenschaft*.

Table 18: Comparative Standards of Living

	France	W. Germany	Italy	Japan	Sweden	UK	USA	USSR
Total energy consumption per head per annum	3305	4202	2381	3070	4900	3740	8290	3650
Total steel used per head per annum	368	538	368	512	463	349	618	566
Passenger cars per 1000 of population	315	326	282	336	346	254	387	22
Persons killed in traffic accidents per annum per 1,000,000	47.6	47.9	44.6	–	–	26.0	–	–
TV sets per 1000 of population	268	308	224	233	324	352	571	215
Circulation of daily papers per 1000 of population	214	289	113	–	572	388	–	397
Doctors per 100,000 of population	163	199	225	118	171	138	159	297
Infant mortality per 1000 live births	12.5	17.4	14.5	10.1	8.7	19.2	15.1	27.7
Average savings per household ($)	3211	1974	1683	–	–	–	–	–
Social protection as % of GNP	23.9	27.4	23.1	–	–	–	–	–
Houses per 1000 of population	337	384	319	–	–	–	–	–

Table 18: (cont.)

Number of hours and minutes of work needed in 1977 to buy:

	1 kg white bread	1kg beef	1 litre whisky	20 cigarettes	Refrigerator	Daily paper	1 litre petrol	100 kw electricity
France	0.16	2.31	3.29	0.08	56.01	0.05	0.08	2.35
W. Germany	0.16	2.0	2.0	0.14	30.34	0.04	0.05	1.51
Netherlands	0.09	1.41	1.51	0.09	28.38	0.03	0.05	2.05
UK	0.10	1.54	3.36	0.20	48.24	0.03	0.06	2.16

Sources: Basic Statistics of the European Community, 1980; Social Indicators for the European Community, 1980.

Table 19: The Fifty Largest Firms in the Federal Republic

Name	Industry	Turnover 1980 (DM m)	Profit (Loss)	Employees
VEBA	Energy/Oil/Chemicals	39,970	479	83,936
Volkswagen	Motors	33,288	302	257,930
Siemens	Electrical	31,960	487	344,000
Daimler-Benz	Motors	31,054	961	183,392
Hoechst	Chemicals	29,915	381	186,850
BASF	Chemicals	29,171	478	116,518
Bayer	Chemicals	28,825	331	181,639
Thyssen	Steel	27,128	144	152,089
RWE	Energy	18,262	489	68,007
Ruhrcoal	Coalmining	16,422	32	136,816
Gutehoffnungshütte	Machinery	15,417	121	86,018
Deutsche BP	Oil	15,201	13	4,340
AEG	Electrical	15,141	−278	145,200
Krupp	Steel/Machinery	13,919	38	85,706
Deutsche Shell	Oil	13,899	246	4,878
Esso	Oil	13,150	430	4,567
Mannesmann	Steel/Machinery	13,110	147	103,491
Bosch	Electrical	11,809	117	120,020
Preussag	Energy/Oil	9,412	89	21,283
Opel	Motors	9,224	−411	59,876
Ruhrgas	Energy	9,122	207	2,938
Metallgesellschaft	Capital Goods	9,047	42	27,220
Ford	Motors	8,692	−463	49,767
Degussa	Chemicals/Non-ferrous metals	8,649	55	20,569
Salzgitter	Steel/Shipbuilding	8,578	−85	56,574
Flick	Holding	8,427	77	46,491
BMW	Motors	8,117	160	43,241
Deutsche Unilever	Foodstuffs	8,095	137	35,334
Hoesch	Steel	7,992	n.a.	46,600
Deutsche Texaco	Oil	7,554	208	4,827
IBM	Electronics	7,380	590	26,362
Mobil Oil	Oil	7,351	294	2,415
Henkel	Chemicals	6,899	86	33,567
Philipp Holzmann	Building	6,266	41	43,400
Hochtief	Building	6,079	124	31,083
Klöckner	Steel	5,561	−11	31,809
Saarbergwerke	Coal/Energy	5,418	5	32,584
Deutsche Babcock	Capital Goods	4,984	24	31,187
VIAG	Steel/Aluminium/Chemicals	4,887	125	26,211
Bertelsmann	Publishing	4,792	56	29,570
KHD	Machinery	4,621	39	29,673
Enka	Manmade Fibres	4,600	−52	43,300
Deutsche Philips	Electrical	4,387	12	28,200
VEW	Energy	4,134	78	7,086
BBC	Electrical	4,018	35	37,615
Neue Heimat	Building/Administration	3,557	26	5,721
SEL	Electrical	3,351	43	33,195
MBB	Aircraft	3,304	50	26,287
Schering	Pharmaceuticals/Chemicals	3,220	68	21,294
Continental	Tyres	3,160	27	30,727

Source: *Die Zeit*, 28 August 1981.

Table 20: The Press in the Federal Republic

At the end of 1980, there were 120 daily papers being published in the Federal Republic, with an overall circulation of 24.15 million copies (higher on Saturdays) and 1200 local editions. For relative costs and coverage, see Table 18. Those with the biggest circulation were:

Name	Circulation '000 (1966 in brackets)		Site of head office	Remarks
Bild	4,710	(4,879)	Hamburg.	Illustrated. Sensational. Owned by Axel Springer.
Westdeutsche Allgemeine Ztg[a]	650		Essen.	Biggest provincial newspaper publishers. Total output 1.3m copies.
Express	435	(226)	Cologne.	
Rheinische Post	351	(314)	Düsseldorf.	Supports CDU.
Süddeutsche Ztg	330	(236)	Munich.	Progressive class daily.
Südwest Presse	314		Ulm.	
BZ (Berliner Ztg)	312	(341)	Berlin.	Owned by Axel Springer.
Frankfurter Allgemeine Ztg (FAZ)	312	(287)	Frankfurt.	Conservative class daily.
Hamburger Abendblatt	281	(333)	Hamburg.	Owned by Axel Springer.
Abendzeitung	265	(291)	Munich.	Same publishers as Süddeutsche.
Kölner Stadtanzeiger	253		Cologne.	Same publishers as Express.
Rheinpfalz	244		Ludwigshafen.	
Ruhr Nachrichten	223	(370)	Dortmund.	
Stuttgarter Ztg	221	(157)	Stuttgart.	Same publishers as Rheinpfalz.
Hannoversche Allgemeine Ztg	204	(206)	Hanover.	
Die Welt	203	(287)	Hamburg.	Conservative. Owned by Axel Springer.

Note: a. Ztg = Zeitung

Table 20: (cont.)

The chief business paper is the *Handelsblatt* which is published in Düsseldorf and appears five days a week with a circulation of 92,000.

The biggest or most significant weekly publications are:

Title	Circulation	Place of Distribution	Remarks
Hör Zu	4,180	Hamburg.	Radio and TV Programmes. Owned by Axel Springer.
Stern	2,000	Hamburg.	Biggest of illustrated weeklies.
Bunte	1,640	Offenburg.	Illustrated weekly.
Brigitte	1,630	Hamburg.	Biggest Women's weekly. Owned by Gruner & Jahr.
Neue Revue	1,600	Hamburg.	Illustrated weekly, once had largest circulation.
Für Sie	1,180	Hamburg.	Women's weekly.
Quick	1,170	Munich.	Illustrated weekly.
Der Spiegel	1,167	Hamburg.	Illustrated news magazine, owned by Rudolf Augstein. See p. 209.
Die Zeit	455	Hamburg.	Leading progressive weekly.
Bayern Kurier	225	Munich.	Closely connected with F.J. Strauss.

NOTES

1. G. Barraclough: *Factors in Modern German History*, p. 17.
2. Gordon A. Craig: *The Politics of the German Army*, p. 16.
3. Sir Arthur Lewis: *Growth and Fluctuations 1870-1913*, pp. 43 and 112.
4. E. Kehr: *Das Primat der Innenpolitik*, p. 165.
5. Baronin von Spitzemberg: *Tagebuch*, p. 416.
6. R.M. Rilke: *Letters to a Young Woman*, 2 February 1923.
7. F.L. Carsten: *The Reichswehr and Politics*, pp. 68 and 140.
8. D. Schoenbaum: *Hitler's Social Revolution*, p. 130.
9. G. Benn: Letter of 12 August 1949.
10. W.L. Shirer: *The Rise and Fall of the Third Reich* (paperback edn), p. 977.
11. W.S. Churchill in House of Commons, 22 February 1944.
12. Goebbels in *Das Reich*, 25 February 1945.
13. A. Speer: *Inside the Third Reich*, p. 588.
14. For evidence as to Hitler's death, see R.G.L. Waite: *Adolf Hitler, The Psychopathic God*, pp. 415-22.
15. W. Leonhard: *Child of the Revolution*, p. 303.
16. W.S. Churchill: *The Second World War*, vol. VI, p. 582.
17. H. Feis: *Between War and Peace*, p. 177.
18. L.D. Clay: *Decision in Germany*, p. 196.
19. W. Abelshauser in *Historische Konjunkturforschung* (ed. W.H. Schröder and R. Spreel), p. 106.
20. See letter from W. Harris-Burland in *The Times*, 27 January 1977.
21. Rolf Zundel in *Die Zeit*, 18 April 1969.
22. G. Brandt: *Rüstung und Wirtschaft in der Bundesrepublik*.
23. Rolf Zundel in *Die Zeit*, 10 May 1974.

The author has set out his views on the relations between the Great Powers during the period 1941-62 in *The Adversaries: America, Russia and the Open World* (London 1981).

FURTHER READING

There are so many books about Germany that it has seemed best to confine the following list (which is far from complete) to secondary works in English. No attempt has been made to cover the military history of the wars or general international history. Many of the books listed themselves contain bibliographies. No book is mentioned more than once.

Chapter 1 and General

Barraclough, G. *Factors in Modern German History* (Oxford, 1946)

Carr, W. *A History of Germany 1815-1945*, 2nd edn (London, 1979)

Clapham, Sir John *The Economic Development of France and Germany*, 3rd edn (Cambridge, 1968)

Craig, G.A. *The Politics of the German Army 1660-1945* (Oxford, 1955)

Dehio, L. *Germany and World Politics in the Twentieth Century* (Eng. transl., London, 1959)

Epstein, K. *The Genesis of German Conservatism* (Princeton, 1966)

Flenley, R. *Modern German History* (London, 1964)

Hamerow, T. *Restoration, Revolution, Reaction: Economics and Politics in Germany 1851-1871* (Princeton, 1958)

— *The Social Foundations of German Unification* (Princeton, 1969)

Henderson, W.O. *The Rise of German Industrial Power 1834-1914* (London, 1975)

Holborn, H. *A History of Modern Germany*, vol. III 1840-1945 (London, 1969)

Kohn, H. *German History, Some New Views* (London, 1954)

Krieger, L. *The German Ideal of Freedom* (Boston, 1957)

Mann, G. The *History of Germany since 1789* (Eng. transl., London, 1968)

Meinecke, F. *The German Catastrophe* (Eng. transl., Harvard, 1950)

Morgan, R.P. *The German Social Democrats 1864-1872* (Cambridge, 1965)

Pflanze, O. *Bismarck and the Development of Germany 1815-71* (Princeton, 1963)

Pounds, N. *The Economic Pattern of Modern Germany* (London, 1963)
Ramm, A. *Germany 1789-1919, a Political History* (London, 1967)
Taylor, A.J.P. *The Course of German History* (London, 1945)

Chapter 2

Balfour, M. *The Kaiser and His Times* (London, 1964; paperback, Harmondsworth, 1975)
Berghahn, V.R. *Germany and the Approach of War in 1914* (London, 1973)
Craig, G.A. *From Bismarck to Adenauer* (Baltimore, 1958)
— *Germany 1866-1945* (Oxford, 1978)
Demeter, K. *The German Officer Corps* (Eng. transl., London, 1965)
Eley, G. *Reshaping the German Right* (New Haven, 1980)
Evans, R. (ed.) *Society and Politics in Wilhelmine Germany* (London, 1978)
Fischer, F. *Germany's Aims in the First World War* (Eng. transl., London, 1967)
— *War of Illusions: German Policies from 1911 to 1914* (Eng. transl., London, 1975)
Geiss, I. (ed.) *July 1914, the Outbreak of the First World War. Selected Documents* (Eng. transl., London, 1967)
Guttsman, W. *The German Social Democratic Party 1875-1933* (London, 1981)
Hartmann, H. *Authority and Organisation in German Management* (Princeton, 1959)
Jacob, H. *German Administration since Bismarck* (New Haven, 1963)
Kennedy, P.M. *The Rise of the Anglo-German Antagonism 1860-1914* (London, 1980)
Knight, M. *The German Executive 1890-1933* (Stanford, 1953)
Koch, H.W. (ed.) *The Origins of the First World War* (London, 1972)
Mayer, J.P. *Max Weber and German Politics*, 2nd edn (London, 1956)
Mommsen, W. (ed.) *The Emergence of the Welfare State in Britain and Germany 1850-1950* (London, 1981)
Mosse, G. *The Crisis of German Ideology* (New York, 1964)
von Müller, G.A. (ed. Goerlitz) *The Kaiser and His Court* (Eng. transl., London, 1961)
Nichols, J.A. *Germany after Bismarck* (Harvard, 1958)
Pulzer, P.J. *The Rise of Anti-Semitism in Germany and Austria* (New York, 1964)

Röhl, J. *Germany Without Bismarck, the Crisis of Government in the Second Reich 1890-1900* (London, 1967)

Rosenberg, A. *Imperial Germany, the Birth of the German Republic*, (Eng. transl., London, 1931)

Samuel, R.H. and R.H. Thomas *Education and Society in Modern Germany* (London, 1949)

Schorske, C. *German Social Democracy 1905-17* (Harvard, 1955)

Steinberg, J. *Yesterday's Deterrent* (London, 1964)

Stern, F. *The Politics of Cultural Despair* (Berkeley, 1961)

— *Gold and Iron: Bismarck, Bleichröder and the Building of the German Empire* (London, 1977)

Stolper, G. *et al. The German Economy, 1870 to the Present*, 2nd edn (Eng. transl., New York, 1967)

Taylor, A.J.P. *Bismarck* (London, 1955)

Turner, L.C.F. *Origins of the First World War* (London, 1970)

Veblen, T. *Imperial Germany and the Industrial Revolution* (New York, 1915)

Woodward, Sir Llewellyn *Great Britain and the German Navy* (Oxford, 1935)

Chapter 3

Angress, W.T. *Stillborn Revolution* (London, 1963)

Bennet, E.W. *Germany and the Diplomacy of the Financial Crisis 1931* (Cambridge Mass., 1962)

— *German Rearmament and the West 1932-3* (Princeton, 1980)

Carsten, F. *The Reichswehr and Politics 1919-33* (Oxford, 1966)

Childs, D. *Germany since 1918*, 2nd edn (London, 1980)

Dorpalen, A. *Hindenburg and the Weimar Republic* (Princeton, 1957)

Dyck, H.L. *Weimar Germany and Soviet Russia 1926-33* (London, 1966)

Eksteins, M. *The Limits of Reason: The German Democratic Press and the Collapse of Weimar Democracy* (Oxford, 1975)

Epstein, K. *Matthias Erzberger and the Dilemma of German Democracy* (Princeton, 1959)

Gatzke, H. *Stresemann and the Re-armament of Germany* (Baltimore, (1954)

Gay, P. *Weimar Culture, the Outsider as Insider* (London, 1969)

Gordon, H. *The Reichswehr and the German Republic 1919-26* (Princeton, 1957)

— *Hitler and the Beer Hall Putsch* (Princeton, 1972)

Hardach, K. *The Political Economy of Germany in the Twentieth Century* (Berkeley, 1980)

Halperin, S.W. *Germany Tried Democracy 1919-33* (London, 1963)

Hiden, J. *Germany and Europe 1919-1939* (London, 1977)

Hunt, R.N. *German Social Democracy 1918-33* (London, 1964)

Lane, B.M. *Architecture and Politics in Germany 1918-45* (Cambridge Mass., 1968)

Nettl, J.P. *Rosa Luxemburg*, 2 vols (London, 1966)

Nicholls, A. *Weimar and the Rise of Hitler*, 2nd edn (London, 1980)

Noakes, J. *The Nazi Party in Lower Saxony 1921-1933* (Oxford, 1971)

Post, G. *The Civil-Military Fabric of Weimar Foreign Policy* (Princeton, 1973)

Ryder, A.J. *The German Revolution of 1919* (Cambridge, 1967)

Stachura, P.D. *Nazi Youth in the Weimar Republic* (Oxford, 1975)

— *The Weimar Era and Hitler, 1918-1933: A Critical Bibliography* (London, 1977)

— (ed.) *The Shaping of the Nazi State* (London, 1978)

Turner, H.A. *Stresemann and the Politics of the German Republic* (Princeton, 1963)

Wheeler-Bennett, Sir John *The Nemesis of Power: The German Army in Politics 1918-45*, 2nd edn (London, 1967)

Wright, J.R.C. *'Above Parties': The Political Attitudes of the German Protestant Church Leadership 1918-1933* (Oxford, 1974)

Chapter 4

Allen, W.S. *The Nazi Seizure of Power: The Experience of a Single German Town* (Chicago, 1965)

Balfour, M. *Propaganda in War 1939-1945: Organisations, Policies and Publics in Britain and Germany* (London, 1979)

— and J. Frisby *Helmuth von Moltke: A Leader against Hitler* (London, 1972)

Bethge, E. *Dietrich Bonhoeffer* (Eng. transl., London, 1970)

Bielenberg, C. *The Past Is Myself* (London, 1968)

Boelcke, W. *The Secret Conferences of Dr. Goebbels 1939-43* (Eng. transl., London, 1970)

Bracher, K. *The German Dictatorship: The Origins, Structure and Effects of National Socialism* (Eng. transl., London, 1970)

Bullock, A. *Hitler, a Study in Tyranny*, revised edn (London, 1964)

Carr, W. *Arms, Autarky and Aggression, a Study in German Foreign Policy 1933-39* (London, 1972)
— *Hitler, a Study in Personality and Politics* (London, 1978)
Carroll, B. *Total War: Arms and Economics in the Third Reich* (The Hague, 1968)
Cecil, R. *The Myth of the Master Race: Alfred Rosenberg and Nazi Ideology* (London, 1972)
— *Hitler's Decision to Invade Russia 1941* (London, 1975)
Conway, J.S. *The Nazi Persecution of the Churches* (London, 1968)
Deutsch, H. *The Conspiracy Against Hitler During the Twilight War* (London, 1968)
— *Hitler and his Generals: the Hidden Crisis January-June 1938* (Minneapolis, 1974)
Dicks, H.V. *Licensed Mass Murder* (London, 1972)
Farquharson, J.L. *The Plough and the Swastika: the NSDAP and Agriculture in Germany 1928-1945* (London, 1976)
Fest, J. *Hitler* (Eng. transl., London, 1974)
Graml, H. *et al. The German Resistance to Hitler* (Eng. transl., London, 1970)
Hale, O.J. *The Captive Press in the Third Reich* (Princeton, 1964)
Hildebrandt, K. *The Foreign Policy of the Third Reich* (Eng. transl., Berkeley, 1973)
Hoffmann, P. *The History of the German Resistance 1933-1945* (Eng. transl., London, 1977)
Kogon, E. *The Theory and Practice of Hell* (Eng. transl., London, 1950)
Lerner, D. *The Nazi Elite* (Stanford, 1951)
Lewy, G. *The Catholic Church and Nazi Germany* (London, 1964)
Manvell, R. and H. Fraenkel *Hermann Goering* (London, 1962)
— *Heinrich Himmler* (London, 1965)
Merkl, P. *Political Violence under the Swastika: 581 Early Nazis* (Princeton, 1975)
Milward, A. *The German Economy at War* (London, 1964)
— *War, Economy and Society 1939-45* (London, 1977)
Nicholls, A. and P. Matthias (eds.) *German Democracy and the Triumph of Hitler* (London, 1971)
Noakes, J. and G. Pridham (eds.) *Documents on Nazism 1919-1945* (London, 1974)
Orlow, D. *The History of the Nazi Party 1919-45*, 2 vols (Pittsburg, 1973)
Peterson, E.N. *The Limits of Hitler's Power* (Princeton, 1964)
Reitlinger, G. *The Final Solution* (London, 1953)

— *The SS, Alibi of a Nation* (London, 1956)

Rich, N. *Hitler's War Aims: Ideology, the Nazi State and the Course of Expansion*, 2 vols (London, 1973)

Robertson, E.M. *Hitler's Pre-War Policy and Military Plans* (London, 1963)

Schoenbaum, D. *Hitler's Social Revolution* (London, 1967)

Schweizer, A. *Big Business in the Third Reich* (London, 1964)

Shirer, W. *The Rise and Fall of the Third Reich* (New York, 1960)

Smelser, R.M. *The Sudeten Problem 1933-1938:* Volkstumspolitik *and the Formulation of Nazi Foreign Policy* (London, 1975)

Speer, A. *Inside the Third Reich* (Eng. transl., London, 1970)

Stein, G.H. *The* Waffen SS, *Hitler's Elite Guard at War 1939-45* (London, 1966)

Steinert, M. *Hitler's War and the Germans* (Eng. transl., Columbus, 1977)

Stevenson, J. *Women in Nazi Germany* (London, 1975)

Taylor, T. *Munich* (New York, 1979)

Toscano, M. *The Origins of the Pact of Steel* (Baltimore, 1967)

Trevor-Roper, H. *The Last Days of Hitler* (London, 1947)

— (ed.) *Hitler's Table Talk* (London, 1953)

— (ed.) *Hitler's War Directives 1939-45* (London, 1964)

Waite, R.G. *Adolf Hitler, the Psychopathic God* (New York, 1977)

Zeman, Z.A.B. *Nazi Propaganda*, 2nd edn (London, 1973)

Chapters 5 to 7

Balfour, M. *Four-Power Control in Germany 1945-6* (in the series Toynbee (ed.) Survey of International Affairs 1939-1946 (London, 1956)

Clay, L.D. *Decision in Germany* (New York, 1950)

Davison, W.P. *The Berlin Blockade* (London, 1958)

Ebsworth, R. *Restoring Democracy in Germany: The British Contribution* (London, 1960)

Feis, H. *Between War and Peace, the Potsdam Conference* (Princeton, 1960)

Gimbel, J. *The American Occupation of Germany: Politics and the Military 1945-1949* (Stanford, 1968)

Grosser, A. *West Germany from Defeat to Re-armament* (Eng. transl., 1956)

Hearnden, A. (ed.) *The British in Germany: Educational Reconstruction after 1945* (London, 1978)

Heidelmeyer, W. and G. Hindrichs *Documents on Berlin 1943-1965* (Eng. transl., Munich, 1965)

Leonhard, W. *Child of the Revolution* (Eng. transl., London, 1957)

Ruhm von Oppen, B. *Documents on Germany 1945-55* (London, 1955)

Smith, B.F. *Reaching Judgment at Nuremberg* (London, 1977)

Snell, J.L. *The Origins of the East-West Dilemma over Germany* (New Orleans, 1959)

Wallich, H.C. *Mainsprings of the German Revival* (New Haven, 1955)

Willis, F.R. *The French in Germany 1945-1949* (Stanford, 1955)

Wiskemann, E. *Germany's Eastern Neighbours* (London, 1956)

Zink, H. *The United States in Germany* (Princeton, 1957)

Chapters 8 to 14

Adenauer, K. *Memoirs 1945-1953* (Eng. transl., London, 1966-8. Later vols not translated)

Becker, J. *Hitler's Children* (London, 1977)

Blair, P.M. *Federalism and Judicial Review in West Germany* (Oxford, 1981)

Brandt, W. *People and Politics* (Eng. transl., 1978)

Braunthal, G. *The Federation of German Industry in Politics* (Ithaca, 1965)

Catudal, H.M. *The Diplomacy of the Quadripartite Agreement on Berlin* (Berlin, 1978)

— *Kennedy and the Berlin Wall Crisis* (Berlin, 1981)

Childs, D. *From Schumacher to Brandt* (London, 1966)

— and J. Johnson, *West Germany, Politics and Society* (London, 1981)

Cullingford, E.C.M. *Trade Unions in West Germany* (London, 1976)

Dahrendorf, R. *Society and Democracy in Germany* (Eng. transl., London, 1968)

Dyson, K.H.F. *Party, State and Bureaucracy in West Germany* (Beverly Hills, 1977)

Edinger, L. *Kurt Schumacher* (Oxford, 1965)

Golay, F. *The Founding of the Federal Republic of Germany* (Chicago, 1958)

Grosser, A. *Germany in our Time* (Eng. transl., London, 1971)

Hallet, G. *Housing and Land Policies in West Germany and Britain* (London, 1977)

Hearnden, A. *Education in the Two Germanies* (Oxford, 1974)

Heidenheimer, A. *Adenauer and the CDU* (The Hague, 1960)

— *The Governments of Germany* (London, 1966)

Hiscocks, R. *Germany Revived* (London, 1966)

Johnson, N. *Government in the Federal Republic of Germany* (Oxford, 1973)

Kitzinger, U. *German Electoral Politics* (Oxford, 1960)

Loewenberg, G. *Parliament in the German Political System* (Ithaca, 1966)

Merkl, P.H. *The Origin of the West German Republic* (New York, 1963)

Morgan, R. *The United States and West Germany 1945-1973* (London, 1974)

Plischke, E. *The West German Federal Government* (London, 1964)

Preece, R.J.C. *Land Elections in the German Federal Republic* (London, 1968)

Pridham, G. *Christian Democracy in West Germany* (London, 1977)

Prittie, T. *Konrad Adenauer* (London, 1972)

— *Willy Brandt, Portrait of a Statesman* (London, 1974)

Richardson, J. *Germany and the Atlantic Alliance* (London, 1966)

Roberts, G.K. *West German Politics* (London, 1972)

Sandford, J. *The Mass Media of the German-speaking Countries* (London, 1976)

Smith, J.E. *The Defence of Berlin* (London, 1963)

Sontheimer, K. *The Government and Politics of West Germany* (Eng. transl., 1972)

Sowden, J.K. *The German Question 1945-1973* (Bradford, 1975)

Spiro, H.J. *The Politics of German Co-Determination* (London, 1977)

Tilford, R. *The* Ostpolitik *and Political Change in Germany* (Farnborough, 1975)

Windsor, P. *Germany and the Management of Detente* (London, 1971)

INDEX

Adenauer, Konrad, Dr: background 155; leader CDU 153, 156, 159, 192; chairs Parl. Council 159-60; and British 155, 210; and Europe 176, 178-91; and ex-Nazis 190; successes 191, 193; and Presidency 194; visits Moscow 196; and nuclear arms 200; and Kennedy 204; and de Gaulle 207-8; 1961 election 206; *Spiegel* affair 209-10; retires 211

Air Force (*Luftwaffe*) 83, 93, 95, 96-7, 106; British 96-7

Air raids, fear of 86, 91; on Guernica 89, Rotterdam 94, Britain 97, Germany 97, 104

Albrecht, Ernst, Dr 251, 252, 257, 265-6

Alliances: Anglo-Japanese 50; Austro-German 38; Franco-Czech 90; Franco-Russian 41, 49; German-Italian 88, 92; Three Emperors 38

Army, Prussian 18, 22, 26-31, 53-5, 58; *see also Reichswehr, Bundeswehr*

Austria 23, 31, 32; Austria-Hungary 38, 49, 51-3, 71; collapse of 56, 59; Republic 64, 74, 87; Hitler seizes 89-90; after 1945 115, 202, 270

Baden 29, 30, 47, 59; Land of B-Württemberg 129, 164-5, 190, 216, 224, 256, 258, 279

Banks 43, 147; *Reichsbank* 70; *Bank Deutscher Länder* 139, 151; *Bundesbank* 139, 187, 214, 229, 232, 239, 242, 253

Barzel, Rainer, Dr 237-9, 252, 257

Basic Law (*Grundgesetz*): Drafting of 158-61; outline of 161-9; Articles (3) 268; (6) 267, 269; (11) 268; (12) 163, 245; (19) 162; (21) 192, 244; (23) 236; (67) 165, 215; (68) 166, 238, 240; (131) 189; amendments 168, 246

Basic Treaty (*Grundvertrag*) 239, 243

Baum, Gerhart 254, 259, 266, 277

Bavaria 12, 29, 30, 67; Land in BRD 115, 127, 129-30, 157, 159-60, 164, 279; Bavarian Party 169; CSU in 210; elections in 216, 242; northern distrust of 243, 257; schools in 267

Benelux 143, 173, 212; Low Countries 15, 95, 132; Belgium 53-4, 56, 59, 64-5, 69, 94-5; Holland 21, 59, 94-5, 130; Luxembourg 94

Berlin: Foundation 18; university 23; in 1848 25; Jews in 36; Congress of 59, 62; in 1918 59, 62; Kapp putsch 66; air raid 97; in 1945 107, 108, 112, 115-16, 141; SPD in 129, 193; communists in 143; CDU in 156; in 1948-9 140-3, 158; relations with BRD 161; status of allies in 179, 202, 224, 234; 1953 rising 184; second crisis 201-5; Wall 205, 212; unrest in 226-7, 253; Four-Power agreement on 235, 248; schools in 267; facts about 279

Bismarck, Otto, Prince von: appointed 27; and unification 27, 29; and Reichstag 30; and Emperor 31; *Kulturkampf* 32; and Socialists 33; introduces tariffs 34; and France 37; and Russia 38-9; resigns 40; quoted 28, 38, 40, 204

Blockade: allied 1914-18 55, 57-8, 65; Hitler's precautions against 86; 1939-45 94; Russian of Berlin 140-2

Brandt, Willy: Lord Mayor of Berlin 193; SPD Leader 206, 213; Foreign Minister 217, 222-3; Chancellor 230-1, 245; foreign policy 232-3, 235, 238; and CDU 237; 1972 election 239, 240; and Schiller 239; and Jusos 242; weaknesses 243, 248, 250; fall 249-50, 252

301